New Casebooks

New Casebooks

New Casebooks

POSTCOLONIAL LITERATURES

ACHEBE, NGUGI, DESAI, WALCOTT

EDITED BY MICHAEL PARKER AND
ROGER STARKEY

First published 1995 by
MACMILLAN PRESS LTD
Houndmills, Basingstoke, Hampshire RG21 2XS
and London
Companies and representatives
throughout the world

ISBN 0–333–60801–1 hardcover
ISBN 0–333–60802–X paperback

A catalogue record for this book is available
from the British Library.

10   9   8   7   6   5   4   3   2   1
04   03   02   01   00   99   98   97   96   95

Printed in Malaysia

Contents

v

Acknowledgements

The editors and publishers wish to thank the following for permission to use copyright material:

F. Odun Balogun, for 'Ngugi's *Devil on the Cross:* the Novel as Hagiography of a Marxist', *Ufahamu: Journal of the African Activist Association,* 16:1 (Spring 1986), 1–24, reprinted by permission of *Ufahamu: Journal of the African Activist Association;* Elleke Boehmer, for 'The Master's Dance to the Master's Voice: Revolutionary Nationalism and the Representation of Women in the Writing of Ngugi wa Thiong'o', *Journal of Commonwealth Literature,* 26:1 (1991), 188–97, reprinted with kind permission of Hans Zell Publishers, an imprint of Bowker-Saur, a Reed Reference Company; Sidney Burris, for 'An Empire of Poetry', *Southern Review,* 27:3 (1991), 558–74, reprinted by permission of the author and the *Southern Review;* Stewart Crehan, for 'The Politics of the Signifier: Ngugi wa Thiong'o's *Petals of Blood',* *World Literature Written in English,* 26:1 (1986), 3–24, reprinted by permission of *World Literature Written in English;* Robin Ikegami, for 'Knowledge and Power, the Story and the Storyteller: Achebe's *Anthills of the Savannah',* *Modern Fiction Studies,* 37:3 (Autumn 1991), 493–507, reprinted by permission of *Modern Fiction Studies,* copyright © 1991, Purdue Research Foundation, West Lafayette, Indiana 47907; Bettina L. Knapp, for 'Fire on the Mountain – a Rite of Exit', *Journal of Evolutionary Psychology,* 8:3–4 (1987), 223–37, reprinted by permission of the author and *Journal of Evolutionary Psychology;* Neil Ten Kortenaar, for 'How the Centre is Made to Hold in *Things Fall Apart',* *English Studies in Canada,* 17:3 (September 1991), 319–36, reprinted by permission of *English Studies in Canada;* Harveen Sachdeva Mann, for

' "Going in the Opposite Direction": Feminine Recusancy in Anita Desai's *Voices in the City*', *Ariel: A Review of International English Literature*, 23:4 (October 1992), 75–95, reprinted by permission of the author and *Ariel: A Review of International English Literature*; Judie Newman, for 'History and Letters: Anita Desai's *Baumgartner's Bombay*', *World Literature Written in English*, 30:1 (1990), 37–46, reprinted by permission of the author and *World Literature Written in English*; Chido Okonkwo, for 'Chinua Achebe: the Wrestler and the Challenge of Chaos', reprinted by permission of the author; Philip Rogers, for '*No Longer at Ease*: Chinua Achebe's "Heart of Whiteness"', *Research in African Literature*, 14:2 (Summer 1983), 165–83, reprinted by permission of the author and *Research in African Literature*; Daizal R. Samad, for 'Cultural Imperatives in Derek Walcott's *Dream on Monkey Mountain*', *Commonwealth Essays and Studies*, 13:2 (1991), 8–21, reprinted by permission of *Commonwealth Essays and Studies*; Elaine Savory, for 'Value Judgements on Art and the Question of Macho Attitudes: The Case of Derek Walcott', *Journal of Commonwealth Literature*, 21:1 (1986), 109–19, reprinted with kind permission of Hans Zell Publishers, an imprint of Bowker-Saur, a Reed Reference Company; Clement H. Wyke, for '"Divided to the Vein": Patterns of Tormented Ambivalence in Walcott's *The Fortunate Traveller*', *Ariel: A Review of International English Literature*, 20:3 (July 1989), 55–71, reprinted by permission of the author and *Ariel: A Review of International English Literature*.

Note: Throughout this Casebook the spellings of the original essays have been deliberately retained.

General Editors' Preface

The purpose of this series of New Casebooks is to reveal some of the ways in which contemporary criticism has changed our understanding of commonly studied texts and writers and, indeed, of the nature of criticism itself. Central to the series is a concern with modern critical theory and its effect on current approaches to the study of literature. Each New Casebook editor has been asked to select a sequence of essays which will introduce the reader to the new critical approaches to the text or texts being discussed in the volume and also illuminate the rich interchange between critical theory and critical practice that characterises so much current writing about literature.

In this focus on modern critical thinking and practice New Casebooks aim not only to inform but also to stimulate, with volumes seeking to reflect both the controversy and the excitement of current criticism. Because much of this criticism is difficult and often employs an unfamiliar critical language, editors have been asked to give the reader as much help as they feel is appropriate, but without simplifying the essays or the issues they raise. Again, editors have been asked to supply a list of further reading which will enable readers to follow up issues raised by the essays in the volume.

The project of New Casebooks, then, is to bring together in an illuminating way those critics who best illustrate the ways in which contemporary criticism has established new methods of analysing texts and who have reinvigorated the important debate about how we 'read' literature. The hope is, of course, that New Casebooks will not only open up this debate to a wider audience, but will also encourage students to extend their own ideas, and think afresh about their responses to the texts they are studying.

John Peck and Martin Coyle
University of Wales, Cardiff

Introduction

MICHAEL PARKER and ROGER STARKEY

I

'One single word make a tremendous difference, that's why you can never be too sure what a word will do.' These words of warning from George Lamming's novel, *In The Castle of My Skin* (1953),[1] spoken by Trumper, a young Caribbean for whom exile proves the keenest teacher, provide an important reminder of the challenge of language, its capacity to chain and change. The purpose of this volume is to consider a number of important postcolonial writers who have been acutely conscious of the formative, political and elusive power of language, and how, as a consequence, their work has engaged their readers in complex cultural narratives, sharpening awareness of the inextricable relationship between language and politics. The manipulation of language to fix and enclose the history of empire, on the one hand, and the potential of language to unfold and address the experience of the colonised, on the other, have stimulated major developments in literatures written in English throughout this century. Postcolonial literatures have emerged from heterogeneous linguistic sources comprised of indigenous languages (oral and written) which colonising languages have attempted to stifle. The opposition of language as stasis and language as growth parallels the conflict between political hegemony and human inventiveness.

Two features of twentieth-century literature converge in the essays that make up this collection: the intensified debate worldwide in literary theories, especially since the mid-1960s,[2] and the developments in postcolonial literatures in English, a symbiotic relationship which has prompted significant re-readings of cultural histories throughout the world. Although India, Africa and the Caribbean have independent, much older aesthetics than European twentieth-century theories in the form of oral folk tradition, myth, ritual and mask, nevertheless, critics of postcolonial literatures written in English have drawn valuable insights from, and found compelling arguments in, amongst others, Saussure's structuralism, Adorno's marxism, Bakhtin's concepts of *heteroglossia* and *carnivalesque*, de

Man's studies of grammar and rhetoric, Foucault's preoccupations with systems of knowledge/power, Barthes' textual decoding, Cixous' notion of subversive writing, Kristeva's analysis of the male symbolic order, Derrida's deconstruction of a transcendental signified, and Spivak's focus on displacement.[3] In contexts of estrangement, dispossession, and the subsequent reconstructions of indigenous literatures, poststructuralist concepts of the *political* nature of the language of race, gender, and class have had profound effects on postcolonial writers preoccupied with subject-identity and oppositional discourses. Literary theories and postcolonial litera- tures have analysed and deconstructed a long tradition of Eurocentric classical, neo-classical and humanist texts, ranging from Greek syllogistic philosophy, the classical/Christian hegemony of Europe, and the medieval construction of the 'infidel', through to the literature of maritime expansion, rationalism, evolutionary theories, and more recent western fictions of Africa as the setting for the white man, a locus for 'adventure' and 'exploration'. Quite rightly these have been seen as cultural histories in which political ideologies have been deeply embedded.

The 'culturally sanctioned habit of deploying large generaliza- tions' within colonial discourse has been commented upon by Edward Said, the Palestinian-American critic. 'Reality is divided into various collectives: languages, races, types, colors, mentalities, each category being not so much a neutral designation as an evalu- ative intepretation.'[4] Such tendencies have had a long tenure, but are particularly commonplace in the period when imperial expan- sion was at its height, the nineteenth century. One cultural theorist whose texts have continued to prove problematic for both postcolo- nial writers and modern critical theorists is Matthew Arnold (1822–88). For Arnold the artistic enterprise was nothing less than a moral crusade, a cultural mission which could only be fulfilled by the implanting of 'the best of knowledge' – that is his own cultural presuppositions, confirmed by his 'reading' of Hellenic culture – from one end of the world to the other. 'The *men* of culture,' he asserted, 'are the true *apostles* [our italics] of quality ... those who have had a passion for diffusing, for making prevail ... the best knowledge, the best ideas of their time.'[5] No small part of the con- tribution of postcolonial literature and theory to contemporary lit- erary studies has involved a deconstruction of such texts, whose views persist all too often in present-day American and European entrepreneurial attitudes to the rest of the world.

The literatures discussed in the following essays exemplify the linguistically complex nature of postcolonial resitings of culture. Chinua Achebe's Nigerian experience and Ngugi's Kenyan Gikuyu world cannot be reduced to a simple, all-containing metonym, 'African'. Anita Desai's fiction textualises the Europeanised cosmopolis of the Indian middle classes, while Derek Walcott's poetry and drama are preoccupied with revisionary significations of the 'New World' that colonialism had previously constructed. Over the centuries large expanses of the world have been dominated and designated by centering languages. The first intervening/middle space was the '*Medi*-terranean'. Subsequently, North European and North American empires exploited their economic and military pre-eminence to rename vast areas of the world such as *India*, *America* (Latin or otherwise), the *West Indies*, *Australia*. As a consequence, indigenous peoples, inheritors of distinctive precolonial languages and cultures, were disinherited, 'placed' within colonial discourse. Their successors in the twentieth century have had to create new languages and new narratives in order to grapple with their complex histories, with what one writer has referred to as 'that wrestling contradiction of being white in mind and black in body'.[6]

European colonists and earlier generations of European writers, of course, had regarded vast regions of the world merely as blank spaces, lands 'without narrative',[7] waiting to be mapped, mined, written into existence. It has only been with the advent of indigenous writers – beneficiaries and blenders of traditions and insights acquired from what Derek Walcott ironically calls 'a sound colonial education' – that these places, their societies and world-views have begun to be inscribed. Particularly since the Second World War, as Edward Said has pointed out, there has been '[a] massive intellectual, moral and imaginative overhaul and deconstruction of Western representation of the non-Western world.'[8] No small contribution to this enterprise has been made by the writers on whom this New Casebook focuses – Chinua Achebe, Ngugi wa Thiong'o, Anita Desai and Derek Walcott – and in whose discourses cultural particularities and diversities are explored.

II

African theory has been the crucible for international debates about the forms and functions of postcolonial literatures. Two significant

strands of thought have developed. On the one hand, the essential-
ist revolutionary aesthetics of such writers as Diop, Fanon,
Chinweizu and Ngugi have emphasised the interconnectedness and
uniqueness of African literary and political discourse. On the other,
polysemic voices as represented by Wole Soyinka have stressed the
plurality of the African cultural experience within a global context.
Between these positions African writers have reconstructed the literary, economic, psychological, social and cultural subject-positions
of their worlds.

In the 'Introduction' to *Towards the Decolonization of African
Literature* (1980), which set as its task the 'probing of the ways and
means whereby Western imperialism has maintained its hegemony
over African literature', the Nigerian critic Chinweizu and his co-
authors define African literature as 'an autonomous entity', and go
on to assert that 'It has its own traditions, models and norms. Its
constituency is separate and radically different from that of the
European or other literatures.'[9] This emphasis upon the authority
of the text to radicalise the reader's awareness within the parameters of their message echoes Ngugi's argument in *Decolonising
the Mind*:

> In the eighteenth and nineteenth centuries Europe stole art treasures
> from Africa to decorate their houses and museums; in the twentieth
> century Europe is stealing the treasures of the mind to enrich their
> languages and cultures. Africa needs back its economy, its politics, its
> culture, its languages and all its patriotic writers.[10]

African literatures, he asserted, could only survive if they were
written in native African languages. Significantly, Ngugi chose to
write *Devil on the Cross* first in Gikuyu in 1980, and then subsequently translated it into English for its secondary audiences in
1982.

The ideological perspective of revolutionary aesthetics derives
from the work of Cheikh Anta Diop on Egypt and the Nile
Valley.[11] In pioneering studies such as *The Cultural Unity of Black
Africa* (1959) and *The African Origin of Civilization* (1974), Diop
reclaimed the cultural centre of the African Nile region for Africa as
a whole from the colonial narratives. Whereas colonial histories
had fixed the 'dark continent' and had anachronistically defined
Egypt in relation to a classical heritage of Greece and Rome, Diop
argued that

literate African cultures of the Nile Valley had taught writing to the Mediterranean cultures of Crete, Greece, and Judaea, had given them their religions and gods, and schooled them in mathematics, astronomy, architecture, and philosophy, and in the other arts and sciences.[12]

As an archaeologist and anthropologist, Diop retrieved a pre-European independent pan-Africanism, initiating a twentieth-century negritudinism,[13] through a politically inspired linguistic agenda, to replace the fragmentation and disintegration of post-independent African states. 'Flight from one's own language', he maintained, 'is the quickest short cut to cultural alienation.'[14] Contentiously for his African critics his theory was seen to sustain a perceived excellence – cultural, political and social – because the value he attributed to Greek civilisation had already been authenticated through European histories.

The acknowledged intervening text in shaping postcolonial aesthetics and cultural theory was Frantz Fanon's *The Wretched of the Earth* (1961). Influential beyond Africa, Fanon's argument that 'blackness' was a white construct of linguistic opposition disguising a deeper cultural opposition of controller/controlled, wealth/poverty, self-fulfilment/self-denial, derived from his experience, as a psychiatrist, of the treatment of North African patients by French doctors in the late 1950s–early 1960s, during the Algerian war of independence. Fanon discovered that patients with physical ailments were being clinically diagnosed as psychologically disturbed because their doctors were not asking the right questions. In ways reminiscent of Freud and Foucault, Fanon saw that personality displacement was culturally induced; illness was reflected in linguistic dysfunction (i.e. the African did not think like the French doctor). The experience and language of the colonized were denied and despised, leaving them marginalised, dispossessed, subjugated within their own land. Africa had become a metonym for a new slavery:

> The emotional sensitivity of the native is kept on the surface of his skin like an open sore which flinches from the caustic agent; and the psyche shrinks back, obliterates itself and finds outlet in muscular demonstrations which have caused certain wise men to say that the native is a hysterical type.[15]

Fanon's deconstruction of so-called respectable ideologies within a tolerant colonialism pointed to the extension of French power during liberation and independence – an alienating vocabulary of the 'other' as 'exotic', as 'curiosities', the strategic vocabulary of patronage. In its place he argues for a structure in which two constructed oppositions could meet, thus liberating both the repressed and the privileged. 'Universality', he claims, 'resides in this decision to recognise and accept the reciprocal relativism of different cultures, once the colonial status is irreversibly excluded.'[16] He emphasises the need to decode embedded assumptions of power, relocating cultural centres and disempowering closed static colonial discourses.

Like Fanon, postcolonial fictions have explored the characteristics of colonial power and the ways in which this power constructs their fictional figures. This is seen, for example, in characters central to their texts like Baba in Anita Desai's *Clear Light of Day*, Sarah in Brian Friel's *Translations*, or Okonkwo in Chinua Achebe's *Things Fall Apart* whose speech impediments reflect a fragmented grasp of the cultures that have shaped them. A different form of impairment is evident within the coloniser's characteristically reductive gaze on Africa as a museum. For example, the Dutch Father Huismans in V. S. Naipaul's 1979 novel *A Bend in the River*[17] collects tribal masks for their aesthetic qualities, yet never actually meets the African peoples nor understands the masking/ disguising/multiplying of meanings. His silent hoarding eloquently reinforces the patronising distance of colonial attitudes towards people who struggle towards an articulation of their confusions. A similar distance can be seen in much of the television representation of Africa by the western media, which portrays Africa in perpetual crisis, and continues to fix the indigenous peoples as passive, infectiously smiling or suffering backdrops for white politicians and aid workers.[18]

Whereas racist colonial regimes and their discourses have asserted that 'Humanity is not one' and privileged the white and the male, postcolonial writers have insisted that the colonised belong to 'the same world and are not absolutely other',[19] and have vigorously affirmed the rights of the silenced to be heard. Such a voice is heard in Tsitsi Dangarembga's novel, *Nervous Conditions*, which derives its title from Jean-Paul Sartre's 'Preface to *The Wretched of the Earth*' and no small part of its ideology from Sartre's and Fanon's theoretical texts, which point to the psychological consequences of colluding with the imperial power: 'The status of "native" is a nervous condition introduced and maintained

by the settler among colonised people *with their consent.*[20] On her
arrival at the Sacred Heart School, where she will be invited to
connive in her exile from her cultural origins and where her
education will be 'finished', Dangarembga's central character,
Tambudzai, is informed by a nun, 'smiling beatifically', that 'All the
first-formers live on this corridor ... And the Africans live in here.'[21]
By its very narrative form, *Nervous Conditions* illustrates effectively
the 'double consciousness' of the colonised, for whereas Tambudzai
the teenage focaliser responds excitedly to her accelerating progress
within the white education system and assimilation of its values,
Tambudzai the adult narrator interjects repeatedly to stress her
later realisations about the nature of the 'game':

> Whites were indulgent towards promising young black boys in those
> days, provided that the promise was a peaceful promise, a grateful
> promise to accept whatever was handed out to them and not to
> expect more.

> Above all I did not question things ... I was not concerned that
> freedom fighters were referred to as terrorists, did not demand proof
> of God's existence nor did I think that the missionaries, along with
> all the other Whites in Rhodesia, ought to have stayed at home I
> simply was not ready to accept that Babamukuru [her 'successful'
> uncle] was a historical artefact; or that advantage and disadvantage
> were predetermined.[22]

In contrast to her is Nyasha, her cousin and much more perceptive
and psychologically distraught alter ego, and her aunt Lucia who,
as a woman, legitimately rebels against continually 'being discussed
in the third person'.[23] Dangarembga's characters, both female and
male, live under a doubly divisive patriarchy, native and colonial.

Whilst still addressing what Sartre called 'a racist humanism',[24]
other writers like Wole Soyinka have urged a plural aesthetic,
directed towards the readers of history and literature focusing, not
on the authority of the author/the state, but on the power of the
reader/the people, accusing nationalist aesthetics of a narrowing
focus. Nelson Mandela's call for a holistic approach in shaping a
democratic pluralism for the future story of South Africa during his
April–May 1994 election campaign has affinities with Soyinka's
revision of revolutionary aesthetics. The African writer's task, like
the politician's, Soyinka argues, is to work towards a future in
which the influence of colonial linguistic, aesthetic and cultural
constructions is modified; African politics are themselves a form of

narrative, and thus shaped by and shaping the narratives of postcolonialism:

> The African writer needs an urgent release from the fascination of the past. Of course, the past exists, the real African consciousness establishes this ... it is co-existent in present awareness. It clarifies the present and explains the future, but it is not a fleshpot for escapist indugence ... A historic vision is of necessity universal.[25]

For Soyinka, African literatures, politicised through their histories, have faced a responsibility for plurality, for polysemic texts which express the voiced and unvoiced stories and intepretations of African conditions before, during and after colonialism. However, both Soyinka's aesthetic of a 'universal historic vision' and Fanon's cultural/political aesthetic of 'reciprocal relativism' emphasise an active engagement with complex networks of political and cultural discourses: the literatures of Africa are already politicised through their oppositional contexts of languages.

Certain revolutionary texts, such as Ngugi's *Petals of Blood* (1977), in their attempt to reclaim African history, can be seen to locate the text in the past, rather than looking to a future which acknowledges the intervention of colonialism in history. When Soyinka stated that Shakespeare 'may turn out to be an Arab after all',[26] he made the important point that a text – literary, social or political – exists at the point of reception; the function of the text is to free itself from history by *present*ing the narrative metonyms, metaphors, oppositions and hidden agendas which encode the ideologies of history through a creative involvement of the reader. Whereas nationalist theories are sometimes accused of centralising the author, as Stewart Crehan argues in his essay (5) on Ngugi,[27] and of locating the reader in the author's frame of reference, Soyinka's echo of Barthes' argument for the death of the author emphasises that interventionist political literature must both draw upon a cultural *langue*[28] and re-*new* its possibilities in the immediate text:

> The African world ... is governed by a ... holistic habit of perception and representation. A blacksmith's poker, an egungun dance, an Ifa prognistic verse, or a royal stool may simultaneously express the history of its makers, their concept of beauty, their propitiation of unseen forces, a statement of cosmic relativity, *and* a mode of experiencing all of them, of harmonising them with the challenge of existence.[29]

The appeal here is that the created object, the text, becomes a multiple signifier of an interactive unity in which the recipient's frame of response and understanding is central for the reconstruction of the text.

III

The determining oppositions of revolutionary nationalist aesthetics on the one hand, cultural pluralism on the other, are responses to historic oppositions of the colonised and colonisers. As such, these responses are at least partly governed by the terms of the dominant discourse. Like poststructuralist feminist theories, the liberating texts are in part defined by the structures of power which they decenter at the time as they create new centres, a condition of all literatures when a language is rescued within a text from the stasis of its history. Derrida indicates the dichotomy:

> Political decentralization, dispersion, and decentering of sovereignty calls, paradoxically, for the existence of a capital, a centre of usurpation and of substitution. ... The modern capital is always a monopoly of writing. It commands by written laws, decrees, and literature. ... Which amounts to recharging writing with the living voice.[30]

Examples of the inevitable difficulty and opportunity for African writers in breaking with the colonial legacy are numerous. In its attempt to 'recharge the living voice' the nationalist African orature aesthetic of Chinweizu and his co-authors is centralised with reference to the colonial culture it subverts. Ngugi in writing of the

> great tradition of European literature [which] had invented and even defined the world view of the Calibans, the Fridays and the reclaimed Africans of their imaginations. Now the Calibans and the Fridays of the new literature were telling their story which was also my story[31]

celebrates the way in which figures from sixteenth- and eighteenth-century European narrative have been relocated to define new Afrocentric *personae*. In the opinion of the critic Simon Gikandi, Chinua Achebe's achievement has been to turn the colonial legacy into fictional opportunity:

Achebe's seminal status in the history of African literature lies precisely in his ability to have realized that the novel provided a new way of reorganizing African cultures, especially in the crucial juncture of transition from colonialism to national independence.[32]

In Ngugi and Achebe sophisticated strategies of narrative disjunctions have realigned African history, including the colonial story, through interwoven textual references to European and precolonial African lore: Kenyan Mau-Mau events woven into the fiction of Ngugi's *A Grain of Wheat* (1967), parodic recreations of colonialists' accounts of *The Pacification of the Primitive Tribes of the Lower Niger* in Achebe's alternative narrative *Things Fall Apart* (1958), a typical example of how the 'colored' is translated into an *'object studied by the Occidental-white.'*[33] Often a network of referential symbols from the European tradition (biblical, classical, rational, imperial) is established which has the effect of reconstructing interpretations of that tradition by juxtaposing it with the story of African texts.

Chinua Achebe's *Anthills of the Savannah* (1987) illustrates well some of these complex interpretative strategies – postcolonial writing rejecting colonialism, postcolonial worlds establishing a new orthodoxy – when he depicts the radical newspaper editor, Ikem Osodi, taking on the corrupt new black postcolonial government led by President Sam, the 'nation's Man of Destiny', in what is clearly a parodic westernised academic setting, the University of Bassa. Instead of delivering the traditional lecture his fictional audience and the reader anticipate, he narrates to the students a story drawn from an oral tradition about 'the Tortoise who was about to die', retold recently to Ikem by a teller of tales currently languishing for his art in the local maximum security prison. Subverting westernised cultural expectations, inherent in terms like 'lecture' and 'university', the text becomes an act of revolt against the hegemonic imprisoning nationalism within the newly-independent fictional African state of Kangan. It undermines the authorial role/the state, the audience's expectations/the people, and the text/the logic of power to renew, remake the tale. Ikem comments,

> Storytellers are a threat. They threaten all champions of control, they frighten all usurpers of the right-to-freedom of the human spirit – in state, in church or mosque, in party congress, in the university or wherever.[34]

A seventeenth-, eighteenth- or nineteenth-century pamphleteer of Europe, or indeed William Blake, would have recognised the lineage: the author imprisoned by cultural bondage; the tale freed from its past to become part of the revolutionary present of dialogues, which are 'infinitely more interesting than monologues',[35] as Ikem says. The passage restores to narrative its metaphoric, metamorphosing function.

This politico-cultural resiting of European texts in postcolonial literatures has had profound implications, not only for the construction of postcolonial literatures, but also for readings of European literature. As the Indian critic, Gayatri Spivak, has demonstrated in her analysis of *Jane Eyre*,[36] and Edward Said in his comments on *Mansfield Park* and *Heart of Darkness*,[37] it should not be possible to read an 'enlightened' English novel without seeing categories of imperial discourse embedded in the alternatives in the texts. African literatures and theories, like many resisting/resiting discourses, are also opening innovative ways of responding to European literature and European traditions of interpretation. Responsive European commentators have recognised the decentralising parameters in which European criticism can operate, confronting rediscovered ways of writing history to destabilise creatively their logocentric systems. Chinua Achebe has warned, however, that 'the European critic of African literature must cultivate the habit of humility appropriate to his limited experience of the African world'.[38] Dated European systems have been superseded by more profound critical positions in Europe itself; but still signifiers describe 'Third World writers' and 'poets in the young countries'.[39] In some cases the novel has been appropriated as a product of the West as if narrative never existed in African culture prior to the twentieth century. There is always a danger that Euro-American theories of literature, developments upon metaphysical positions from Greek to Cartesian philosophy, could become a new kind of dominant discourse constructing postcolonial literatures as inventively struggling against recent history to reconstruct an indigenous and essentially 'African' culture. In other words, a new opposition could be created in the West in which postcolonial literatures become the object of a critical gaze (admiring but untouched) of texts struggling against powerful outsider forces, ignoring the fact that postcolonialism is as much a European condition as it is a description of former colonies, even whilst new technological/media networks create new global dominations. Paradoxically, one result of such an approach would be to create a new orthodoxy, a new canon of postcolonial 'correctness' denying the plurality of voices within postcolonial discourses

IV

If African literatures and criticism written in English reveal at their extremes oppositional directions – one inwardly located in an essentially African history, the other outwardly embracing and reshaping 'recent' African history towards a plural future – Indian literature and criticism in English are historically more closely tied to the discourses of Europe. Whilst nineteenth-century travellers appeared in Africa with the paraphernalia of explorers, their counterparts went to India as if to another home. This domestication of the 'orient' coupled with a discourse of the 'inscrutable' nature of its peoples has been analysed by Edward Said in his *Orientalism* (1978). The 'orient' is a western construct as much intended to define, internalise and valorise western discourses as it has defined the east – a global cultural stereotype.The Marabar Caves in E. M. Forster's novel *A Passage to India* (1924), for example, are imagined initially as a locus for romance, but subsequently translated, like India itself, into something repellent, maddening, destructive of identity under disoriented western eyes:

> Crammed with villagers and servants, the circular chamber began to smell. She lost Aziz in the dark, didn't know who touched her, couldn't breathe, and some vile naked thing struck her face and settled on her mouth like a pad ... For an instant she went mad, hitting and gasping like a fanatic. For not only did the crush and stench alarm her; there was also a terrifying echo.[40]

Central to Said's thesis is the textual nature of place and placement, of 'us' and 'them', 'west' and 'east', 'the rigidly binomial oppositions of "ours" and "theirs" with the former always encroaching on the latter (even to the point of making "theirs" exclusively a function of "ours")'.[41] Such are the defining relatives in European vocabularies.

Western constructs of eastern tales of cruelty, of 'pleasure domes' and 'perfumed gardens'of escapist and erotic delight – such as those created by Richard Burton in his translation of *The Arabian Nights* (1885–88) – fed nineteenth-century prejudices: for to construct narrative closure was to control and desire the story. Indian critics, such as Pathak, Sengupta and Purkayastha in their essay, 'The Prisonhouse of Orientalism', have argued that the construction of an acquiescent east created a space in which others – the British, French, Germans, Dutch and Portuguese – could speak, act and manage. For them, the problem is one of reclaiming and renegotiating their Indian experience: 'Identity is a matrix of subject positions which may contradict one another. Indian subject identities are constituted in a multiciplicity of discourses rising out of structures of religion, class, caste and gender.'[42] The narrator in Salman Rushdie's *Midnight's Children* (1981), reflecting upon his own confusing hybridity and that of the world, exclaims at one point:

> O eternal opposition of inside and outside! Because a human being, inside himself, is anything but a whole, anything but homogeneous; all kinds of everywhichthing are jumbled up inside him, and he is one person one minute and another person the next.[43]

Gayatri Spivak describes 'India' as a limiting metonym for 792 million people, the 'India' of western discourse which reduces the continent to the scale of 'Proust's Paris. It's very small.'[44] Spivak's recognition of the strong ties which continue to exist with European intellectual life finds fictional reinforcement in the 'small world' and confining spaces inhabited by Anita Desai's characterisations, who struggle to find identity within highly complex Indian cultures, subtly Europeanised Indian contexts.[45]

Some traditional criticism of Anita Desai's fiction reflects a problem with this 'small world'. Her novels are 'located' within an English nineteenth-century author-centered tradition by 'realist' criticism. She is praised for the description of Indian urban 'realities', especially that of Indian educated society. The possibility of seeing 'India' in her novels as a construct, is not explored, nor is the textual complexity of her novels acknowledged by such criticism. Established critical practice sanctions her by tying the analyses of her novels to a canon of 'great writers'. Her novels are urbanised, simplified, examples of psychological depth, whereas the important emphasis is the interplay of strategies of characterisation which create the problematic nature of any textual 'fixing'. Often titles reach beyond logocentric norms[46] to metonyms of plurality which imply metaphoric expansion: *Voices in the City, Baumgartner's*

Bombay, Where Shall We Go This Summer? and *Clear Light of Day.* In the last 'silence' is the final telling voice, the interpretative gap in which 'there seemed no need to say another word' as the fictive illusions the principal characters, Bim, Tara, Raja and Baba, had each separately created for themselves and others were punctured. The characterisations are constructs of multiple voices which impede rather than reveal meaning. The metaphor of an all-invasive cacophony frequently imposes itself upon the narrative:

> the mosquitoes that night were like the thoughts of the day embodied in monster form, invisible in the dark but present everywhere, most of all in and around the ears, piercingly audible. ... Now ... they rose in swarms, humming away, turning their backs on her.[47]

Desai's work acts as a filter and amplifier for a babble of competing voices and discourses. She is drawn towards the polyphonic model provided by T. S. Eliot and his attempts to contain and pattern the evanescence of words in time. Many of her central characters – Nanda Kaul in *Fire on the Mountain*, Tara in *Clear Light of Day*, Baumgartner in *Baumgartner's Bombay* – are, like Eliot, émigrés/exiles in search of a signifying moment.[48]

An illustration of the self-analytic nature of her fiction through juxtapositions of European and Indian discourses can be found in *Where Shall We Go This Summer?* (1975) Sita hears the prayer of Rekha:

> There seemed to be no relationship at all between that heavy, brooding body and the voice that greeted the sun like some goddess's, like some inhuman, unsubstantial creature's, and finally woke the *chelas* so that they came stumping up the stairs to sway and sing and clap to the music till they were in a state near that of the dervishes; that later rang out on All India Radio every morning, all over the country, singing the first pure *bhajan* of the day.[49]

The value of this passage is that it illustrates how Desai involves the reader in the textual problems of a narrative which refuses to create a stereotypical goddess out of Rekha, whilst it recognises that through her prayer she becomes a goddess to her audience. The passage encloses her substantial identity as a woman ('heavy, brooding body') within the enclosures of the room. Her 'voice', which is 'like some goddess's', is transposed/recreated by others through ritualistic body-language, reflecting traditions of the past, and then through radio waves, reaching to unheard audiences beyond her. She becomes the story that others make of her prayer. The textual 'reality' of Rekha, therefore, is a complex of her identity as a woman, the Indian culture she shares, and her prayer which others transform through ritual into new languages.

Such passages are typical of Desai's strategy in portraying urban domesticity, an essentially patriarchal world which strives to fix women in motherhood and placid contentment, whilst undermining the reader's search for a fixed subject-identity by suggesting widening spaces into what 'seems'. 'Reality' in Desai's novels is always linguistically elusive, never specific. The reader is 'placed' to unravel the threads that weave the text, engaged with textual closures and openings, with the stasis (*Where Shall We Go This Summer?*) and the ecstasy (*Fire on the Mountain*) of cultural discourses problematically defining individuated subject-positions.[50]

Anita Desai's novels focus on an Indo-European world whilst involved with the 'Indianness' of her characters. This suggests that a critique is shaping in her novels – an engagement with a set of precolonial Indian discourses. The would-be poet and intellectual, Raja, in *Clear Light of Day*, reads Tennyson and Swinburne, is scornful of Hindi and is contemptuous of a populist theory, yet his love for the Urdu language and culture reveals a desire to reach for precolonial roots: '"Look", he said again and wrote out a few lines in the Urdu script with a flourish that made them [his sisters] quiver with admiration'[51] – another passionately bodily signifier, like that of the dervishes. Raja, whose name suggests multi-imperial origins, is one of the perennial outsiders, off-centre like Deven in *In Custody;* [52] both yearn for a purer, more refined time – an imaginary past, somewhere other than here and now.

Desai's focus on the outsider, the expatriate, the marginalised, suggests a mixed cultural assimilation of discrete centres where the metonym of 'India' as a homogeneous unit fades as characters attempt unsuccessfully to re-establish 'home'. Spivak's remarks are once again relevant here:

> I don't write a great deal about 'India', but I am very happy that it's placed within quotation marks here. 'India', for people like me, is not really a place with which they can form a national identity because it has always been an artificial construct. 'India' is a bit like saying 'Europe'.[53]

In a similar fashion, Desai's novels thwart metonymic terms to construct metaphors of symbolic networks, 'dream-web[s]',[54] which cross cultural divides with paradoxical positions of subjects alienated within their 'home'.

Thus, reinforcing her fictional critique, Desai's characterisations and locations bear the imprint of a long tradition of colonising presences from a hybrid past. *Baumgartner's Bombay* (1988) is the story of a Jew brought up in pre-war Berlin, who, after being sent into exile in India to escape the Nazis, ends up being killed by a German in post-war, post-independence India. 'Strongly marked by repetition', as Judie Newman's essay points out,[55] it is a novel about recurring cycles of violence and dispossession, 'of global war, the colonial war ... religious war. Endless war.'[56] Amongst the European exiles, caught in what Baumgartner sees as 'a great web in which each one was trapped',[57] is a Jesuit, who will only eat bananas or peanuts because they are 'not touched by their hands'; striving to protect his subjectivity within the hard shell of European culture, he is imprisoned and homeless.[58] His closure is echoed in the lengthy narrative interpellation of Baumgartner's near-imprisonment in Nazi Germany as a Jew and his actual confinement in India as a 'German'. During his captivity

> Although a part of him greedily, hungrily took in every morsel of information that came his way of the situation of the Jews in Germany, of their disappearance, of the labour camps, of Nazi propaganda, another part frantically built a defensive barrier against it. It was as if his mind were trying to construct a wall against history, a wall behind which he could crouch and hide, holding him to a desperate wish that Germany were still what he had known as a child and that in the dream-country his other continued to live the life they had lived there together.[59]

The characterisation of Hugo Baumgartner as doubly exiled, in Europe and then in India, emphasises his confusing self-identity, his inability to find 'the shelter [which] was once there but is there no longer'.[60] An overwhelming sense of absence is established immediately in the novel's opening scene when Lotte, a long-time German friend and fellow refugee, reads some letters discovered by Baumgartner's dead body, and stares at the familiar formlessness around her: 'A blank sky, as always, with neither colour nor form. Empty. Afternoon light. Daylight. Perpetual light. And blankness.'[61] 'Indigestible and inedible',[62] Baumgartner's search for identity is ultimately defined as 'a meaning to the meaningless'.[63]

India is perceived in Desai's novels as an interactive narrative, inscrutable not with the neat constructions of exoticism, mystery and excitement, nor with a story of precise beginnings and endings, but through portrayals of outcasts like Lotte where no centre defines the code. India, for the outsiders, becomes a place where they are criminalised, marginalised, 'other': Baumgartner in death finds home in a foreign country, visited and wanted most when he has no more identity. He is always at the entry and exit points of his language, never in it: 'He realised ... that silence was his natural condition.'[64] The interaction between sections of Indian narrative and that of Europe is just one instance of what Homi K. Bhahba identified as the pull between the regulatory closed systems of institutionalised perceptions and the separate narratives which voice the 'other', those outside the systems who yet exist within it.[65]

V

The Caribbean's cultural plurality has made it one of the discursive centres for the African, the Afro-American, the European and the Pacific world as result of the central work of C. L. R. James, Aimé Césaire, George Lamming, Leopold Senghor, Kamau Brathwaite, Jamaica Kincaid, Michelle Cliff and Derek Walcott. Caught between western constructs of an African past and an American future, its literature creates a hybrid present from the African diaspora. Lines of travel from Europe westwards and beyond are subverted: the story of the silent 'other' place and gender which precedes the nineteenth-century narrative of *Jane Eyre* is written in the twentieth century with Jean Rhys's *Wide Sargasso Sea*. As with African and Indian fictions, much of the writing from and about the 'New World' reflects a preoccupation with the alienated, the outsider. Mervyn Morris textualises the problem of hybrid identity in 'To An Expatriate Friend':

> New powers re-enslaved us all:
> each person manacled in skin, in race,
> You could not wear your paid-up dues;
> the keen discrimination typed your face.[66]

Historically, the texts of Europe have been far-reaching in fixing a construct of an island-paradise. One of the earliest and most enduringly influential of these, Shakespeare's *The Tempest* (1610–11?), may have derived part of its origins in stories, brought back to

London a year later, of the 'miraculous deliverance'[67] of the crew and passengers – Virginia-bound colonists – aboard the *Sea-Adventure*, savaged in a storm off the Bermudas in July 1609. The scene of Shakespeare's drama is significantly described as 'an uninhabited Island', a bewitched and calibanised location. There a sprite is imprisoned by a 'beast' – Prospero's 'educated' perception of Caliban – a creature who 'proves himself to be' irredeemable, ineducable when he later lecherously preys on the wondrous vision from 'civilisation', Prospero's daughter, Miranda. The 'beast', therefore, must be tamed. By learning the language of subjugation and subservience, Caliban becomes a prisoner. Indeed, the nature of his imprisonment is, like Friday's,[68] above all linguistic: Prospero promises him a hope, which is glimpsed and then cruelly denied. Ultimately it is the resisting language of Caliban which tells in *The Tempest*. European humanism is examined and undermined through its oppositional constructs of the bestial set against reason, ugliness with beauty, untamed nature with civilisation, in attempting to *re*-create its own version of Eden.

Derek Walcott in his poetry rewrites the myth yet again:

> Adam had an idea.
> He and the snake would share
> the loss of Eden for a profit.
> So both made the New World. And it looked good.[69]

For Walcott the signification of a 'New World' already has the inscriptions of a future mapped by the earliest European languages. Though the Caribbean can now be recognised as a locus for the worst aspects of imperial history – enslavement of what were defined as the 'other', forced transportation, extinction of indigenous peoples, piracy, rape and territorial appropriation – in the past it has been the source of much western fiction about the lure and fascination of dangerous pleasures, and islands of treasure. As with the terminologies of the 'dark continent', the 'orient', referred to earlier in this essay, so with the construction of the 'West Indies'; a European vocabulary constructs a Eurocentric view of 'the other' both in terms of place and identity.

The marks of Europe have been impressed upon the terrain of the Caribbean, duplicating problematic meanings of selfhood, identity. In Walcott's lines, below, traces of the precolonial identity remain to trouble the living stream of the present:

There were still shards of an ancient pastoral
in those shrines of the island where the cattle
drank their pools of shadow from an older sky[70]

Questions of identity surface in one of Walcott's earliest extended pieces, 'Origins', where there is a developed consciousness of a Caribbean/Caliban self, 'Nameless ... among olives of algae', in contrast to the named classical heroes – Hector, Achilles, Aeneas, Ulysses. Walcott repeatedly reaches back past the colonial era and its literature to a classical and pre-classical, hybrid point of origin and authority, a 'Greek and African pantheon'[71] in search of validation through the power to name, instead of being named.

The mind, among sea-wrack, sees its mythopoeic coast,
Seeks, like the polyp, to take root in itself.[72]

The dialogic of 'Origins' brings together Egypt, Greece, Guinea, Caribbean, 'stitching two worlds', like 'The retching hulks of caravels', which sewed together Europe, Africa and the Americas in their sickening trade. Walcott's ambition to 'purify the language of the tribe', to 'use my hand' to give 'voice to one people's grief',[73] is signalled in parts IV–VII, with the important semantic shift away from 'I' to 'we' and 'our'. 'Origins' celebrates forebears and their forbearance, nets their lost voices, and offers rites of atonement to

... those whose back on hillsides buckles on the wind
To sow the grain of Guinea in the mouths of the dead,
Who, hurling their bone-needled nets over the cave mouth,
Harvest ancestral voices from its surf ...
Whose sweat, touching earth, multiplies in crystals of sugar.[74]

Derek Walcott in both his poetry and drama juxtaposes the textual richness of language/race/geography with the discriminating oppositions of black/white. His play *Dream on Monkey Mountain* (1970) opens with 'the white disc of an African drum', and a dancer shadowed by a crouched figure, whose face is symbolically 'halved by white make-up'.[75] An almost naturalistic scene then follows introducing the audience to the figure of Makak, a black charcoal-burner, jailed for being drunk and disorderly – a man who has visions. Quickly, however, the play-journey shifts into dream sequences to fragment 'normality', to break with images of heroic pilgrimages, in order to restate the inner quest for human worth in a culture subjugated by imperial claims. The odyssey back to Africa posited by Makak and imagined by his followers in the play, coupled with the problematic decapitation of the White Goddess[76] – an enabling and disabling emblematic figure who both inspires and enslaves Makak – violently disrupts the language and symbols of colonialism so that both colonised and coloniser may rediscover a lost compassion.

Walcott's repeated allusions to biblical and Shakespearean narratives in *Dream on Monkey Mountain* and playful acknowledgement of Homer revealed as a contemporary Caribbean figure in his long poem *Omeros* (1990) through the travels of Achille, Hector, Helen and Philoctete, exemplify the intertextual nature of much of postcolonial writing, in particular its involvement with the discourses of earlier stories from classical Europe, rewritten and absorbed into new contemporary complexities of alienation. Fiercely atavistic symbols of natural survival

> There's a race of beetles whose
> nature is to bleed
> the very source
> that nourishes them, till the host
> is a rattling carapace[77]

mark a yearning of the exile for home

> when he'd weep in the window for their tribal shame.
> A shame for the loss of words, and a language tired
> of accepting that loss, and then all accepted.[78]

Omeros as a text rewrites the history of Achilles signified by his death and crystallisation in seas that bore and continue to bear invaders to the shores of the poem/island. Walcott's metaphors mimic the absolutes of the invasive language of colonialism to parody, defy and deconstruct absolutes of heroism:

> He wept again, though why, he was unsure,
> At dazzling visions of reflected tin.
> So Heaven is revealed to fevered eyes,
> So is sin born, and innocence made wise,
> By intimations of hot galvanize.[79]

VI

This is not to say that postcolonial literatures do not have problems of their own. Whereas postcolonial writers have seen their principal targets as being paternalistic colonial discourses and have created dialogic narratives to subvert monologic imperialism, there has been a tendency among male writers to ignore the continued enslavement of women within indigenous, essentially patriarchal cultures, as Ngugi's fiction demonstrates. The essays in this volume by Boehmer (7), Mann (8) and Savory (13)[80] contribute to important debates about the reductive portrayal of women in male postcolonial literatures. It is possible to see in Achebe's Beatrice in *Anthills of the Savannah* a significant departure in her naming the girl-child of Elewa and Ikem 'Amaechina' (*May-the-path-never-close*), 'a boy's name' which '*Girl fit answer am also*'[81] in spite of tribal custom's deference to the father's choice. Judie Newman's essay (10) forcefully opens the texts of Anita Desai's Indian women to a discourse which has parallels with the writings of Toni Morrison, Maya Angelou, Buchi Emecheta and others. Elaine Savory's essay on Walcott defines male attitudes to women which have parallels in 'Je n'aime pas Afrique' by the Guadeloupian poet Paul Niger:

> Moi, j'aime ce pays, disait-il, on y trouve,
> nourriture, obéissance, poulets à quatre sous, femmes à cent ...
>
> (As for me, I just love this land, he said, you can find there
> food, deference, chickens for four sous, women a franc ...[82]

Many of Walcott's poems do appear to recycle archetypal, male-constructed images of women, and indeed not only fail to give women a voice, but at times fail to recognise women as human. In his *Another Life* (1973), for example, the narrator recalls his adolescent lust for the painted

> shepherdesses of Boucher and Fragonard
> and I raved for the split of their arses,
> their milk-jug bubs[83]

but his 'adult' poetry too often retains similarly reductive, reifying attitudes to his female characters, fixing them, while feeding off them. In the satirical poem, 'New World', Eve is excluded altogether; a carve up occurs between Adam and the snake.[84] Not surprisingly, given its title, 'A Lesson for This Sunday' focuses upon Sin, and is also set in a Caribbean Paradise. The narrator idly swinging in his hammock becomes aware of two children experimenting scientifically with yellow-wing butterflies. Cruelty is not just a feature of colonist–colonised relations, the text recognises, but a fact of the human condition, of the 'Heredity of cruelty everywhere.' In the poem, however, it is the girl-child's cruelty that is singled out, as if it were somehow greater. 'The girl, in lemon frock', 'herself a thing of summery light / Frail as a flower in this blue August air', is fixed both as predator (compared to a mantis) and victim of Time ('and everywhere the frocks of summer torn'), as evanescent as the butterfly she destroys.[85]

Patriarchal attitudes are not just dealt out to the young. In 'A Letter from Brooklyn' an old friend of his dead father writes a kindly letter about him, and though she is given a voice in writing, each of her lines is subjected to a patronising commentary:

> 'I am Mable Rawlins,' she writes, 'and know both your parents';
> He is dead, Miss Rawlins, but God bless your tense;
> 'Your father was a dutiful, honest,
> Faithful, and useful person.'
> For such plain praise what fame is recompense.[86]

She is reduced to a 'veined hand', and a face he cannot remember; her 'spidery style' inscribes a text he has difficulty reading. She becomes translated in the second half of the poem into a Muse figure/an ageing humble Penelope, one 'who spins the blessings of her years / Not withered of beauty if she can bring such tears.' Yet another translation can be seen in 'Nights in the Gardens of Port of Spain' where night is feminised, 'burning to be the bitch she will become', associated with 'secret and sweat' and an 'impenetrable musk'.[87] Although clearly the 'impenetrable' has sexual connotations – it is a typical example of what Dale Spender calls 'man-made' language – at the same time perhaps it gives a clue as to Walcott's difficulties in his representation and understanding of women, as texts which cannot be read.

VII

The informing principle throughout this collection, therefore, is that postcolonial literatures are interpretative discourses, reshaping the languages whence they arise, disclosing to former colonising cultures redefinitions of centralising literary, cultural and political histories. The 'outsider' inside the text; the 'dispossessed' in possession of language; the 'alienated' decentering discourses of power; the 'disempowered' recentered in their own empowering texts. Through defamiliarisation these literatures marginalise the closed interpretative frames of European histories of the 'other'. Walcott's reworking of Homer, Achebe's resiting of Conrad, Desai's interpolation of T. S. Eliot re-place dominant European narratives which have spoken to each other for centuries. The postcolonial enterprise is concerned with the 'forging of a language that [goes] beyond mimicry, a dialect which ha[s] the force of revelation as it invent[s] names for things … which finally [settle] on its own mode of inflection.'[88] Whereas limiting European stereotypes of oppositional writings speak of 'minority discourses' (even women's writing is so described), in erstwhile colonised worlds a vast body of postcolonial literatures gives voice to 'minorities', who are in fact majorities. The 'marginalised', who have their own discursive centres, are creating new pluralities for aesthetics and politics.

Postcolonial narratives have made keener the insights of twentieth-century studies of defamiliarisation, fantasy, dream and myth. Strategies so often naturalised into a new canon by western critics as 'modernist', 'deconstructionist', 'absurdist' – and thereby tolerantly absorbed as 'acceptable' within a western 'pluralism' – have become essential tools reflecting actual displacement in postcolonial politics. In a world absurdly governed – as much in postcolonial cultures as in the West – estranging strategies may be the only serious form of response. This is the literature of the dispossessed repossessing fragmented realities. That enshrining symbol of imperial values in the English nineteenth-century novel – the 'home' – is empty. In a radical deconstruction of western history and reconstruction of complex narratives, postcolonial literatures – along with the literatures of subjugated classes globally – sharpen a forceful paradox: that the fundamentally provincial nature of imperial acculturation has stimulated postcolonial writers to shape a richer plurality in their own histories, pointing to new and diversified syncretisms on the basis of a shared quest for meanings/roots which are ultimately elusive. We are all exiles in our languages, warned

> That in the future time each must learn to live
> Beadless in a foreign land; or perish.

Or each must learn to make new jouti,
Arrange them by instinct, imagination, study
And arbitrary choice into a pattern
Pleasing to the self and to others
Of the scattered tribe; or perish. Each
Will be barren of ancestral memory
But each endowed richly with such emptiness
From which to dream, surmise, invent, immortalise.[89]

NOTES

1. George Lamming, *In The Castle of My Skin* (first publ. 1953; Harlow, 1992), p. 289. Lamming was born in Barbados in 1927 and wrote this award-winning novel about growth and change in the colonial Caribbean soon after emigrating to Britain in 1950. His other major novels include *The Emigrants* (1954) and *Natives of My Person* (1972).

2. The mid-late 1960s saw the publication of a number of influential structuralist and poststructuralist theoretical texts, emanating from France, including Michel Foucault's *The Order of Things* (1966), Roland Barthes' *Criticism and Truth* (1966), 'Death of the Author' (1968) and *S/Z* (1970), and Jacques Derrida's *Of Grammatology* and *Writing and Difference* (both 1967).

3. Amongst the useful readers containing their work are *Modern Literary Theory*, ed. Philip Rice and Patricia Waugh (London, 1989), *Modern Criticism and Theory*, ed. David Lodge (London, 1988), and *A Critical and Cultural Reader*, ed. Antony Easthope and Kate McGowan (Buckingham, 1992). For useful introductions to each of these named theorists' work, see Terry Eagleton's *Literary Theory: An Introduction* (Oxford, 1983), Terence Hawkes's *Structuralism and Semiotics* (London, 1977), Catherine Belsey's *Critical Practice* (London, 1980) and Jonathan Culler *On Deconstruction* (London, 1982).

4. Edward W. Said, *Orientalism: Western Concepts of the Orient* (1978; rpt. Harmondsworth, 1991), p. 227.

5. Matthew Arnold, *Culture and Anarchy*, ed. J. Dover Wilson (1869; rpt. Cambridge, 1969), p. 70.

6. Derek Walcott, 'What the Twilight Says: An Overture', in *Dream on Monkey Mountain and Other Plays* (London, 1972), p. 12.

7. See Neil Kortenaar's essay , pp. 31–51 in this volume.

8. Edward W. Said, *Culture and Imperialism* (London,1993), p. xxi.

9. Chinweizu, Onwuchekwa Jemie and Ihechukwu Madubuike, *Toward the Decolonization of African Literature: African Fiction and Poetry and Their Critics* (1980; rpt. London, 1985), p. 4.

10. Ngugi wa Thiong'o, *Decolonising the Mind* (Harare, Zimbabwe, 1987), p. xii.

11. Cheikh Anta Diop was born in Senegal in 1923, and is generally regarded as one of the important African scholars of this century. He worked for his PhD at the Sorbonne where his ideas, reassessing African civilisation, were viewed as too controversial to be acceptable. His later years saw him at the forefront of Moslem scholarship in Senegal, and in the 1970s he was influential in forming a nucleus of black writers in the United States. He died in 1986.

12. Chinweizu, Jemie and Madubuike, *Decolonization of African Literature*, p. 26.

13. Cheikh Anta Diop, *The African Origin of Civilization: Myth or Reality* (Westfort, USA, 1974; first publ. as *Nations negres et culture* by *Présence Africaine*, 1955). 'Négritude,' said Diop, 'was originally a West Indian creation' intended to mobilise black activists against colonialism in every sphere of life. Diop attributed it to the Martinique writer Aimé Césaire, acknowledging Sartre's popularisation of the term in his *Black Orpheus* (cf. 'Conversations with Cheikh Anta Diop', pp. 403–8; details below in note 14).

14. Carlos Moore, 'Conversations with Cheikh Anta Diop', *Présence Africaine*, no. 149–150 (1 & 2 Quarterlies, 1989), 407.

15. Frantz Fanon, *The Wretched of the Earth*, with Preface by Jean-Paul Sartre, trans. Constance Farrington (Harmondsworth, 1990); first publ. as *Les Damnés de la Terre* (1961), p. 44.

16. Frantz Fanon, *Toward the African Revolution* trans. from French by Haakon Chevalier (London, 1967 first publ. as *Pour la Révolution Africaine* (François Maspero, 1964), p. 44.

17. V. S. Naipaul, *A Bend in the River* (1979; rpt. Harmondsworth, 1980), pp. 69–70, 86–9.

18. Interestingly the name given to the mission to send British soldiers to help in the relief effort to Rwanda in August 1994 was 'Gabriel', a reference which places the Europeans on the side of the 'angels'. Rarely is sufficient attention given by the European or American media to the developed West's economic role in the impoverishment of Africa during and after the colonial era.

19. See Neil Kortenaar's essay in this volume, p. 32. For the problematic portrayal of women by male postcolonial writers see below pp. 21–2.

20. Jean Paul Sartre, Preface to *The Wretched of the Earth*, p. 17. The same passage is quoted as an epigraph in Derek Walcott's *Dream on Monkey Mountain and Other Plays*, p. 277.

21. Tsitsi Dangarembga, *Nervous Conditions* (London, 1988), p. 194.

22. Ibid., pp. 106, 155, 160.

23. Ibid., p. 131.

24. Sartre, Preface to *The Wretched of the Earth*, p. 22.

25. Wole Soyinka, *Art, Dialogue & Outrage: Essays on Literature and Culture* (Ibadan, 1988), p. 19.

26. Ibid., p. 220.

27. See pp. 101–26 in this volume.

28. *Langue* is Ferdinand de Saussure's term for a potentially limitless language-system constantly adapting to new cultural forces: cf. his *Course in General Linguistics* (London, 1978), passim.

29. Soyinka, *Art, Dialogue & Outrage*, p. 108.

30. Jacques Derrida, *Of Grammatology*, trans. by Gayatri Chakravorty Spivak (Baltimore, MD, 1976; first publ. as *De la Grammatologie*, Les Editions de Minuit, 1967), p. 302.

31. Ngugi wa Thiong'o, 'Moving the Centre: Towards a Pluralism of Cultures', *Journal of Commonwealth Literature*, 26:1 (1991), 200.

32. Simon Gikandi, 'Chinua Achebe and the Post-colonial Esthetic: Writing, Identity, and National Formation', *Studies in Twentieth Century Literature*, 5:1 (Winter 1992), 30–1.

33. Said, *Orientalism*, p. 228.

34. Achebe, *Anthills of the Savannah*, p. 153.

35. Ibid., p. 154.

36. See Gayatri Chakravorty Spivak, 'Three Women's Texts and a Critique of Imperialism', *The Feminist Reader*, ed. Catherine Belsey and Jane Moore (London, 1989), pp. 175–83.

37. Said, *Culture and Imperialism*, pp. 24–9.

38. Chinua Achebe, 'Where Angels Fear to Tread', *Nigeria Magazine*, 75 (Lagos, 1962); repr. in Chinua Achebe, *Hopes and Impediments: Selected Essays 1965–87* (London, 1988), p. 49. Georg M. Gugelberger importantly analyses the signification 'Third World Literature' as a conveniently amorphous phrase with embedded, unstated power assumptions in 'Decolonizing the Canon: Considerations of Third World Literature', *New Literary History*, 22:3 (Summer 1991), 505–24.

39. Cited in Achebe, *Hopes and Impediments*, p. 56.

40. E. M. Forster, *A Passage to India* (1924: rpt. Harmondsworth, 1961), p. 145.

41. Said, *Orientalism*, p. 227.

42. Sakia Pathak, Saswati Sengupta and Sharmila Purkayastha, 'The Prisonhouse of Orientalism', *Textual Practice* (1991), 5:2, pp. 195ff, esp. p. 214.

43. Salman Rushdie, *Midnight's Children* (1981; rpt. London, 1982), pp. 236–7.

44. Gayatri Chakravorty Spivak (ed. Sarah Harasym), *The Post-Colonial Critic: Interviews, Strategies, Dialogues* (London and New York, 1990), p. 81.

45. Even in an English novelist like Forster his problematic characterisation of Aziz in *A Passage to India* reveals another voice beyond the texts of English legality, another man not tied to a subjugated observed role, but attempting to adopt his own subject-position. Aziz is invariably comic or inefficient, as in his attempts to organise the visit to the Marabar caves, which admittedly reduces the English to farce as well – see *A Passage to India*, pp. 316–17, for an example of one of the points at which Aziz rejects the English surfaces. Salman Rushdie's *Midnight's Children* is relevant here: the narrator recalls schoolday 'mimicry of European literature. ... Perhaps it would be fair to say that Europe repeats itself, in India, as farce' (p. 185).

46. *Logocentrism* is Derrida's term for a (western) desire to fix an ultimate meaning to existence. *Metonym* indicates a relatively close association between one word and another: stereotypes and generalisations are examples.

47. Desai, *Clear Light of Day* (Harmondsworth, 1980), pp. 152–3. Compare the description of the silence following Kurt's murder of Baumgartner broken suddenly by '[t]he cats ... leaping like black flares around his feet, yowling maniacally. Jumping over them, he turned to the shelf, sweeping off all the tarnished silver trophies with ringing sounds of metal on metal, clanging and clanking, one against the other' (*Baumgartner's Bombay*, p. 219).

48. Both *Baumgartner's Bombay* and *Clear Light of Day* are introduced with epigraphs from T. S. Eliot's *Four Quartets*.

49. Anita Desai, *Where Shall We Go This Summer?* (1975; rpt. 1982, New Delhi, Bombay), p. 78.

50. Baba in *Clear Light of Day* longs for the illusory freedom from his home since childhood in lyrics from the west: 'Then [he], shaded and sequestered in his own room, played "Don't Fence Me In" once too

often. It was what Bim needed to break her in two, decapitated with anger. Clutching at her throat, she strode into his room and jerked the needle-head off the record and twisted back the arm' (p. 163).

51. Desai, *Clear Light of Day*, p. 47.

52. Deven longs for the beauty, the aristocratic power he sees embodied in the Urdu verse of Nur, as an escape from what he sees as his tawdry, banal existence as a teacher of Hindu and as a husband with an unhappy wife.

53. Spivak, *The Post-Colonial Critic*, p. 39.

54. A similar critique can be found in Salman Rushdie's work. For the reference to 'dream-web' see *Midnight's Children*: 'Do Hindus not accept – Padma – that the world is a kind of dream; that Brahma dreamed, is dreaming the universe; that we only see dimly through that dream-web, which is Maya' (p. 211).

55. See pp. 195–208 below.

56. Desai, *Baumgartner's Bombay*, p.180.

57. Ibid., p. 173.

58. Ibid., p. 89.

59. Ibid., p. 118.

60. Seamus Deane, 'Unhappy and at Home', an interview with Seamus Heaney, *The Crane Bag*, 1:1 (Dublin, 1977), 67.

61. Desai, *Baumgartner's Bombay*, p. 4.

62. Ibid., p. 190. 'Indigestible, inedible Baumgartner. The gods had spat him out. *Raus*, Baumgartner, out.'

63. Ibid., p. 230.

64. Ibid., p. 117.

65. Homi K. Bhabha, *Nation and Narration* (London, 1990), pp. 297ff.

66. Included in John J. Figueroa, *An Anthology of African and Caribbean Writing in English* (London, 1988), p. 248.

67. Shakespeare, *The Tempest*, ed. Robert Langbaum (New York, 1964), p. xxiii.

68. Daniel Defoe, *Robinson Crusoe* (1719: rpt. Harmondsworth 1994), pp. 202–9.

69. Derek Walcott, *Collected Poems 1948–1984* (London, 1992), p. 301.

70. Ibid., p. 383.

71. Ibid., p. 12.

72. Ibid., p. 14.

73. Ibid., p. 360.

74. Ibid., pp. 15–16.

75. Walcott, *Dream on Monkey Mountain and Other Plays*, p. 212.

76. In the above, Makak's attempted exorcism of the colonial presence figured in the beheading of the 'White Goddess' prompts the Corporal to assert that the white woman is:

> but an image of your longing, as inaccessible as snow, as fatal as leprosy, Nun, virgin, Venus, you must violate, humiliate, destroy her. ... She is all that is pure, all that he cannot reach She is the white light that paralysed your mind, that led you into this confusion (pp. 318–19).

77. Derek Walcott, *Omeros* (London, 1990), p. 240.

78. Ibid., p. 248.

79. Walcott, *Collected Poems 1948–84*, p. 36.

80. See the essays in this volume, pp. 143–53, 155–75, 245–57.

81. Achebe, *Anthills of the Savannah*, p. 222.

82. Quoted in M. T. Bindella and G. U. David, *Imagination and the Creative Impulse in the New Literatures in English*, Cross/Cultures 9 (Amsterdam, 1993), p. 83.

83. Walcott, *Collected Poems 1948–84*, p. 202.

84. Ibid., pp. 300–1.

85. Ibid., pp. 38–9.

86. Ibid., pp. 41–2.

87. Ibid., p. 67.

88. That image of 'forging' inevitably invites comparisons with Joyce, an entirely appropriate role model for Walcott and many other postcolonial writers. (Indeed in *Omeros*, Walcott actually names him as 'our age's Omeros'.) One recalls Stephen Daedalus's announced mission at the end of *Portrait of the Artist as a Young Man* 'to forge in the smithy of my soul the uncreated consciousness of my race' (London, 1977, p. 228). The voice of Joyce surfaces again in *Another Life*, when the narrator remembers a

> ... plaster-of-Paris Venus
> which his yearning had made marble, half-cracked
> unsilvering mirror of black servants. (*Collected Poems*, p. 147)

an image which brings to mind Stephen's telling comparison of Irish art – and by extension perhaps the art of many other colonial and postcolonial cultures – with 'the cracked lookingglass of a servant' (*Ulysses*, Harmondsworth, 1986, p. 6).

89. David Dabydeen, *Turner: New & Selected Poems* (London, 1994), pp. 33–4.

1

How the Centre is Made to Hold in *Things Fall Apart*

NEIL TEN KORTENAAR

A whole volume has been written by Emmanuel Meziemadu Okoye[1] on the encounter between traditional Igbo religion and Christianity in the novels of Chinua Achebe, a volume which concludes that Achebe has done his research and that his depiction of the colonization of Igboland is historically accurate. Fiction, of course, cannot be judged by its verifiability; it expresses not what happened but what might have happened. Precisely because it must be plausible, however, fiction has to meet standards of correspondence and be adequate as an image of the human experience of the world.[2] Okoye's desire to establish the accuracy of Achebe's fiction is not misplaced. However, if we consider the novels as historiography and judge how faithful they are to the past, it is not just the details of culture and of incident that must be considered. The writing of history has two components: it depends on verifiable facts and it arranges those facts in a narrative. How does Achebe establish his narrative authority when writing about a period more than fifty years in the past, and more particularly about a worldview that has lost its original integrity?

Things Fall Apart ends with the decision taken by a historian to recount the process whereby a whole world was overturned. The narrative this historian will write is not, however, the one the reader has just finished reading, but a less objective and necessarily less accurate narrative. In the final pages the new District Commissioner walks away from the site of Okonkwo's suicide and

31

wonders whether to make Okonkwo's death a chapter or a paragraph in his projected book, *The Pacification of the Primitive Tribes of the Lower Niger*. This appeal to an obviously false authority deploys irony to establish Achebe's own credentials as a historian of Igboland.[3] We do not ask why we should trust the narrative we have just read: the District Commissioner's projected history and by implication other texts on Africa stand condemned as manifestly untrustworthy, and that is enough. We deconstruct what is told us of the District Commissioner and reconstruct a higher level where we join the author in seeing around the Europeans. But where exactly is this higher level?

In *Things Fall Apart* the District Commissioner's false narrative assumes the otherness of the Africans. Humanity is not one. What the District Commissioner finds of interest in Okonkwo's suicide is its mystery: its impenetrability as an example of the foreignness, the difference of supposed primitives. By fitting Okonkwo into a comprehensible narrative, the Commissioner establishes both Okonkwo's essential otherness and his own heroic character – his narrative says in effect, 'I have travelled through Africa and seen such things for myself' – thus eliminating the threat of that difference. To underline the falsity of this version of events Achebe must reestablish the humanity of his Africans, must insist that Africans live in the same world and are not absolutely other.

The effect of Achebe's plain style – in spite of what Weinstock and Ramadan argue,[4] it is singularly stripped of symbol – is to stress the everyday ordinariness of Igbo life. This world is comprehensible. The transition in the book from pre-colonization Africa to an Africa that has felt the European presence is, in terms of style, unremarkable. Indeed, because the transition is so fluid, Achebe has to draw our attention to it by means of divisions: the encroachment of the European missionaries takes place while Okonkwo is in exile, during the division identified as Part Two.

C. L. Innes has pointed out how in *Things Fall Apart* when Mr Brown the missionary and Akunna, one of the great men of the village of Umuofia, discuss God, they misunderstand each other.[5] But more remarkable is how they can discuss and learn from each other at all, as clearly they do: their mutual tolerance and their open-mindedness are applauded by the author and contrasted with the fanaticism of Mr Smith and of Okonkwo. The report of the discussion between Mr Brown and Akunna sounds like the published proceedings of a modern conference on inter-faith dialogue, full of a confidence that beneath the differences of language and ritual there is a common quest for God and a common view of human nature. There can only be discussion where there is an agreement more fundamental than the subjects of dissension. Argument is only possible where there are common terms. Mr Brown does not speak of Christ; Akunna does not speak of Ani the goddess of the land. Instead they speak in much more general terms of God and sound like nothing so much as eighteenth-century deists.

Achebe goes further in making African and European the same in a later novel, *Arrow of God*, which is generally considered a more complex, satisfying novel, with richer characterization and greater unity of plot than *Things Fall Apart*, but which is for that very reason less interesting. In that novel the narrative moves freely and alternately into the minds of both Igbos and Englishmen. Their thoughts, their desires, and their strategies are remarkably similar. The ease with which the narrative moves between the two communities is matched by the ease with which characters travel from one world to another. They misunderstand each other to be sure, but Europe and Africa are contiguous in time and space. By implication the story of each fits metonymically into a larger narrative, the history of modern Africa generally. Rather than a conflict between two worlds, we have a conflict between individuals who are very similar but who cannot see into each other's hearts. The unforeseen results of this mutual blindness recall similar tragedies in novels by Hardy.

The problem with seeing two cultures as occupying the same world is that they can then be measured against each other and one preferred to another as a reflection of that world. To measure them is to assume a scientific objectivity that allows the observer to stand outside both. But in this case scientific objectivity is a mode of knowledge associated with one of the cultures to be measured. Achebe cannot appeal to the scientific model of knowledge and still be fair to the Igbos about whom he is writing. What Timothy Reiss calls the analytical-referential model of knowledge, the way of knowing asssociated with science and modern historiography, sees language as a tool that, placed between the observer and the world observed, allows the observer to know the world as it truly is and to manipulate it.[6] It is inseparable from Europe's claim to know fully the world and other societies, in a way that other societies with other modes of knowing are never allowed to know Europe.

Achebe believes, with Reiss, Foucault, and Lévi-Strauss, that the West's knowledge of the world is as culture-based and time-bound as any other mode of knowledge. The title *Things Fall Apart* refers to the Yeatsian prophecy of the decline and fall of the current incarnation of the West. In using it to speak of the collapse of the Igbo world, Achebe plays with cultural equivalence. One mode of knowledge is forced to give way before another, but not because the other has a stronger claim to be able to know the world. Both are time-bound, culture-bound; either may fall apart. At one moment of history the Igbo world-view gave way before the Western analytical-referential model. The triumph of one world-view does not imply its greater fitness in an evolutionary sense; given different circumstances, the encounter could have had other results. In Nadine Gordimer's *July's People,* for instance, it is the self-assured, bourgeois world of white South Africa that is falling apart, giving way before an African world it cannot comprehend.[7]

To emphasize the exclusivity of the two worlds, Achebe often leaves Igbo words untranslated. These foreign traces in an English text refer metonymically to a whole world that cannot be adequately translated, a world that Achebe implicitly shares with the characters he writes about. The non-Igbo reader, by implication, can only achieve a mediated knowledge of that world. There is no model that will contain both worlds.

However, there is in this glorious relativity an *aporia* that Foucault, Lévi-Strauss, and Reiss only overcome by openly admitting. The analytical-referential model continues at the present moment as the dominant mode of knowledge: it includes us and we are unable to see around it. It is incontrovertible because we look at it only through the lenses that it provides. Achebe is writing of a moment of epistemic rupture, when one mode of knowledge gives way before another. But how can he do justice to both? Reiss believes that we cannot understand Greek tragedy, for instance, because the Greek epistemic mode within which the tragedies were written is not ours. How then can the Igbo world be made intelligible once it has bowed before another *episteme*?

The difficulty is signalled in chapter 9 of *Things Fall Apart,* which describes how a year before the present of the novel a medicine-man exorcised Ezinma, Okonkwo's daughter. Ezinma was an *ogbanje,* a malicious spirit that had been born many times to the same earthly mother, only to die and return to the world of the unborn each time the mother came to love it. Ezinma was ordered to reveal where her *iyi-uwa* was buried, the stone representing her link to the world of the unborn. This she did and the medicine-man dug it up: Ezinma would now stay in the land of the living. Achebe's narration recounts what happened without comment or irony: the reader must suspend disbelief and enter into the Igbo world-view. So too, later in the book, a militant Christian who dared to kill a sacred python falls ill and dies. The traditionalists accept that the gods were protecting their own, let the reader think what he likes. However, although there is no rhetorical irony in the presentation of the *ogbanje* scene, there is an irony implicit nonetheless.

In the present of the novel, a year after the exorcism, Ezinma's mother wakes Okonkwo to tell him his daughter is suffering from *iba*. The glossary at the end of the book tells the non-Igbo reader that *iba* is fever. The word is presumably not translated because 'fever' in English has the wrong connotations: it would be thought of as something to be diagnosed, then treated with medicine. Okonkwo's people see in *iba* a manifestation of spiritual disorder: the mischief of an *ogbanje* or the perversity of one's *chi*. Ekwefi, Ezinma's mother, is terrified.

The chapter opens with the buzzing of a mosquito in the ear of Okonkwo, who recalls a story his mother told him about why Mosquito buzzes near Ear, who had once refused to marry him. The inclusion of this story can be ascribed to the encyclopedic thrust of the narrative: in *Things Fall Apart* details are relevant not because they further the plot or reveal character but because they contribute to the display of Igbo culture. However, the irrelevant on one plane may assume significance on another. Mosquitoes have a meaning for both Achebe and the reader that they do not have for Okonkwo. The chapter, by making mosquitoes and *iba* contiguous, even if not explicitly linking them as cause to effect, acknowledges a connection where the characters themselves do not see one. Achebe and his reader both know Ezinma's fever would be diagnosed as malaria by a doctor, and the recurring deaths of an *ogbanje* considered a superstitious explanation of a high infant mortality rate more appropriately responded to by modern medicine.

We cannot say Achebe is exchanging ironic glances with his reader over the heads of his characters. The reader, if at all involved in Okonkwo's world, is likely to miss the reference to malaria. Yet I believe my reader will agree that the mosquitoes are significant and point to a foreign *episteme* that is otherwise absent. In Wayne

Booth's terms the irony is covert, but stable and finite.[8] If reconstructed it constitutes an invitation to the reader to join the author
at a level of understanding higher than that of the literal account.
When later in the novel the killer of the python is himself killed the
reader suspends disbelief: we are given only the Umuofia point of
view, and though another explanation is conceivable, it is not suggested. But in the exorcism of the *ogbanje* a second, irreconcilable
way of looking at things is offered and we are reminded that no
reader of the novel, and Achebe himself, believes entirely in the
existence of *ogbanjes*. Achebe shows us Okagbue the medicine-man
actually finding Ezinma's *iyi-uwa*, yet is careful to indicate that
Okagbue is digging in the pit alone when he announces his find: the
reader may think what he will.

The exorcism of the *ogbanje* is recalled in an explanatory retrospective; it is thus twice distant in time from the reader – it occurs
before the present of the novel, which is already set in the past. In
another novel such distancing might make it easier to accept the
inexplicable and the uncanny without question. In the homeostatic
world of Umuofia, however, where nothing seems ever to change,
the distance is removed. The exorcism appears related synchroni-
cally to the events of the present of the novel: specifically to the
execution of Ikemefuna, Okonkwo's adopted son. When Okonkwo
is woken up to respond to Ezinma's *iba* it is the first time he has
been able to fall asleep since his participation in Ikemefuna's death
three nights before. It is not an *ogbanje* but guilt that haunts him.

There is, moreover, present in the account of Ezinma's exorcism
a potential figure of doubt: Nwoye, Okonkwo's son. The reader has
already seen Nwoye ill at ease with traditional metaphysics. When
his friend was executed to fulfil the ordinance of the oracle, Nwoye
felt something give way inside him 'like the snapping of a tightened
bow': he had experienced a similar chill when he heard the crying
of infant twins abandoned in the evil forest. That was in chapter 7.
In chapter 9 we are told that one year earlier, at the time of the
digging up of Ezinma's *iyi-uwa*, Nwoye 'stood near the pit because
he wanted to take in all that happened'.[9] Did he see Okagbue find
the stone that had always been there or did he see him plant a
stone? This is not an idle question. If Nwoye saw the stone found,
then he would have had to deny much that he once knew when
later he joined the Christians, who dismissed Igbo religion as so
much supersition. If he saw the stone planted, then his crisis in faith

over the death of Ikemefuna can be seen to have had its seeds in an earlier time.

In another chapter Achebe shows us the *egwugwu* judging a marital dispute: the glossary at the back defines these, with thorough-going unbelief, as masqueraders impersonating ancestral spirits. We are told that the women of Umuofia never asked questions about the *egwugwu* cult. They 'might have noticed that the second *egwugwu* had the springly walk of Okonkwo', and they might have noticed 'that Okonkwo was not among the titled men and elders' (pp. 63–4), but if they did, they kept these thoughts to themselves. Perhaps it was never possible that any reader of the novel should believe that the *egwugwu* were ancestral spirits returned to earth, but it is clear that the narrative itself does not believe. The reference to a possible doubt among the women spectators advertises the distance of the narration from faith in the world it describes.

Abdul JanMohamed explains the ambivalence in this scene by invoking a 'double-consciousness'. Achebe's characters, says JanMohamed, like all people in an oral society, make no distinction between the worlds of the secular and the sacred. However, this lack of discrimination would make the Umuofians appear 'foolish' to modern readers, so Achebe makes his characters aware of the border between secular and sacred, but quick to repress what they know.[10] JanMohamed's implication is that modern Western-educated readers know more than did the traditional Umuofians, and so can judge the Umuofians as 'foolish' or at least ignorant. JanMohamed is right about the 'double-consciousness' in *Things Fall Apart*, but it is not limited to the characters; a double-consciousness characterizes the narrative as a whole. As we saw in the *ogbanje* episode, two world-views are present even when the characters are not aware of them. It is in the reader, rather than in the characters, that a double-consciousness is created.

This 'double-consciousness' is perhaps inevitable when writing about a society that did not itself know writing, or when using English to describe an Igbo-speaking world. Achebe's solution, as Abdul JanMohamed has detailed, was to forge a written style that as much as possible echoed oral story-telling. The abundance of proverbs and the absence of original imagery are only the most obvious features. More significant is the flatness of the style: it is repetitive and additive, and it refuses to subordinate or privilege narrative elements. Everything is thus made equal and there is a seeming lack of direction. The flatness of character also echoes oral narration: Okonkwo's psychology goes largely unexamined and he is a type, both larger and flatter than life. Only thus, by telling Okonkwo's story as the kind of story Okonkwo himself knew, can Achebe be fair to an oral culture. To bring to bear on Umuofia the novelistic techniques of bourgeois Europe, designed to explore the interior individual, would be unjust, because they would suggest that writer and readers know more about Umuofians than the Umuofians know about themselves.

JanMohamed describes the syncretism that results from writing about an oral culture that did not know writing, but the asymmetry involved in writing the history of a society that did not conceive of itself historically has not been sufficiently explored. An example of this asymmetry is the following passage, in which Elizabeth Isichei in her *History of the Igbo People* explains the powers ascribed to the *dibia*, the Igbo priest:

> I think that it is possible that Igboland's *dibia* were developing real skills – or sciences – in the sphere of what we would now call extra-sensory perception. The imposition of colonial rule has basically put an end to these skills, and deflected Igbo intellectual energies into such 'modern' spheres as medicine or physics. It is possible that in doing so it cut off a real and original advance of the human mind, and impoverished the total development of human knowledge.[11]

Isichei is writing a history of the Igbo people in order to prove that they have a history. Igbo knowledge must therefore qualify as real knowledge by European definitions, meaning it must be a science, verifiable and replicable. Igbo science was advancing because, Isichei affirms, the human mind does not stand still but is engaged in a progressive evolution. In other words, a history could be written of Igbo experiments in extra-sensory perception if the records existed. However, in portraying the *dibia* as scientists Isichei is ignoring what the Igbos saw as true about themselves. She denies the reality of the Igbo gods and implies that while the *dibia* thought they were praying they were actually doing something else that only we moderns can appreciate.

The narrative voice in *Things Fall Apart*, too, occasionally lapses into the knowing tone of an anthropologist; for instance, he will explain, 'Darkness held a vague terror for these people, even the bravest among them' (p. 7). The narrator and his modern audience, presumed to be unafraid of darkness, believe they can know 'these people' more fully than these people know themselves.

Chinweizu, Jemie, and Madubuike argue that since most Africans believe in spirits and the efficacy of magic, one should expect to find magic in the African novel.[12] They further argue that there is no shame in believing in magic: Westerners are just as fervent in their belief in favourable and unfavourable omens. The Nigerian critics may be right about Westerners, but by their reasoning one would expect to find magic occupying a large role in the Western tradition of the novel. One does not, and the reason is that the realistic novel as established in the nineteenth century appeals for its authority to history writing, and modern historiography is based on the analytical-referential model of knowing. In novels we are invited to judge characters who believe in omens or in magic as superstitious.

Of course, Africans need not write realistic novels in the Western tradition. The metamorphoses in Amos Tutuola's novels belong to another world-view altogether, one that eschews cause and effect and inner and outer as explanations of events. Achebe's problem is that he wants to show that Africa has a history, as Europe has a history, and so he does not want to insist on the difference of Umuofia. Instead he invokes a double-consciousness.

In the *ogbanje* episode that we looked at, the analytical-referential model underlies the traditional Igbo model. But the one is not allowed to contain the other. Achebe wants his readers both to remember what we know and to forget what we know, or rather he wants his readers to suspend disbelief, not as in a fantasy that is without implications for our life in the world, but to suspend disbelief and yet continue to judge.

How we are to suspend disbelief even as we judge can be seen in a short story entitled 'The Madman',[13] in which Achebe presents a series of disputes demanding adjudication. Where one can stand outside and survey the two sides of a dispute, judgment is easy. Nwibe, an upright citizen, puts an end to the quarrel between his two wives by labelling one mad, the other one foolish for arguing with a mad woman, and bidding them both be silent. A quarrel between the local madman and the market women over the rightful possession of the market stalls where the madman sleeps is judged without difficulty by the reader: the madman is in the wrong because he is mad. However, when the madman steals Nwibe's cloth while the latter is bathing and the naked citizen chases the now clothed madman, the townspeople judge incorrectly. They assume Nwibe, who is naked, is the mad one. The family consult two medicine-men: one says Nwibe cannot be treated; the other, less famous and less strict, agrees to attempt a cure. Nwibe is cured and the townspeople praise the successful medicine-man.

Most readers will be confident they share Achebe's own judgment on the story: Nwibe was not truly insane and the medicine-man who cured him was a lucky confidence-man. The humour of the story lies in the fact that while we see that Nwibe is a victim of circumstances – he is a modern figure in an absurd universe – the townspeople do not believe in chance but believe everything has significance. The author invites his readers to see around the characters.

However, as soon as we have seen around the townspeople, the validity of our stance is called into question. How can we judge sanity or insanity across cultures? The townspeople assume Nwibe was insane when he ran into the sacred precincts of the market; we attribute the sacrilege to Nwibe's uncontrolled rage. But if he was not insane when he ran naked into the market, the townsfolk reason, the gods would certainly have taken away his wits as a punishment. Nwibe himself accepts that he was insane. And it is quite possible that Nwibe really was insane, whether driven to insanity by the gods or by the horror of what he had done. Who is to stand outside the difference of opinion between the reader and the characters and to judge?

The definition of madness is culture-specific. The townspeople see a naked man and assume he is mad, nakedness being part of the code for madness. Nakedness itself is defined by cultural context. In the market Nwibe's wife hurriedly removes her topcloth to cover her husband: behaviour that would be made in many a non-African context. One cannot stand outside and pontificate on differences between cultures; the best one can do is appreciate where the difference lies.

This double-consciousness, whereby we judge and suspend judgment at the same time, leads to a certain unease. One student of mine objected that she could not even be sure the original madman in the story was really mad. True he talked to the highway, but she could not be sure that kind of communication with the world outside himself did not indicate a poetic sensibility the Igbo townspeople lacked. How is one to judge? Her suggestion will be felt by most readers to be a misreading, but it is a useful one, because it challenges us to justify the judgments that we have been invited to make. Achebe intends for us to judge – or the story would lose its humour – but also to doubt our judgment.

This discussion of radical doubt sounds like many another contemporary critical celebration of a post-colonial text. Abdul JanMohamed praises Achebe's 'syncretism'; Homi Bhabha argues that the indeterminacy of the post-colonial text makes it more valuable than the European critical approaches that privilege representation.[14] My discussion, however, is intended to show that this quality of instability is as much a fault as it is a virtue, and that it is neither virtue nor fault, but a necessary condition of Achebe's text.

Paul Ricoeur argues that the proper way to consider the past is not as the same nor as different, but first as the same, then as different, and then in terms of an analogy parallel to the past: as a narrative.[15] *Things Fall Apart* is about epistemic rupture, but rupture threatens to make narrative, which implies continuity and development, impossible. Yet the novel insists that the Igbos have a story. This needs to be insisted on, for in the District Commissioner's eyes Okonkwo has no narrative of his own. The imperialists brought history to Africa, but, as Fanon observes of colonial settlers, it is not the history of the plundered country that they made, but the history of the mother country.[16] They could not make African history, because Africa was a blankness in the imagination, a land without narrative. George Allen, as the author of *The Pacification of the Primitive Tribes* is identified in *Arrow of God*, sees in Africa an invitation to make history extended to all 'who can deal with men as others deal with material'.[17] Narrative is thus a product of European agents acting on raw material extracted from Africa: a literary parallel to the processes of colonialism more generally.

Edward Said argues that if non-European peoples are to be written about with justice it must be in a narrative in which they are themselves the agents.[18] They would then be seen as the makers of their own world. JanMohamed, however, following Jack Goody and Walter Ong,[19] characterizes oral societies as homeostatic: that is, oral cultures without written records testifying to the past tend to ignore the ways in which the past was different from the present and conceive of the world as always the same. Of course, people who have not built empires and did not have written records have nevertheless a past that can be unearthed by archaeologists and ethnographers. But to tell their story as history is to describe them in a way they themselves would never have recognized.

The problem with writing Igbo history is not just that the records are missing. The records are missing because the Igbos did not have writing, and, if one follows Walter Ong, it is writing that produces the self-consciousness of historical agents. Hayden White, in agreement with Hegel, argues that some periods, however event-filled, lack objective history for the very reason that people in those periods lacked the self-consciousness to produce written history.[20] Ahistorical peoples may accomplish much, but no narrative can be written about the unself-conscious.

The District Commissioner, George Allen, was making history. He acted always with an idea as to how he would narrate the story of his actions afterwards. And the narrative of his own actions he fitted into the larger narrative of the British involvement in Africa. That in turn he saw as part of the narrative of British history, which was part of a yet larger narrative project, the unfolding of human potential. Allen has an eye on this larger narrative and the contribution he can make to it, which will be rewarded with a place when the history of the epoch comes to be written. Allen's own narrative, it is plain, is blind to others and self-deluding. Even a fellow British colonialist, twenty years later, when *Arrow of God* is set, will find Allen's narrative insufferably smug. Where Allen saw glory Achebe and we see sordid conquest and imperialist greed. But the point is that because Allen and his contemporaries emplotted their own lives as narratives, it is possible for the historian who follows to emplot those lives as narratives. Where the Europeans in Africa saw epic, the modern historian sees irony, but that the historian's configuration of events is possible at all is only because the British prefigured their own lives in a narrative.[21]

Is Okonkwo the hero of his own life, to use David Copperfield's words? Okonkwo does emplot his life according to a certain narrative pattern. He designs his life according to the upward curve of a romance: the hero of lowly origins overcomes great obstacles to prove his nobility. He rejects one kind of tale – the stories of animals, told by women – and delights in tales of tribal wars and military prowess (p. 38). His faith that this is the story he is intended to live out is the guiding principle of all his actions.

The notion of emplotting one's life as a narrative is expressed by the Igbos as wrestling with one's *chi*. The term *chi*, as Achebe points out in an article on the subject,[22] is rich in suggestive meaning. One definition seems to be that the *chi* is the writer of one's life story, and one must wrestle with one's *chi* to give the story the shape one wants. A strong man emplots his own life – when he says yes, his *chi* says yes also. Yet the narrative of one's life may not be the narrative originally emplotted – one cannot wrestle with one's *chi* and hope to win, as Okonkwo finds out. The upward curve that Okonkwo emplots takes a sharp downward turn and becomes the inverted U of tragedy. However, the reason Okonkwo has a story at all, even though not the story he intended, is because he self-consciously thinks of his life in terms of a story.

But is Okonkwo's emplotted story an example of historical narrative? Is it not more accurately an example of mythic thinking? Peter Munz distinguishes between cyclical myth, that is, myths of eternal return, and linear myth (or history), narrative that incorporates a sense of uni-directional time.[23] *Things Fall Apart* introduces Okonkwo by relating how he gained fame by wrestling Amalinze the Cat in one of the fiercest fights Umuofia had seen since 'the founder of their town engaged a spirit of the wild for seven days and seven nights' (p. 3). Okonkwo lives in the same world as the mythical or semi-mythical founder of Umuofia, in the same space as spirits of the wild.

According to Lévi-Strauss, past and present are joined in myth, 'because nothing has been going on since the appearance of the ancestors except events whose recurrence periodically effaces their particularity.'[24] Thus every wrestling match would be a ritual repetition of the original fight between man and nature, man and spirit. At the same time, in myth the past is disjoined from the present because the original ancestors were of a nature different from contemporary people: they were creators and their successors are imitators.[25] The ancestors set the rules that moderns must follow. In *Things Fall Apart* the ancestors return in the shape of egwugwu to render judgment in modern disputes.

Ricoeur lists three instruments of thought that allow the writing of history. They are the calendar, the succession of generations, and, above all, the survival of archives, documents, and traces of the past.[26] These make possible extrapolations from the individual's story to the story of the world, to history. At least two of these connectors are not present in the Umuofia consciousness.

References to time in *Things Fall Apart* are to seasons, to moons, to weeks, and to time that has passed since memorable events occurred. There is no calendar measuring an absolute scale, for such calendars are the product of literate societies. Instead, time is cyclical, observing the recurrence of the seasons and the market days. We can date *Things Fall Apart*, locate Okonkwo's story in relation to events happening elsewhere, because at the end of the book the Europeans appear. In the first two-thirds of the book we are shown a society such as we suppose might have existed at any time in the last three hundred years (they have guns, but have not met Europeans). At the end of the novel, however, when the missionaries arrive, there are references to the queen of the English. Since Victoria died in 1901, the narrative must be set in the late nineteenth century. There is a slight contradiction here. Okoye establishes that the events on which *Things Fall Apart* is based, specifically the killing of a solitary white man on a bicycle and the retribution exacted by British forces, occurred in 1905. That is the year of the large-scale British expedition to subdue Igboland. JanMohamed too assumes the novel is set in 1905. Of course, what Achebe has written is fiction and does not have to be faithful to the calendar in the same way as history has to be. But in not being faithful to dates he suggests his narrative has come loose from history, as in a way it has. The time frame by which these events can be dated and related to other events – the scramble for Africa, the Boxer Rebellion in China, the Boer War in South Africa, or the discovery in 1899 by Sir Ronald Ross that the malaria parasite is transmitted by anopheles mosquitoes – is unknown to Okonkwo.

In Ricoeur's opinion the dominant connector between the individual and history is the trace. The French means 'track' or 'spoor', as well [as] 'trace'; synonyms include 'vestige' and 'remains'. The trace is something that exists here and now and yet points to something that exists no longer.[27] There are traces in *Things Fall Apart* that indicate to the reader, but not the Umuofians, that change has occurred in Umuofia. Okonkwo's gun – he points it at one of his wives in a moment of anger – indicates that European encroachment has begun. Firearms were introduced into Igboland by way of the coastal trade with Europeans only in the seventeenth century; not until the nineteenth century did they become widespread.[28] Okonkwo takes snuff from a snuff bottle with a spoon, unaware that his ancestors did not always do so. The women in his community grow cassava and maize, products originally brought from the New World by the Portuguese.[29] These traces signal to the reader, but not to Okonkwo, that the approach of the Europeans is inevitable, has indeed already begun.

The Igbos might still have a history even if they are not aware of making history. Hayden White argues that once one people has entered history, has learned to see itself historically, then mankind as a whole has entered history; a historical consciousness implies a progressive integration of the world. It cannot be otherwise if we are one species. Those who do not enter history as makers enter as the victims of the makers.[30] Eric Wolf, in *Europe and the Peoples Without History*, has written of the integration of the world into a single history, not the history of progress postulated by Europe, but the history of makers and victims implied by the development of capitalism.[31]

One could read the first two thirds of *Things Fall Apart* as a synchronic presentation of a whole society. References to past and present events are commingled because there has been no change and thus there is no significance to time passing. The novel takes on a diachronic presentation only when the missionaries appear, bringing change and, just as importantly, the notion of change. Such a reading implies that the Umuofia community was an ahistorical organic whole disrupted and set upon the path of history by the brutal entry of the Europeans. According to this reading traditional Igbo society has an end, but no beginning or middle, and therefore cannot be fitted into a proper narrative. Indeed the end is better seen as the beginning, as the Igbos' entry into history.

This reading stresses that Umuofians are not proper individuals, not true narrative agents, but rather they fulfil defined roles in a community structure. James Olney finds in Okonkwo 'the generalized portrait of a man whose character is deliberately and significantly without individualizing traits'.[32] He concludes, 'Thus one must read Okonkwo's fate, he being representative and typical, as nothing less than the symbolic fate of the traditional Ibo society with the advent of the white man.'[33] Olney, eager to prove his thesis that African narrative stresses the type rather than the individual, summarizes Okonkwo as follows: 'We learn of Okonkwo, and this is really about all, that he is physically powerful, ambitious, generous and honest, proud, quick to anger, hard-working, a great wrestler.'[34]

Okonkwo is all those things and not much more than those things. Nor, as Olney points out, does Okonkwo change in the course of the narrative.[35] However, there is something that Olney leaves out because it does not fit his thesis, a detail that does not fit with Okonkwo's representative status and that makes him an individual in time, and this is his relationship with his father.

The succession of generations is the third of Ricoeur's connectors between the life of the indvidual and history. Okonkwo is not the quintessential African of Olney's and George Allen's imagination, fulfilling the role of dutiful son, honouring the ancestors and maintaining their common wisdom. It is true that Okonkwo identifies with the ancestors to the point of donning a masquerade costume and becoming one of the *egwugwu*. On the other hand, Okonkwo has made rejection of his father the principle of his life. He is a self-made man. Because Unoka, his father, was a failure, always in debt and without status, Okonkwo has had to forge his own career. Okonkwo, the mainstay of tradition, has inherited nothing, but has as it were engendered himself.

The contradiction is signalled in the text when Nwoye, Okonkwo's son, abandons the traditional ways and joins the Christians. Okonkwo is enraged: why, he cries in his heart, should he be cursed with such a son? (p. 108). If all male descendants were to follow Nwoye who would there be to offer sacrifices to the ancestors? 'He saw himself and his fathers crowding round their ancestral shrine waiting in vain for worship and sacrifice and finding nothing but ashes of bygone days, and his children the while praying to the whiteman's god' (p. 108). Okonkwo forgets that, even if Nwoye were to prove completely loyal, Okonkwo would never join his father round an ancestral shrine. Unoka died of a noxious swelling disease that made it impossible for him to receive the necessary burial. Instead he was put out in the Evil Forest to die. Unoka's spirit cannot join the ancestors and cannot be reborn; he is doomed to wander the world as a ghost. Okonkwo, upstanding titled man that he is, has an altar to the ancestors in his compound, but his father is not among the ancestors worshipped there. Okonkwo, who imagines himself and his father haunting the cold ashes of an abandoned altar, is not really as concerned with the fate of tradition as he is with the flouting of his own will; it is not the rights of ancestors that he cares about, but his own rights as a father to dictate to his son.

Okonkwo the wrestler patterns his life on the model of the founder – he proves his own greatness by re-enacting the achievements of the founder. We have here a notion of time that stresses repetition, the return of the same: wrestling is a ritual that repeats the founding of the village. But Okonkwo's motivation is not merely obedience to the universal law; it is the restoration of what has been lost and what in every generation has always been lost. He is himself a would-be founder. The established pattern has been flouted by Unoka and is only reasserted by Okonkwo. The narrative of his life both follows the model of the successful man laid down by tradition and establishes that model. It sets down the law: if Nwoye follows it, all shall be well; if he does not there will be trouble. To establish his own authority as lawmaker Okonkwo appeals to the divine origins of the law, declares he is merely following traditional custom. But in this case traditional custom is an assertion of Okonkwo's own will.

Okonkwo wants the narrative of his life to correspond to the truth of traditional wisdom and at the same time to guarantee that truth. But what his narrative shows is that the search for absolute and fixed truth is itself the product of Okonkwo's upbringing, and must be understood in its context. Okonkwo, who sets himself up as defender of community values, totalizes those values and in so doing betrays them. When Okonkwo's adopted son Ikemufuna is sentenced to death by the oracle, Okonkwo accompanies the executioners. He does this to prove his fidelity to the oracle. He sets divine authority above personal sentiment. But this is the loyalty of the doubter who must prove to himself his uncompromising faith. In participating in the execution Okonkwo flouts the advice of the elder Ezeudu. The law is not universal and absolute, but made by men operating in historical circumstances. This Ezeudu understands. The law will be obeyed, but it need not be carried out by Okonkwo personally. Okonkwo, however, misunderstands the law. He wants it to be universal and to govern all situations. It does not.

The oral world of Umuofia is not wholly based on repetition and stability: there is an instability implicit, the instability of narrative. The succession of generations marks change, and this is most evident in the rejection of Okonkwo's law by his son Nwoye, who converts to Christianity. Christianity is brought by the Europeans, as history itself appears to be. But Christianity is portrayed as a fulfilment of historic trends among the Igbos; Nwoye has sought something other and thinks he has found it in Christianity. He has had doubts about the religion of his fathers; the songs of the Christians fill his soul with sweetness and peace; they answer to a need in his soul. Similar doubts are expressed by Obierika, who comes to destroy Okonkwo's compound after his friend has been exiled for an offence that was purely accidental. Achebe is anxious to show that Igbos make their own choices, are not victims of history, but makers of history. There is continuity and development, not just repetition and rupture. The Igbos chose Christianity, as Nwoye did, or rejected it, as Okonkwo did, because they were aware of themselves making their own world in time.

The title of the novel establishes that Okonkwo's whole life will be seen from the perspective of his end. But that end is not gratuitous; it is of a piece with his life. To appropriate what Louis O. Mink has written of the narrative unity of Oedipus's life:[36] Okonkwo who hangs from the tree at the end is the son of man who could not be properly buried, the warrior who must forever prove his own courage, the wealthy man who has taken the second highest title in the land, the short-tempered husband quick to suspect insubordination and to beat his wives, the wearer of a spirit mask, the father who is rejected in his turn by his son, the man who wrestles with his *chi*, and the killer of the white man's messenger. He is alive and he is dead, and he could not be anywhere else than hanging on that tree.

The coming of the Europeans is not portrayed by Achebe as arbitrary, a *deus ex machina* dropped from another realm. It fulfils in inevitable fashion the tragic narrative he has been telling. The narrative of traditional Igbo society can only now be told with an eye to the end, the coming of the colonizers. But that does not mean Igbo history is derivative. It is no different from the history of eighteenth-century France, which is always written and can only be written with 1789 in mind, even though those who lived at the time may have not seen the revolution coming. Umuofia's responses to the coming of the Europeans are the responses of self-conscious narrative agents to the circumstances in which they find themselves.

Ricoeur makes a useful distinction betwen seeing history as a totality and seeing it as a totalization. We can no longer, with Hegel, see history as a totality that can be expressed as the development of the Spirit, or as any other single concept. Universal history can mean tyranny if it means the hegemony of a particular society, and that is what seeing history as a totality is likely to mean.[37] Not only is it wrong to see history as a totality, but it is no longer even possible. We must make do, not with a totality, but with a totalization, an imperfect mediation of an horizon of expectation (the future) an area of experience (the past and the present).[38] It is with such a totalization that Achebe is concerned.

In *Things Fall Apart* the author disappears behind an omniscient narrator who claims to know all sides. We should be suspicious of such objectivity; suspicious but not wholly sceptical. The objectivity can be justified if we keep in mind the writer who writes about the past with one eye on the present. *Things Fall Apart* is the work of a young Igbo in pre-independence Nigeria who must establish the common humanity of Africans and the difference of traditional African culture, and who must show history made by Africans in order to inspire them to make history. The needs of the present determine how the history is written, but that does not make the history false. An aphorism of John William Miller puts it well:

> There can be only one point of view from which history can be written, and further, there is such a point of view. Obviously something of this sort is necessary if history is to avoid dogmatic assertions of what really happened or refusal to say what really happened. Whatever the one point of view may be through which history needs to be written if it is to escape subjectivity, it seems that it, too, is a historical resultant. Thus the one necessary point of view from which history is to be written is itself the outcome of history.[39]

From *English Studies in Canada*, 17: 3 (September 1991), 319–36.

NOTES

[Neil Ten Kortenaar's essay explores the problems of historicity raised by and within *Things Fall Apart*. It focuses on the problems of writing and reading the narratives of individuals within a society governed by mythic forms at a point when they are to be overtaken by western inscriptions of history. The essay reflects new historicist views that no history is stable; therefore, no viewpoint is omniscient. Eds]

1. Emmanuel Meziemadu Okoye, *The Traditional Religion and its Encounter with Christianity in Achebe's Novels* (Berne, 1987).

2. Paul Ricoeur, *Temps et récit III: Le temps raconté* (Paris, 1983), p. 278.

3. Among the difficulties involved in writing about Igboland is orthography. Achebe's first novel betrays the time of its writing because it still uses the orthography bestowed on the name of his people by the British: Ibo. But the 'β' of Ibo is but an approximation of a sound not found in English. In orthography as it has been standardized since the writing of *Things Fall Apart* this sound is represented by the letters gb in combination. This is not two consonants but one; using two letters

to represent one sound (approximately á, a voiced bilabial fricative) is a tactic that makes possible the writing of the Igbo language on a typewriter. The name of the ethnic group is thus written Igbo in the group's own language. English has adopted this revised spelling, in spite of the problem of pronunciation for English speakers, as part of the larger movement that considers it proper that a people name themselves.

4. Donald J. Weinstock and Cathy Ramadan, 'Symbol and Structure in *Things Fall Apart*', *Critical Perspectives on Chinua Achebe*, ed. C. L. Innes and Bernth Lindfors (Washington, DC 1978), pp. 126–34.

5. C. L. Innes, 'Language, Poetry, and Doctrine in *Things Fall Apart*', *Critical Perspectives on Chinua Achebe* (cf. note 4), pp. 111–25.

6. Cf. Timothy J. Reiss, *The Discourse of Modernism* (Ithaca, NY, 1982).

7. Nadine Gordimer, *July's People* (New York, 1981).

8. Cf. Wayne Booth, *A Rhetoric of Irony* (Chicago, 1974).

9. Chinua Achebe, *Things Fall Apart* (1958; London, 1988), p. 59. All further references to the novel are placed in parentheses in the essay.

10. Abdul JanMohamed, 'Sophisticated Primitivism: the Syncretism of Oral and Literate Modes in Achebe's *Things Fall Apart*', Ariel, 15: 4 (1984), 33.

11. Elizabeth Isichei, *A History of the Igbo People* (London, 1976), p. 124.

12. Chinweizu, Onwuchekwa Jemie and Ihechukwu Madubuike, *Towards the Decolonisation of African Literature* (Washington, DC, 1983).

13. Chinua Achebe, 'The Madman', *Girls at War and Other Stories* (London, 1972), pp. 1–10.

14. Homi K. Bhabha, 'Representation and the Colonial Text: Some Forms of Mimeticism', *The Theory of Reading*, ed. Frank Gloversmith (Brighton, 1984), pp. 93–122.

15. Ricoeur, *Temps et récit III*, pp. 219–27.

16. Frantz Fanon, *The Wretched of the Earth*, trans. Constance Farrington (Harmondsworth, 1967), p. 40.

17. Chinua Achebe, *Arrow of God* (1964; London, 1974), p. 33.

18. Edward Said, *Orientalism* (New York, 1978), p. 240.

19. Cf. Jack Goody, *The Domestication of the Savage Mind* (Cambridge, 1977); and Walter Ong, *Orality and Literacy* (London, 1982).

20. Hayden White, *The Content of the Form* (Baltimore, MD, 1987), p. 12.

21. Ricoeur, *Temps et récit I* .

22. Chinua Achebe, '*Chi* in Igbo Cosmology', *Morning Yet on Creation Day* (Garden City, NY, 1975), pp. 93–103.

23. Peter Munz, *The Shapes of Time* (Middletown, CT, 1977) pp. 119–26.

24. Claude Lévi-Strauss, *The Savage Mind* (London, 1986), p. 236.

25. Ibid., p. 236.

26. Ricoeur, *Temps et récit III*, p. 153.

27. Ibid., pp. 177ff.

28. Isichei, *A History of the Igbo People*, pp. 75–6.

29. Ibid., p. 8.

30. White, *The Content of the Form*, p. 56.

31. Cf. Eric Wolf, *Europe and the Peoples Without History* (Berkeley, CA, 1982).

32. James Olney, *Tell Me Africa* (Princeton, NJ, 1973), p. 167.

33. Ibid., p. 171.

34. Ibid., p. 167.

35. Ibid., p. 169.

36. Louis O. Mink, 'History and Fiction as Modes of Comprehension', *New Directions in Literary History*, ed. Ralph Cohen (Baltimore, MD, 1974), pp. 107–24.

37. Ricoeur, *Temps et récit* III, p. 312.

38. Ibid., pp. 359ff.

39. John William Miller, *The Philosophy of History* (New York, 1982) p. 188.

2

No *Longer at Ease*: Chinua Achebe's 'Heart of Whiteness'

PHILIP ROGERS

Obi Okonkwo, the antihero of Chinua Achebe's *No Longer at Ease*, is preeminently a man of words and books, a product of 'mission-house upbringing and European education'.[1] Only in his willful, self-destructive individualism does he resemble his warrior grandfather, Ogbuefi Okonkwo, the hero of *Things Fall Apart*. In this he is, as a village elder observes, 'Okonkwo *kpom kwem*, exact, perfect' (p. 53). This single likeness is strikingly ironic, because in all other aspects of their characters the grandfather and grandson differ absolutely. Okonkwo the Great lives by the sword and perishes by the sword (p. 138). A man of violent action, he was unable to express himself in words: 'He had a slight stammer and whenever he was angry and could not get his words out quickly enough, he would use his fists.'[2] Obi, in contrast, is the man of nothing but words, whose downfall is precipitated by his inability to act: 'Paralysed by his thoughts' (p. 169), he destroys himself through inaction. Living by the book, he ultimately dies by it.

Throughout *No Longer at Ease* Obi is presented both in terms of his relation to 'book'[3] and to particular books – especially the canon of literary modernism he studied in England and to which, as antihero of an ironic and allusive novel, he himself belongs. Obi's perception of his world and his attempts to make sense of his experience – 'exegesis' Achebe calls it (p. 46) – are pervasively literary.

Achebe's literary allusions and Obi's literary sensibility combine to provide a counterpoint of subtle and invariably ironic commentary on Obi's behavior. The heart of his action – and more significantly his inaction – is revealed in the reflected light (or darkness) of several major antiheroes of modern literature: Evelyn Waugh's Tony Last (*A Handful of Dust*), Joseph Conrad's Mr Kurtz (*Heart of Darkness*), Graham Greene's Scobie (*The Heart of the Matter*), W. H. Auden's Icarus ('Musée des Beaux Arts'), and T. S. Eliot's personae from 'The Waste Land', 'The Love Song of J. Alfred Prufrock', and, of course, 'The Journey of the Magi', which provides Achebe's title.[4] These works possess significant common themes and in several instances allude to one another, creating in *No Longer at Ease* a substructure of allusion within allusion. *A Handful of Dust* points to 'The Waste Land',[5] *The Heart of the Matter* to *Heart of Darkness*. Achebe's ironic annexation of Conrad's imagery of hearts, centers, and emptiness from *Heart of Darkness* inevitably brings to mind Eliot's use of Conrad in 'The Hollow Men'. 'Musée des Beaux Arts' similarly parallels 'The Journey of the Magi'; the contrasting attitudes of young and old toward the nativity in 'Musée' mirror the ambiguous reaction of Eliot's magi to the same event.[6] The clustered meanings of these interrelated allusions focus on Obi, revealing more of his nature and plight – the hollow heart of his whiteness – than Achebe's typically reticent narrative comments.

That Achebe wishes to present Obi Okonkwo above all as a man of words is evident in his treatment of the major crises of Obi's childhood, all of which relate to the world of 'book' and suggest that European education and values constitute the germ of his later alienation and betrayal of his parents' world.

As the son of a Christian convert, Obi is heir to his father's values and is shaped by their influence. Isaac Okonkwo is a Christian, but his beliefs comprise far more than his religion: 'Mr Okonkwo believed utterly and completely in the things of the white man. And the symbol of the white man's power was the written word, or better still, the printed word' (p. 126). His father's religion has little enduring effect on Obi, but the influence of his devotion to the word and white power it symbolizes is indelible. Achebe's description of Isaac's book-filled room suggests that for the first generation of converts, veneration of print is little more than logolatry: 'The result of Okonkwo's mystic regard for the written word was that his room was full of old books and papers … from obsolete cockroach-eaten translations of the Bible into the Onitsha dialect to yellowed Scripture Union cards of 1920 and earlier. Okonkwo never destroyed a piece of paper' (p. 127). To the naïve convert, the written word symbolizes only white power; Isaac's print fetish augments this symbolism and burdens his uncritical belief in the white man with ominous associations of decay and inanity. Obi's experience in *No Longer at Ease* reveals the implications of this double meaning: the word of white power also portends black spiritual decay and death. ...

Of all Achebe's literary allusions in *No Longer at Ease*, his use of Conrad's *Heart of Darkness* is by far the most elaborately ironical and systematically patterned. It constitutes in fact a polemical parody of Conrad in which Obi plays the role of a black Kurtz in Achebe's 'Heart of Whiteness'.[7] The stages of Obi's experience exactly parallel Kurtz's. Both are quasi-literary men, writers of idealistic articles, who travel from Europe imbued with optimistic theories about the future of Africa. In the tests of real experience, however, their idealism proves insubstantial and they are shown to be hollow men. The discovery that there is 'nothing within' them, that their beliefs are merely illusions, leads them to violate the very principles which they had set forth in their essays. Kurtz had theorized that the African's awe of the white man (Kurtz, that is) would enable him to exert a powerful moral influence over the 'savages': 'By the simple exercise of our will we can exert a power for good practically unbounded,' wrote Kurtz in his report to the International Society for the Suppression of Savage Customs.[8] Kurtz, of course, discovers that the will he chooses to exercise manifests itself rather differently in deeds from its expression in words and becomes himself the object of fetishism, leading presumably to the further degradation (in Conrad's terms) of the Africans he had come to civilize.

Obi had theorized that the elimination of bribery and corruption from Nigeria's civil life would necessarily follow when young, Europeanized university men (Obi, that is) took over the senior posts in the civil service. Like Kurtz, he formulates his theory in a paper, which he delivers to the Nigerian Students Association in London (p. 38). Obi's theory, like Kurtz's, proves to be merely words when he himself becomes a bribe taker. Significantly, when Obi discovers he cannot refuse the bribe, he tries to hide the pile of money – and the failure of his theory – from himself by covering it with newspaper (p. 168). The gesture recalls Obi's burying his idealistic 'Nigeria' poem in the Housman volume and also the piles of empty words – yellowed and cockroach-eaten religious tracts – mouldering ineffectually in his father's bedroom. Truly for both Kurtz and Obi, 'Between the idea / And the reality ... Falls the Shadow' of the word.[9]

In his application of *Heart of Darkness* to his own world, Obi assigns the role of Kurtz to his English boss, Mr Green, who, in Obi's analysis, had succumbed not to the darkness of 'weird ceremonies and unspeakable rites' but to 'the incipient dawn' of African liberation (p. 106). Obi, of course, sees himself not as Kurtz, but in the more flattering role of an African Conrad who will one day write a novel about Green as Kurtz. He affects an analytical detachment from Green that recalls the bitter ending of *Things Fall Apart* in which the District Commissioner coolly reflects on the possibility of writing about the fate of Ogbuefi Okonkwo in his projected book, *The Pacification of the Primitive Tribes of the Lower Niger*. Mr Green does have a counterpart in *Heart of Darkness*, but in accordance with Achebe's turning of Conrad's world upside down, white Green plays a black role, rather than that of the white Kurtz, while Obi plays the role of the analytical white, who, like Kurtz or the DC, can reduce complex human experience to words and books. This reversal is seen when Obi marvels at Green's devotion to duty: 'Obi could not understand it. Here was a man who did not believe in a country and yet worked so hard for it. Did he simply believe in duty as a logical necessity? ... He was like a man who had some great and supreme task that must be completed before a final catastrophe intervened' (p. 105). Obi's bewilderment at Green's incomprehensible devotion to duty exactly parallels Marlow's amazement at discovering restraint and discipline among the African workers on his river boat: 'Restraint! ... Was it superstition, disgust, patience, fear – or some kind of primitive honour? ... these chaps had no earthly reason for any kind of scruple.'[10]

The polemical aspect of Achebe's parody of *Heart of Darkness* is most apparent in his attributing to whiteness and light the deadly qualities Conrad gave to darkness.[11] Early in the novel the association of light with white civilization is subjected to an ironical undercutting. Obi, on his departure for England, is seen by the African Christians as one who will return (like Mr Kurtz) bearing the torch of civilization. He will fufil the prophecy: 'The people which sat in darkness / Saw a great light, / And to them which sat in the region and shadow of death / To them did light spring up' (p. 8). Of this prayer Achebe notes that the only 'darkness' observable on this occasion was self-inflicted, the kind caused by the shutting of Christian eyes in a prayer so prolonged that when it was over, 'people blinked and rubbed their eyes to get used to the evening light once more' (p. 9). Ironically the converts themselves are the ones who choose to 'sit in darkness'. A similar irony occurs in the account of Lagos Obi hears from a soldier: 'There is no darkness there', he relates, but then proceeds to give unwitting evidence of the profound spiritual darkness of the Africans in this well-lit white world: 'If you see a whiteman,' the soldier adds, 'take off your hat for him. The only thing he cannot do is mould a human being' (p. 14). Achebe shows the persistence of this kind of psychological darkness in Hon. Sam Okoli's rapt admiration of western technology: 'White man don go far, we just de shout for nothing' (p. 68). 'Our people have a long way to go' (p. 69), Okoli concludes, a self-judgment echoed by Obi (p. 36).

Achebe's reversal of Conrad's imagery of light and darkness is most clearly seen in his contrasting of Lagos, the black city, with Ikoyi, its white (senior service) suburb; here darkness is associated with community, fertility, and life – whiteness with isolation, sterility, and death (p. 18):

> Going from the Lagos mainland to Ikoyi on a Saturday night was like going from a bazaar to a funeral. And the vast Lagos cemetery which separated the two places helped to deepen this feeling. For all its luxurious bungalows and flats and its extensive greenery, Ikoyi was like a graveyard. It had no corporate life – at any rate for those Africans who lived there. They had not always lived there, of course. It was once a European reserve. But things had changed, and some Africans in 'European posts' had been given houses in Ikoyi. Obi Okonkwo, for example lived there, and as he drove from Lagos to his flat he was struck again by these two cities in one. It always reminded him of twin kernels separated by a thin wall in a palm-nut shell. Sometimes one kernel was shiny-black and alive, the other powdery-white and dead.

The two halves of the palm kernel perfectly represent the two halves of Obi's divided life; it is his misfortune that the direction in which he is traveling, both in this quotation and in his life, is from the fertile black seed to the sterile white one.[12] The most dramatic, and in fact the culminating image of the destructive force of whiteness is seen in Obi's mother's dream (p. 135):

> 'I dreamt a bad dream, a very bad dream one night. I was lying on a
> bed spread with white cloth and I felt something creepy against my
> skin. I looked down on the bed and found that a swarm of white ter-
> mites had eaten it up, and the mat and the white cloth. Yes, termites
> had eaten up the bed right under me.'

In her dream, rapacious whiteness devours the bed of maternity; as in
the image of the blighted white palm nut, the undermining of the
mother's bed hints at the destruction of the very basis of fertility and
continuity.[13] This second image of Obi's mother as victim makes
explicit what was implied in her being wounded by his school razor:
she is the victim of the white world, whose agent is her own son.

That exposure to whiteness destroys black fertility and sexuality
is suggested too in the way Achebe exemplifes Obi's feeling for his
native language. We see in several episodes that Obi has lost his
facility in Ibo while in England. The damage he sustains because of
this loss is subtly presented. For Obi, English lacks the emotional
power and immediacy of Ibo; when his thoughts turn to women
and the erotic, he 'said words in his mind that he could not say out
aloud even when he was alone. ... He could say an English word,
no matter how dirty, but some Ibo words simply would not proceed
from his mouth' (p. 45). His separation from his mother tongue is
thus also a separation from the emotional basis of his own feelings
and personality.

The collapse of Obi's values at the end of the novel is conveyed in
a sexual metaphor that epitomizes the effect of the white world on
Obi: emasculation. Pondering the events that brought about the
submission of his people to white rule (and which led to the suicide
of his heroic grandfather), Obi is tranquil. He even feels 'a queer
kind of pleasure' when he thinks of how the white man captured
and broke the guns of Aninta, an event explicitly symbolizing 'the
emasculation of the clan by the white man's religion and government' (p. 166).

Achebe's parody of Conrad necessarily requires that England be a
Heart of Whiteness for Obi, as indeed it is. Marlow's misty evoca-
tion of his pilgrimage through the unearthly, bewitched darkness of
the Congo jungles is echoed in the Umuofians' notion of Obi's trip
to England as a pilgrimage to a realm less geographical than metaphysical: 'a man gets to the land of spirits when he has passed seven
rivers, seven forests and seven hills. Without doubt you have visited
the land of spirits' (p. 51). To them England is also 'the place where

learning finally came to an end' (p. 9), a designation whose ominous finality not only mirrors the mental repose implied in Obi's name (Obiajulu, 'the mind at last is at rest' [p. 6]), but also corresponds to Marlow's view of Kurtz's Inner Station as an ultimate point in human experience, 'the centre of the earth', 'the farthest point of navigation and the culminating point of my experience'.[14]

While in England Obi succumbs to Whiteness and like Kurtz goes native: he decides to take a degree in English. In Nigeria he had told his Umuofian sponsors that he would study law so as to help them with village business. The significance of this shift of academic interests is suggested in the heavily ironic praise Obi receives when he returns and is numbered among true Umuofians: 'We are not empty men who become white when they see white, and black when they see black' (p. 53). Achebe suggests that Obi has indeed seen white and become just such an empty man. As the elders of Umuofia observe, 'When a new saying gets to the land of empty men, they lose their heads over it' (p. 48). When he must argue against his father's values he discovers this emptiness, that 'there was nothing in him' (p. 137) to challenge his father. His heart has become like the dead white kernel within the palm nut. The hollow-heart metaphor, of course, pervades *Heart of Darkness* and is implicit in its title. Kurtz himself, like Obi, is 'hollow at the core'[15] which explains (as all English majors, including Obi, know) T. S. Eliot's use of 'Mistah Kurtz – he dead' as the epigraph of 'The Hollow Men'. While the metaphors are superficially the same, the values associated with them are transposed: for Achebe the dark heart, like the dark, living seed of the palm nut, represents the core of enduring, if threatened, African values and vitality. Of the many incidents and proverbs demonstrating the coherence and life of the African community, the most specific in its moral application and relevance to the heart theme is 'The Song of the Heart', which Obi hears in his home village (p. 129):

> *He that has a brother must hold him to his heart,*
> *For a kinsman cannot be bought in the market,*
> *Neither is a brother bought with money. ...*
> He who has brothers
> Has more than riches can buy.

What has become of Obi's heart in the heart of whiteness? Becoming white when one sees white obviously entails more than acquiring a taste for Housman and Eliot; Achebe suggests that the changes wrought in Obi are profound and fundamental ones. The change in Obi is more than losing touch with his family and his mother tongue: it also implies the acquisition of white values. Mr Kurtz is undone by 'the fascination of the abomination', the pleasure of presiding at weird rites in which he is the object of worship. In appropriate contrast to the temptations of the 'primitive', Obi succumbs to the very values Conrad and contemporary British culture saw as distinctly civilized – the pragmatic devotion to efficiency and to work, getting the job done. As Marlow notes, 'What saves us is efficiency – the devotion to efficiency.'[16] The temptations of secular pragmatism are less lurid than Kurtz's, but more insidious in their ultimate effect on the heart. We see from Obi's behavior when he returns from England that he is guided almost exclusively by utilitarian concerns. On a superficial level this is evident in his impatience with traditional attitudes toward hierarchy and ceremony. He wishes to dispense altogether with the forms of respect and status. At his welcoming ceremony, he is the only one not dressed for the occasion. When he delivers his speech, his style is plain and simple, 'is and was', not the rhetorical display of erudition the occasion traditionally calls for. These deviations from tradition are, of course, humorous ones. As the novel progresses, however, we see that Obi's European values affect more than his manners. In the crucial episode of his not attending his mother's funeral, he makes his decision according to the baldest of utilitarian motives (pp. 160–1):

> What was the point of going to Umuofia? She would have been buried by the time he got there, anyway. ... Obi wondered whether he had done the right thing in not setting out for Umuofia yesterday. But what could have been the point in going? It was more useful to send all the money he could for the funeral instead of wasting it on petrol to get home.

Mr Green would not dispute such an eminently practical decision. That utilitarian values pervade even the deepest levels of Obi's mind is seen in the way his memory of his mother changes after her death. He no longer dreams of her coming toward him, her bleeding hand extended. This image fades and is replaced by the abstract conception of her efficiency and productivity – as 'a woman who got things done' (p. 165). The memory that he specially cherishes is of her having decapitated the sacred he-goat of Udo, one of the great gods of Aninta, when she caught him eating her precious yams. This memory cancels the intimate linking of mother and son that the earlier one of her bleeding possessed and also significantly depicts her in a role congenial to Obi's white values – as a profaner of African tradition. From being the victim of the razor she becomes herself the wielder of the destructive blade. Obi in effect transforms her into an image of himself.

The episode of Obi's arrest and trial – the novel's frame – nicely focuses the ironies that pervade the novel. The judge and the European community cannot understand how a young man of Obi's education can have committed such a crime. That his education has in fact led him to commit the crime is incomprehensible to them. The final page of the novel relates Obi's arrest; here Achebe gently reminds the reader of Obi's grandfather and the ending of *Things Fall Apart*. Once again, an Okonkwo is being arrested. The arresting officer is performing precisely the role of the court messenger Okonkwo decapitates; taking Obi into custody, he is compared to 'a District Officer in the bush reading the Riot Act to an uncomprehending and delirious mob' (p. 170). The final image of Obi shows him to be hollow to the last, struggling as he is sentenced, to conceal a tear under a false smile, a whimper that recalls by contrast the bang of *Things Fall Apart*. To criticize *No Longer at Ease* because Obi lacks 'a graspable self' and the center of the novel reveals only 'a disturbing void'[17] is in my view to misconstrue its mode, a little like complaining that Gulliver or Candide are too naïve to be believable. The novel lacks the beauty and the power of *Things Fall Apart*, but Achebe is faithful to history: Obi's is a mean and empty world. His void is meant to disturb, for the novel's title in fact describes not the dilemma of its insensitive antihero, but rather the reader's response to him and his world.

From *Research in African Literature*, 14: 2 (Summer 1983), 165–83.

NOTES

[This essay contributes to an established discussion of Achebe's intertextual references to European culture, including Achebe's own essay on Conrad – cf. note 7 below. Rogers' analysis illustrates a reading of the novel as a fictional critique of western influences on the world of its characters, especially of Nigerian-born Obi, remade but destroyed, deconstructed by the polarities in his history. In this sense the novel itself is viewed as a deconstructionist text, whilst the essay adopts a socio-realist approach in its analysis. Eds]

1. *No Longer at Ease* (London, 1960), p. 71. All further references to this work appear in parentheses in the text.

2. *Things Fall Apart* (London, 1958), p. 2.

3. 'Book' is the generic pidgin term denoting the white world of European values and education. In this novel its use is always pejorative. To the lorry driver, Obi is 'too too know', one of the 'book people' (p. 43). Obi's friend Joseph notes its limitations: 'You know book, but this is no matter for book' (p. 71). The President of the Umuofia Progressive Union chides Obi: 'You are very young, a child of yesterday. you know book. But book stands by itself and experience stands by itself' (p. 82).

4. Evelyn Waugh, *A Handful of Dust* (Boston, 1977); Joseph Conrad, *Heart of Darkness*, ed. Robert Kimbrough (New York, 1971); Graham Greene, *The Heart of the Matter* (London, 1971); W. H. Auden, *Collected Poems*, ed. Edward Mendelson (New York, 1976); T. S. Eliot, *Collected Poems 1909–1962* (New York, 1963).

5. 'I will show you fear in a handful of dust'. *The Waste Land*, line 30. Achebe's allusions to T. S. Eliot are discussed by Roderick Wilson in 'Eliot and Achebe: An Analysis of Some Formal and Philosophical Qualities of *No Longer at Ease*', *Critical Perspectives on Chinua Achebe*, ed. C. L. Innes and Bernth Lindfors (Washington, DC, 1978), pp. 160–8. Wilson deals primarily with allusions to 'The Waste Land' and hints at, but does not pursue, the relationship of Obi to Mr Kurtz and to 'The Hollow Men.' Wilson discusses neither the Waugh allusion to 'The Waste Land' nor Obi's memories of Prufrock. Another complex use of allusion – Achebe's linking of 'The Hollow Men' with 'The Journey of the Magi' – is briefly noted by Rosemary Colmer, ' "The Start of Weeping is Always Hard": The Ironic Structure of *No Longer at Ease*', *Literary Half-Yearly*, 21 (1980), 135.

6. 'When the aged are reverently, passionately waiting
For the miraculous birth, there must always be
Children who did not specially want it to happen.'
(W. H. Auden 'Musée des Beaux Arts', ll. 5–7)

7. Achebe's reason for wishing to set Conrad on his ear are fully (and I think convincingly) explained in his essay, 'An Image of Africa', *Massachusetts Review*, 18 (1977), 782–94.

8. *Heart of Darkness*, p. 51.

9. 'The Hollow Men,' ll. 72–3, 75.

10. *Heart of Darkness*, pp. 42–3.

11. A good example of Achebe's penchant for reversals is his humorous idea of sending African Peace Corps volunteers to the United States to revive the extended family. (See 'An Image of Africa', p. 794.)

12. The significance of Obi's direction at this point is noted by Carroll. See David Carroll, *Chinua Achebe* (New York, 1970), p. 70.

13. The image of white termites devouring the emblems of Africa's past is also central to one of Achebe's finest poems, 'Dereliction', *Beware, Soul-Brother and Other Poems* (Enugu, 1971), p. 36.

14. *Heart of Darkness*, pp. 13, 9.

15. Ibid., p. 59.

16. Ibid., p. 6.

17. David Carroll, *Chinua Achebe*, p. 87.

3

Knowledge and Power, the Story and the Storyteller: Achebe's *Anthills of the Savannah*

ROBIN IKEGAMI

Many critical discussions of Chinua Achebe as storyteller centre on the ways in which he deliberately draws upon an African oral tradition to enhance his efforts to depict different tensions – such as that between precolonial Ibo ways of thinking and Christian missionary notions, or between men and women, or between generations. Such critics point to Achebe's use of proverbs, different speech rhythms, and repetition,[1] but they do not explicitly address in any detail the role of storytelling itself as a political or social act – as a demonstration of knowledge and an exercise of power – within the novels. Although each of Achebe's five novels demonstrates his own power as a storyteller and reveals his view of the complex and often problematic relation between knowledge, power, and storytelling, nowhere does Achebe more minutely examine the nature of that relation than in his latest novel, *Anthills of the Savannah* (1987). My endeavor in this paper is to examine both Achebe's storytelling and his view of the act of storytelling as manifested in his most recent novel to determine the ways in which power and knowledge impinge upon stories and their tellers.

Unlike his previous novels, *Anthills* features characters who are concerned neither with negotiating a way between black society and white government (as in *Things Fall Apart, No Longer at Ease,* and *Arrow of God*) nor with making a direct transition from colonialism to self-government (as in *A Man of the People*); instead, these characters are occupied with finding a way of establishing and maintaining a successful form of postcolonial self-government. Rather than trying to fill in the skeletal structure of government left by colonialism, they attempt to construct a new government out of their history, a contemporary African government. The relation between knowledge and power in *Anthills,* then, is particularly problematic, for the characters have a great deal of various kinds of knowledge, and they believe that they have a certain amount of power as well. But they recognize that the possession of that knowledge and power is not necessarily enough to ensure either their own well-being and survival or those of their society.[2] They are almost perpetually in a state of confusion because the extent of their knowledge and power is always in question, not only in their own minds but in the minds of others as well. Thus the trope of storytelling and Achebe's own storytelling also demonstrate that confusion.[3] Each of the main characters – Chris, Ikem, the president, and Beatrice – participates in the storytelling. Unlike the stories we find in the earlier novels, these stories are not seen as sources of solutions to problems; no one views them as coherent wholes that offer reassurance or advice. The stories in *Anthills* only suggest more questions for the characters. Thus the concept of knowledge is problematized; what makes for knowledge, how it is acquired, how it is or should be used – all are questions with which the characters, and Achebe himself, struggle throughout the novel.

Significantly, the limits and complexities of the power of storytelling and storytellers in Anthills may be, at least in part, attributed to the historical setting of the novel.[4] The book's characters represent a generation of Africans that has never experienced life without numerous uncertainties; unlike the characters in the earlier novels, the main characters in *Anthills* have not maintained close connections with a traditionally ordered society. Significantly, *Anthills* takes place during a time when colonialism is neither an impending threat nor a concrete presence; rather, colonialism is something of a haunting but distant memory, the remnant of a past the novel's leading characters would like to transcend but which has in some overt as well as covert ways influenced the concept of government current through most of the novel. But the early forms of precolonial government are also only a vague memory, like colonialism, influencing although not dominating newer constructions of institutional power. The characters know about the overthrow of different institutions of power, and consequently, they realize that power is not a stable entity. Previous forms of government, whether colonial or precolonial, are suspect in this novel; indeed, all constitutions of power are suspect.

The president, for example, is extremely insecure about both his claim to the office and his ability to keep the position. This self-doubt becomes almost immediately apparent in the first chapter, for we find that the president seems to worry as much about maintaining control of his own cabinet – made up of mostly longtime companions – as providing leadership for his country. We discover details such as the president's adoption of the title 'His Excellency', the obsequious Chief Secretary's arrangement of the president's shoes under the table,[5] and the orderly's 'quivering hands' (p. 9), demonstrating the ways in which the president seeks to safeguard his position through intimidation and exhibition. Much of his ability to preserve his position depends upon his capacity to tell believable stories and to sort through the stories of others. He is always gathering information from various people, listening to and deciphering their stories, and he also tells stories, giving out information or allowing the release of selected pieces of information. The problem, for the president as for the other characters in the book, lies in figuring out which stories to believe and in making one's own stories credible. The opening conversation between the president and his oldest friend, Chris, points out a connection between political power and the power of storytelling; it shows a man who fears losing both. With more than a little frustration, the president tells Chris, 'The matter is closed, I said. How many times, for God's sake, am I expected to repeat it? Why do you find it so difficult to swallow my ruling. On anything?' (p. 1). We later discover that it is not only the president's rulings that Chris, and others, have difficulty believing, but his descriptions and interpretations of events as well. The president's reaction to the essentially conciliatory visit from the representative of Abazon is a further proof of his insufficient capacity to rationally interpret a story; he sees the visit as a threat of insurrection. His paranoia interferes with his ability to listen to and tell a story, and the depth of his paranoia is most clearly evidenced by his readiness to suspect Chris not only of disrespect but of insurgency.

Suspicion and paranoia are not the sole property of the president, however. Chris and Ikem are also subject to such feelings, and, as in the case of the president, those feelings interfere with their story-telling and interpreting abilities. For instance, despite his descriptions of the other cabinet members, which he insists spring from 'detached clinical interest' (p. 2), Chris suspects the motives of virtually everyone in the book, including himself. He questions Professor Okong's role in 'the birth and grooming of a baby monster [the president]' (p. 10), and, pondering the state of his nation's government, Chris wonders, 'why then do I go on with it now that I can see' that governing is not a game (p. 2). Chris's suspicions and resulting confusion about the power dynamics at work in his society undermine his ability to remain a 'detached' and 'clinical' storyteller. Significantly, his first conversation with Ikem, his subordinate although also his good friend, greatly resembles the opening conversation he has with the president. Ikem questions Chris's orders, and Chris tells him, 'We have gone over this matter a million times now if we've gone over it once; and I'm getting quite sick and tired of repeating it' (p. 25). Implicit in Chris's statement to Ikem, as in the president's to Chris, is a suspicion of disloyalty, of a lack of respect for his authority. Chris and Ikem engage each other in a battle similar to the confrontations between Chris and the president, and in both cases what is at stake is a credible story. Just as Chris wonders about the president's state of mind in the face of new-found power, Ikem doubts Chris's integrity: 'he probably believes the crap too. Amazing what even one month in office can do to a man's mind' (p. 35). Ikem alludes to the stories that the president either manufactures or encourages in order to maintain power – the stories which Chris, in his capacity as Commissioner of Information, helps to perpetuate.

Chris and Ikem are in certain ways very different types of story-tellers. Chris is interested in fact, and he sees power as closely linked with a comprehensive knowledge of facts. He wants to present a story that is believable because it is objective, factual. Hence we find in his first narration an insistence upon his objectivity and aloofness from the events he reports. But his privileging of objectivity is Chris's greatest weakness as a storyteller, a weakness he does not realize until too late. In a different context, Achebe describes this kind of objectivity, 'which asks a man to cut his own throat for the comfort and good opinion of another', as a 'malady'.[6] From the beginning, Achebe points out the symptoms of Chris's malady, for sprinkled throughout Chris's testimony are – in addition to the president's suspicions of Chris's objectivity – phrases which undermine his posture of indifference. Chris continually asserts the importance of his role in the movement that brought the president to power, his role in the selection of the cabinet, and his role as a voice of reason in deliberations over national policy. He is concerned with demonstrating his access to and possession of facts; for him, the factual story is the powerful, convincing, story. To further emphasize the problem with Chris's storytelling, Achebe places Ikem's philosophy of storytelling in opposition, demonstrating that Chris's approach is often an impediment to constructive change.

Ikem always questions the source of the so-called facts and suspects claims of objectivity. Ikem recognizes that Chris is not a detached observer, that Chris's stories are influenced by a fear of the facts that compromises his integrity, for Ikem advises Chris, 'Stop looking back over your shoulder' (p. 42). Ikem privileges passionate engagement in storytelling: 'Those who mismanage our affairs would silence our criticism by pretending they have facts not available to the rest of us. ... Our best weapon against them is not to marshal facts, of which they are truly managers, but passion. Passion is our hope and strength ...' (p. 35). Thus Ikem reveals here in his first narration that his view of storytelling is quite different from that which Chris holds, and his assessment of the state of their society also varies somewhat from Chris's. Whereas Chris views the nation's political situation as something out of control, particularly out of his control, Ikem sees it as still salvageable 'if we put our minds to it' (p. 42). Both, however, invest storytelling with real power – Chris initially sees it as something to be neutralized, and Ikem sees it as something to be exploited – which is why both reveal a feeling of urgency in telling their stories and anxiety over the stories of others. As Ikem says in his lecture at the university of Bassa, 'storytellers are a threat. They threaten all champions of control' (p. 141).

The threat Ikem speaks of is one that many of the characters in the novel sense; they fear the story yet desire its power for themselves or their cause. One of the ways in which the characters try to appropriate the power of storytelling is by using stories of each other's past to try to figure out the present. Many of the characters share a past, and each at different times contemplates that past in an attempt to understand present relationships as well as the political situation. But their past knowledge of each other, the old stories, only leads to more confusion. Unlike the stories of Winterbottom's past or the stories of Ezeulu's past that help other characters as well as the reader to understand better some of the motivations and tensions at work, the stories of shared experiences in *Anthills* complicate rather than clarify understanding. Mad Medico, for instance, tells Beatrice that she should have known Chris and Sam (the president) five years earlier because they 'were much nicer people then' (p. 54), but we never really find out in what ways they were nicer. Indeed, one of the central questions in the novel focuses on how the past became the present: how did the characters become what and who they are and, relatedly, how did the nation become what it is?

The ways in which characters deal with the past provide some insight into who they are whom they have become. The president, for example, fears the past. He sees stories about it as a threat, and this point of view contributes to his deteriorating relationship with Chris. He recalls with approval the advice of President Ngongo: 'Your greatest risk is your boyhood friends. ... Keep them at arm's length and you will live long' (p. 22). Chris's knowledge of his past is a knowledge the president wants to suppress, hence the numerous confrontations and suspicions. But the president does not understand that knowledge and power make up not a simple equation but a complex dynamic. As Clarke observes in *Arrow of God,* 'Did knowledge of one's friends and colleagues impose a handicap on one? Perhaps it did. If so it showed how false was the common assumption that the more facts you could get about others the greater your power over them. Perhaps facts put you at a great disadvantage; perhaps they made you feel sorry and even responsible.'[7] And indeed, Chris and Ikem in their own way feel 'sorry and even responsible' for what has become of Sam and for what has become of their country. But Chris especially, because of his greater emphasis on facts, is subject to such feelings. Many of Chris's soliloquies focus on his responsibility for the state of the nation and its leadership, and initially there is little sorrow and more self-aggrandizement. Even under the ironic tone he adopts in the opening chapter, Chris's conceit shows through, but his attitude gradually turns into genuine self-blame as the novel progresses.

The problematic relationship between power and knowledge as manifest in stories of the past is particularly evident in the episode in which Chris tells Beatrice about his schooldays with Ikem and Sam. He characterizes Ikem as the brightest, Sam as the 'all-rounder' (p. 59), and himself as 'in the middle' (p. 60). Chris tells the story to provide some illumination of the present, attempting to use facts from the past to create an objective explanation for the current state of affairs. He attributes the president's shortcomings to Sam's too successful past: 'He never failed once in anything. Had the magic touch. And that's always deadly in the long run. He is paying the bills now, I think. And if we are not lucky we shall pay dearly' (p. 60). Ironically, Chris's story does not explain what he means for it to explain – that is, the state of the country and in particular the character of the president. He ultimately confesses that he does not really know why or how things turned out as they did (p. 61). The story does, however, throw some light on Chris's personality, particularly his conceit and lack of self-awareness. Once again we discover that Chris is not the detached, disinterested storyteller he seems to think he is, for, as Beatrice points out, 'The story of this country, as far as you are concerned, is the story of the three of you [Chris, Ikem, and Sam]' (p. 60). And in Chris's own characterization of himself – 'I have always been the lucky one' and 'in the middle' (p. 60) – we find that he believes himself to be not only an aloof storyteller but also an aloof subject. That is, he sees himself as above the events he relates; he is 'the lucky one', and those who are not lucky 'shall all pay dearly'. Further, he is a fence-straddler, 'in the middle', and thus is not fully committed to either Sam's point of view or Ikem's. Chris eventually learns that such an attitude, and such a position, are luxuries that the current society cannot afford or allow. There is no such thing as an impartial storyteller in this society, and Chris eventually realizes that he must take a stand.

But even storytellers who take a stand from the very beginning of the novel are subject to suspicion and doubt. Ikem, for instance, continually asserts the storyteller's obligation to speak out against injustice, to tell stories with which one is passionately engaged, stories in which one has a stake. Ikem insists that the storyteller should tell stories without allowing fear of the consequences to interfere (p. 42), and he blames Chris for compromising in the face of such fear. But like Chris, Ikem also holds himself somewhat above the events he discusses in his stories. His distance, however, is due not to a false belief in his own disinterest but to his valorization of the role of the artist. Initially, that valorization is somewhat naïve and optimistic, for at first he thinks that the storyteller provides the only real means of saving the world simply because the storyteller can furnish the stories that will solve all. Once again, Beatrice pulls back the conceit and reveals the complications beneath. She discovers 'the chink in [Ikem's] armoury of brilliant and original ideas', pointing out to him that, although he has written a novel and a play on the Women's War, 'he has no clear role for women in his political thinking' (p. 83). Until his suspension from the *Gazette*, Ikem assumes that he can speak for others without listening to or seriously considering their views, just as until Ikem's arrest Chris assumes that the story of the nation is the story of himself and his two closest friends. What Chris and Ikem ultimately learn is that the storyteller, in Ikem's words, 'must listen to his characters who after all are created to wear the shoe and point the writer where it pinches' (p. 88). What they learn, in other words, is that storytelling is not a simple procedure of gathering and dispensing facts or of sharing and eliciting passions, that the power of storytelling does not lie solely in the acquisition of a knowledge of facts or passions. They learn that the power of storytelling, like other powers, is diffuse and thus cannot be located in any one place or person, in any single method.

Just as the characters in the novel struggle with suspicions about storytellers and their stories, we as readers struggle with similar suspicions. Like the characters, we too are thrown into a state of confusion; we suspect everyone's stories and wonder whom to believe. To some extent, it is essentially a matter of the old question regarding the reliability of the narrator. Here, however, we have several narrators, two of whom (Chris and Ikem) are singled out as 'witnesses'. Achebe's use of the term 'witness' in the heading of both Chris's and Ikem's initial narrations undermines our faith in their stories.[8] It encourages us to approach these sections with some caution, like a jury assessing testimonies, and to beware of identifying too quickly with either man. Although their later narrations are unlabled, and we must ascertain the narrator's identity from the context and narrative style, their first narrations put us on guard. Unlike Achebe's earlier novels, with untitled chapers and narration that slips in and out of various consciousnesses (with the exception of *A Man of the People*) which is a first-person narration), *Anthills* overtly draws attention to the subjectivity of storytelling. And, oddly enough, the overt attention complicates rather than simplifies the process of interpreting both the individual narrations and the overall story. Despite the self-interest inherent in each testimony, Achebe points out that there is validity in every point of view:

Chris's factual approach does keep the peace for some time, and Ikem's passionate approach does bring about some constructive change.

But the selection entitled simply 'Beatrice' poses a different sort of problem. Achebe does not term Beatrice a 'witness', so how are we to take her narration? He invests a great deal of himself in Ikem – compare, for instance, Ikem's assertion that the storyteller should '[m]arch to the stake ... and take the bullet in [the] chest' (p. 42) with Achebe's contention that the writer's place in the African movement toward independence 'is right in the thick of it – if possible, at the head of it'.[9] However, Achebe also seems to endorse Beatrice's criticisms of Ikem's political and aesthetic ideologies. Her analyses of Ikem and for that matter of Chris as well, are without the kind of undercutting irony or contradiction we find in the other narrations; indeed, her analyses generally prove accurate. She admires Ikem and loves Chris, but she also gets at the heart of the problems in their modes of storytelling. Despite her personal involvement with the two men, she recognizes and identifies the particular conceit that damages their storytelling, and she tries to help them toward a clearer understanding of their flaws.

Although it is Beatrice who not only assists in the formation or clarification of the understanding of Chris and Ikem, it is also she who helps us, explaining many of the contradictions or puzzles in the novel. For instance, Beatrice resolves the contradictory intepretations of Chris's last words. Emmanuel takes Chris's last words to be a simple joke – 'The Last Grin' – through which Chris meant to soothe the young student leader, but Adamma suggests that Chris 'did not finish' his statement (p. 213). Beatrice brings together Emmanuel's and Adamma's intepretations, asserting that Chris's last words were a joke but a joke that was both bitterly political and personal rather than merely soothing: 'The last green bottle. It was a terrible, bitter joke. He was laughing at himself' (p. 214). She thus invokes her more intimate and extensive knowledge of Chris and causes us to recall Chris's own explanation of the green bottles: 'The trinity who thought they owned Kangan as BB once unkindly said? Three green bottles. One has accidentally fallen; one is tilting. Going, going, bang' (p. 176). In this way, Beatrice asserts her power as storyteller, emphasizing her greater knowledge and deeper insight but also her unique capacity to bring together disparate elements and form them into a new kind of story, a point I shall return to shortly.

We must also notice Achebe's skillful manipulation of details here, for in Chris's last words Achebe reminds us of the significance of Chris's metaphor. Chris unwittingly prophesies his own death; he dies because of a gunshot, a bang. The metaphor also brings together the three friends and emphasizes their similarities instead of their differences. They are united in their arrogance and in their fates. Ikem accidentally falls, for according to the new release he was 'fatally wounded by gunshot' in a scuffle (p. 156) – although the accuracy of the report is highly suspect. On another level, Chris had meant to protect him from such a fall but accidentally knocks him down with his complacency. The president is tilting, for his regime is very unstable and, as far as Chris and Ikem are concerned, his psyche is rather unstable as well. By the end of the novel, it seems that Sam also probably falls victim to a gunshot. Further, Achebe unites the three by means of prophecy; it is, after all, a capacity they share. Ikem appears to virtually read the president's mind in some of the *Gazette's* controversial editorials, and Chris and Sam see, each in his own way, the threat of the ultimate downfall of the government. And the last grin is not without its significance as well, for it underscores the ambiguity that runs throughout Achebe's novel, and that points out the impossibility of reaching anything resembling positive knowledge. As he demonstrates in Beatrice's stories, Achebe here brings together seemingly disparate elements, creating 'a purposive unity', to borrow a phrase from Chidi Amuta's formulation of the revolutionary role of art.[10]

Beatrice as storyteller plays a crucial part in Achebe's delineation of his vision, his story. Although she is, perhaps, the most reliable narrator in the novel, Beatrice is not without flaws herself. She, like Chris and Ikem, initially lacks a certain degree of self-knowledge. She does not know the 'traditions and legends of her people because they played but little part in her upbringing. She was born as we have seen into a world apart. ... So she came to barely knowing who she was. Barely, we say though, because she did carry a vague sense more acute at certain critical moments than others of being two different people' (p. 96). Beatrice is both 'demure damsel' and priestess (p. 96), both woman and seer, both English and African. Like Chris and Ikem, Beatrice gradually comes to know herself better. But Beatrice has a more profound understanding of both her personal history and her cultural roots, and she is able to perceive the connections between not only the immediate past but also the distant past and the present. Like Chris and Ikem Beatrice can make prophecies that come true; she tells Chris, 'And I see trouble building up for us. It will go to Ikem first. No joking, Chris. He will be the precursor to make straight the way. But after him it will be you. We are all in it ...' (p. 105). Again, we see that Beatrice's focus is always on the whole not just individual parts; her concerns are not based solely in egotistical interests, like Chris's and Ikem's initially are, but in the connections between people, the interconnectedness of all. Further, Beatrice's prophecies are more genuine in the sense that they originate in neither an attempt to second-guess the future, as Ikem's do, nor in a joke, as Chris's prophecy does. Beatrice's look into the future comes out of her understanding of various pasts – the country's, Ikem's, Chris's – and her analysis of the present.

The prophetic capacity of each of the major characters represents the movement of the entire novel and reveals something of Achebe's purpose in writing the book. It looks to the future, in every character, in every story, in the title of the novel itself. In Ikem's 'Hymn to the Sun' Achebe reveals the significance of the novel's title and points out the importance of stories for the future: anthills survive 'to tell the new grass of the savannah about last year's brush fires' (p. 28). Because, as the elder from Abazon says, 'the story is everlasting' (p. 114), the power of the story (and the storyteller) lies in its ability to bring past, present and future together. We see this power dynamic at work throughout the novel. For instance, Ikem's 'Hymn to the Sun' – which itself brings together old proverbs and modern politics – lives on after his death, teaching Chris about the necessity of engagement in storytelling and the danger of complacency: 'And now the times had come round again out of storyland. Perhaps not as bad as the first times, yet. But they could easily end worse' (p. 194). The warning that the future could be worse than the past – alluding to both colonialism and the corrupt dictatorship before the coup that put Sam in the presidency – is one which Chris finally acknowledges, for he passes the poem to Emmanuel saying, 'You must read this' (p. 196). Although such a warning is implicit in Achebe's storytelling as well, it is the consideration, the inclusion, of the past in order to come to terms with the present and look toward the future that Achebe emphasizes here and throughout the book. Ikem and Chris together with Beatrice teach Emmanuel about politics, about dying, about unifying people and ideas, through their stories. But in the final analysis it is Beatrice who teaches us the most about a future story and a future kind of storytelling.

What the character of Beatrice enables Achebe to do is to suggest a new means of storytelling, a new kind of storyteller, on which the next generation can base its future. In many ways *Anthills* is a search for the type of storytelling that in some real way represents a contemporary African nation. Achebe alludes to this sort of endeavor when he speaks of his use of the English language: 'I feel that the English language will be able to carry the weight of my African experience. But it will have to be a new English, still in full communion with its ancestral home but altered to suit its new African surroundings.'[11] Beatrice, although she initially lacks a complete knowledge of it, feels the ties to her cultural heritage and its contribution to who she is now and whom she may become. She recalls her mother's stories and her father's maxims (p. 100), and she realizes the effects that her personal and national history have had on her life: 'So, two whole generations before the likes of me could take a first-class degree in English, there were already barely literate carpenters and artisans of British rule hacking away in the archetypal jungle and subverting the very sounds and legends of daybreak to make straight my way' (p. 100). Unlike many of the other characters, Beatrice acknowledges her debt to the past and contributions of the present. And her storytelling demonstrates that acknowledgement, for Beatrice frequently invokes the past – in the form of childhood memories and traditional proverbs and myths, for example – as she tells her stories. Beatrice's storytelling suggests the dialectical aesthetic Amuta envisions.

Through Beatrice, Achebe describes a form of storytelling that recognizes the necessity and desirability of selectively and purposefully incorporating various ways of telling a story – whether proverbial, factual, passionate. Beatrice's storytelling represents a movement toward a creative amalgamation of facts and passions, past and present, people and ideas. She continually insists on the reconstruction of either/or situations, but it is not an insistence that comes out of the stereotypical female-as-peacemaker model. Beatrice does not advocate compromise necessarily, but deliberate and progressive reformulations of oppositions. Here is a form of storytelling that seeks to actively bring about change. It is not the sort espoused by one of the elders from Abazon: 'there are those others whose part is to wait and when the struggle is ended, to take over and recount its story' (p. 113). Such a view removes the storyteller from the struggle, and although Beatrice does recount Chris's story at the end of the novel, her narration is not a passive act.

Through it, she tries to show the way toward building a better future: 'Chris was sending us a message to beware. This world belongs to the people of the world not to any little caucus, no matter how talented' (p. 215). It is doubtful that Chris came to any such realization about the people of the world – it is so far removed from the way of thinking he displays throughout the book – but Beatrice's intepretation is important because it demonstrates her desire to make a story not only mean something but do something. Her focus on 'the people' is typical of her mode of storytelling for, like Ikem, Beatrice wants to create and tell stories that lead to real political, economic, and social changes, but unlike Ikem she also wants to make those intrinsically connected to the people they serve. As she tells Emmanuel, 'Ideas cannot live outside people' (p. 207).

Achebe's own manner and philosophy of storytelling seems closely aligned with Beatrice's, for he too sees the role of the writer as one of action rather than reaction.[12] The elder from Abazon states that 'it is only the story that can continue beyond the war and the warrior. ... The story is our escort; without it, we are blind' (p. 114), but throughout the novel Achebe demonstrates that not all stories are equally valuable or useful for any given purpose. Because he believes that 'the writer's role is more in determining than merely in reporting',[13] he, through Beatrice, suggests a kind of storytelling which looks ahead to a new future for Africa. In Beatrice's attempts to bring together elements of the past and present, we get a glimpse of Achebe's belief that 'our most meaningful job today should be to determine what kind of society we want, how we are going to get there, what values we can take from the past, if we can, as we move along.'[14] Beatrice suggests a way of getting this job done, and it is most clearly demonstrated in the naming ceremony.

Beatrice brings together past and present in the naming ceremony for Elewa and Ikem's daughter. Beatrice adapts the ancient rite to contemporary circumstances, creating a new hybrid with which to greet the future. As she did with Chris's and Ikem's modes of storytelling, she finds the flaw in the traditional naming ceremony, pointing out that it wrongly privileges masculine knowledge over maternal knowledge because it gives the father the responsibility of naming the child. This is not a simple inversion of Okonkwo's problem, making feminine knowledge all important, but a recognition of the problematic nature of knowledge. Beatrice points out how difficult it is to know anything, even the proper name to give a child. Although she challenges men's access to knowledge – 'What does a man know about a child anyway that he should presume to give it a name' – she also acknowledges that women do not have absolute knowledge either: 'It is really safest to ask the mother' (p. 206). For Beatrice, determining what is true knowledge comes down to a question of probability rather than absolutes. She names the baby 'AMAECHINA: May-the-path-never-close' (p. 206), symbolizing open access to knowledge, communication between past and present, and once again unification of apparent opposites, this time by giving a masculine name to a female child. For Beatrice, the story always combines different, seemingly irreconcilable, elements in an amalgamation that unifies and yet still preserves the identities of the individual elements. Taking Beatrice's cue, Elewa's uncle reminds the company to remember the children and the 'useless old people' when making plans for their future world (p. 211). The path should 'never over-grow' (p. 206) to block the link between past and present or to blur the distinctiveness of individual components. In other words, the new storytelling, as represented by Beatrice, must always remember its past even as it looks to the future. This idea is not new to Achebe; his earlier novels incorporate traditional proverbs and myths to tell stories of the present and allude to the future. However, in *Anthills* the sense of nostalgia which we find in the earlier novels is gone, and the focus is on the future – a future that acknowledges the past but insists on moving forward.

Achebe's agenda in *Anthills* is to effect change through a new kind of storytelling. It seems an uncharacteristically romantic notion for Achebe, and the last chapter is not without some irony, but the predominant theme of the book focuses on changing the world with words, through storytelling. Despite the romanticism, Achebe is realistic about the possibility. The closing lines of the book come from the very logical and practical Elewa (herself a link between past and present, having experienced a more traditional upbringing), and they add a bit of pragmatism to Beatrice's overly enthusiastic 'Oh my Chris!' speech. Elewa worries, 'What kind trouble you wan begin cause now? I beg-o. Hmm!' (p. 216), ending the novel on an uncertain note and thus reiterating the book's refusal to supply us with pat answers. We get Beatrice's brand of storytelling for the future, a storytelling that tries to resolve apparent oppositions while preserving individual elements, and we get a newborn child who represents a resolution of opposites in its name. However, Elewa's closing lines undercut the satisfaction ostensibly offered by such resolutions by reminding us that Kangan is still in trouble (a new government has not yet been installed) and that story-telling always causes some kind of trouble for someone. In the context of the novel, and considering also Achebe's essays on the role of the writer, causing trouble is not necessarily a bad thing. Thus the novel offers us a view of the storyteller as a person who recognizes the diffusion of power throughout society and uses that recognition to tell stories which effect change – stories, in other words, which cause trouble. John Povey suggests that these lines represent a rhetorical question Achebe poses to himself: 'Perhaps Achebe is in a state where he feels that his judgment of events is "hmm". But then again, perhaps he is contemplating what trouble he can begin to cause!'[15] It seems to me that Achebe is doing both. He demonstrates the uncertainty of knowledge inherent in any kind of storytelling by showing how difficult it is to actually know any-thing – facts, passions, even best friends. And he demonstrates the ways in which that kind of suspicion about knowledge, about pat answers and strict distinctions between (for instance) what is and is not 'true', gives the storyteller a kind of power to change the world. And changing the world is precisely what Achebe tries to do in all of his stories.

From *Modern Fiction Studies*, 37: 3 (Autumn 1991), 493–507.

NOTES

[Ikegami's essay contributes to the critical debate about the function of story in African societies today; and it is especially valuable as a study of *Anthills* as a self-reflexive text, a story about storytelling. It develops recent critical thought about the destabilising nature of multiple narrative and the problematics of narrative in relation to a post-independent African novel. Eds]

1. See, for example, articles by Karl H. Bottcher, 'The Narrative Technique in Achebe's Novels', *Journal of the New African Literature and the Arts*, 13/14 (1972), 1–12; Solomon O. Iyasere, 'Narrative Technique in *Things Fall Apart*' in *Critical Perspectives on Chinua Achebe*, edited by C. L. Innes and Bernth Lindfors (Washington, DC, 1979), pp. 93–110 (first publ. in *New Letters*, 40: 2 [1974], 73–93); Solomon O. Iyasere, 'Oral Tradition in the Criticism of African Literature', *Journal of Modern African Studies*, 13 (1975), 107–19; Eldred Jones, 'Language and Theme in *Things Fall Apart*', *Review of*

English Literature, 5: 4 (1964), 39–43; Eugene McCarthy, 'Rhythm and Narrative Method in Achebe's *Things Fall Apart*', *Novel*, 18 (1985), 243–56; Emmanuel Obiechina, 'Structure and Significance in Achebe's *Things Fall Apart*', *English in Africa*, 2: 2 (1975), 39–44; Felicity Riddy, 'Language as a Theme in *No Longer at Ease*', in *Critical Perspectives on Chinua Achebe* (cf. above), pp. 15–59 (first publ. in *Journal of Commonwealth Literature*, 9 [1970], 38–47).

Iyasere's 'Oral Tradition' (above) is especially helpful in identifying some of the characteristics of traditional African oral narratives.

2. Characters in Achebe's previous novels saw power as locatable even though power in precolonial Ibo society was flexible and integrated, which interestingly suggests the notion of power in modern European society described by Foucault:

> Power's condition of possibility, or in any case the viewpoint which permits one to understand its exercise ... must not be sought in the primary existence of a central point, in a unique source of sovereignty from which secondary and descendent forms would emanate; it is the moving substrate of force relations which, by virtue of their inequality, constantly engender states of power, but the latter are always local and unstable.

(Michel Foucault, *History of Sexuality*. vol. I: *An Introduction*, trans. Robert Hurley [New York, 1978], p. 93; first publ. as *Histoire de la sexualité* I. *La Volunté de savoir*, Bibliothèque des histoires [Paris, 1976].)

3. Bruce King sees the confusion as a flaw, asserting that the book is 'needlessly complex and trite – and responsive to current fashions' (Bruce King, 'Postcolonial Complexities', review of *Anthills of the Savannah* by Chinua Achebe, *Sewanee Review*, 96 (1988), lxxiv. I contend that the confusion is purposefully deployed and that the novel's responsiveness to 'current fashions' is a deliberate reflection of late twentieth-century life and art and politics in Africa as Achebe sees them.

4. For a discussion of the parallels between Nigeria and fictional Kangan, see Larry Diamond, 'Fiction as Political Thought', review of *Anthills of Savannah* by Chinua Achebe, *African Affairs*, 88 (1989), 435–45.

5. Chinua Achebe, *Anthills of the Savannah* (Garden City, NY, 1988), p. 7. All further references to the novel will be found in parentheses in the text.

6. Chinua Achebe, *Morning Yet on Creation Day* (Garden City, NY; revised and enlarged edn 1976), p. 68.

7. Chinua Achebe, *Arrow of God* (New York, 1974, 2nd edn), p. 106.

8. Diamond identifies Achebe with Ikem ('Fiction as Political Thought,' review of *Anthills of the Savannah* by Chinua Achebe, *African Affairs*, 88 [1989] 435–45, here p.433), but I will argue that Achebe to some extent identifies with many of the storytellers in the book and that, although he invests a great deal of himself in Ikem, he invests as much or more in Beatrice.

9. Interview, *Palaver: Interview with Five African Writers in Texas*, ed. Bernth Lindfors et al. (Austin, TX, 1972), p. 6.

10. Chidi Amuta, *The Theory of African Literature: Implications for Practical Criticism* (London, 1989), p. 121.

11. *Morning Yet on Creation Day*, p. 84.

12. *Palaver: Interview with Five African Writers in Texas*, p. 11.

13. Ibid., p. 11.

14. Ibid., p. 12.

15. John Povey, review of *Anthills of the Savannah* by Chinua Achebe, *African Arts*, 21: 4 (1988), 21–3.

4

Chinua Achebe: the Wrestler and the Challenge of Chaos

CHIDI OKONKWO

I ORDER AND THE FRONTIERS OF CHAOS

The central problem of Chinua Achebe's fiction is the perennial cycle of creation of order from chaos and the dissolution of order into chaos. This theme reflects Achebe's desire to use literature to contest Europe's disguise of colonialism as a civilising mission. By associating Africa with an absence of order, of soul, humanity itself, colonialist discourse had rationalised colonial conquests as a consecration of cosmos out of chaos, and thus invested the conqueror-as-Jehovah with absolute ownership rights over the creation. 'You do not walk in, seize the land, the person, the history of another, and then sit back and compose hymns of praise in his honour,' Achebe argued in 1990. 'You construct very elaborate excuses for your action. ... Finally, if the worse comes to the worst, you will be prepared to question whether such as he can be, like you, fully human.'[1] *Things Fall Apart* (1958) and *Arrow of God* (1964) were accordingly designed to challenge colonialist myths of Africa's inability to create order out of chaos. At the same time, with the passage of direct colonial domination, the problem assumed the new form of how to create a national order out of the anarchy of nation-states created by colonial masters to serve their own long-term interests. This second dimension of the problem is explored in

No Longer at Ease (1960), *A Man of the People* (1966) and *Anthills of the Savannah* (1987).

Persisting through all these texts is the use of wrestling metaphor to define different levels of conflict in terms of society's efforts to push back the frontiers of chaos. Ideally, the wrestler archetype represents society's hero challenging anarchic forces in symbolic re-enactment of the 'passage-rites of hero gods' in cosmogonic myth. Chaos has been described by Wole Soyinka, who makes the challenge a central issue in his first novel, *The Interpreters* (1965), as 'a chthonic realm, a storehouse for creative and destructive essences' which 'required a challenger, a human representative to breach it periodically [for] the well-being of the community'.[2] Though derived from the mythology of Soyinka's Yoruba rather than Achebe's Igbo culture, this fully captures the essence of the Igbo myth and ritual at the core of Achebe's exploration.

The ambiguity of creation and destruction, life/birth and death, is fully exploited in Achebe's integration of various mythologies to explore society in motion. Igbo mythology furnishes tales of intrepid adventurers who journey beyond the frontiers of order and engage spirit beings in combats from which they win wealth, fame or both. From Judaeo-Christian eschatololgy come paradigms within which historical events can be imaginatively 'intepreted as representations of an eternal struggle in which the world order is defended against chaos'.[3] As reworked in W. B. Yeats's 'The Second Coming' and T. S. Eliot's 'The Journey of the Magi', they provide a flexible frame for integrating past, present and future, ends and beginnings, into a model of society's ritual passage from the overthrow of indigenous cultures to the massive disillusionment provoked by the fraudulence of independence. Yeats's poem provides both the title and the controlling motif for *Things Fall Apart*, while Eliot's does the same for *No Longer at Ease*. But, in combination with indigenous models, their influence also pervades the whole of Achebe's major fiction. This essay examines their exploitation as structural devices and prefiguration motifs to explore the various manifestations of society's response to the challenges of chaos.

II THE WRESTLER, ORDER AND ORIGINATION

Consistent with its cultural-nationalistic inspiration, *Things Fall Apart* opens on an image of the hero as archetypal wrestler and creator of order:

> Okonkwo was well known throughout the nine villages and even beyond. His fame rested on solid personal achievements. As a young man of eighteen he had brought honour to his village by throwing Amalize the Cat .... in a fight which the old man agreed was one of the fiercest since the founder of their town had engaged a spirit of the wild for seven days and seven nights.[4]

By defining Okonkwo's wrestling within a mythical paradigm of the combat between a human hero and a monster or spirit of the wild,[5] the passage symbolically establishes the thematic thrust of the novel: the people of Umuofia through the representative figure of their ancestral hero had fought and conquered chaos to establish a civilisation without the help of the European civilising mission.

Going further, *Arrow of God* looks forward to an issue which Achebe has been stressing more forcefully in recent years, namely, the democratic basis of many indigenous African social organisations before they were undermined by dictatorial colonial regimes.[6] The six-village clan of Umuaro was founded in the mythical past, expressed in remarkably accurate palaeontological imagery as 'when lizards were still few and far between', to counter the threat of annihilation posed by Abam warriors.[7] Following their federation, they created a powerful. protective deity, Ulu, and assumed the new name and identity of Umuaro.[8] The Coming of Ulu became an annual ritual (complete with a validating myth) during which the cosmicization is symbolically re-enacted, with the Chief Priest of Ulu, Ezeulu, impersonating the god. In this role, Ezeulu's subjugation of the four days of the Igbo week corrresponds to the wrestling feat of the ancestral hero in *Things Fall Apart*, and accounts for his perennial concern that certain acts might be 'an augury of the world's ruin'[9] or cause 'the collapse and ruin of all things'.[10]

Achebe presents the rural cosmos as maintained through ritual observances whose internal contradictions make the order vulnerable to chaotic forces. Umuofia, for instance, alienated some citizens by branding them as ritually unclean; it also oppressed women who either had no male children or had given birth only to twins. Naturally, these disaffected people proved receptive to Christian missionaries' appeals. In *Arrow of God*, the creation of Ulu provokes the enmity of the autochthonous deities of the land, especially the deity of the chief village, Umunneora. Though Achebe rarely employs name symbolism beyond strict denotation, the word 'Umunneora' is a notable exception. 'Umunneora' translates into 'Children-' or 'Offspring of the Universal Mother', the primary originative force unifying within itself the Sky God Idemili and the

Earth Mother or Goddess, both of whom are represented by the Sacred Python.

Through such ironies, too, Achebe's protagonists become both challengers and carriers of chaos. In *Things Fall Apart*, Okonkwo's frequent acts of abomination against the Earth goddess, such as beating his wife during the sacred Week of Peace and participating in the ritual sacrifice of a boy with whom he has established a fatherson relationship, threaten the clan with annihilation by the defiled deity. Even his offer of military resistance to the white man, whom he correctly identifies with chaos, threatens to unleash the very chaos he hopes to keep at bay, for the trigger-happy colonial regime needs just such an excuse to subject Umuofia to Abame's fate of extermination. By contrast with Okonkwo who is conceived in classical heroic terms as a man of action, a vainglorious warrior, Ezeulu is 'an intellectual'.[11] His position also carries the irony of the Champion-as-Scapegoat who 'should go ahead and confront danger before it reaches the people'.[12] Yet when the need arises for him to fulfil this role, the very intellectual endowments which equip him for the role also impel him to subvert it.

Arrow of God opens with Ezeulu performing one of the lunar rituals for taming chaos and responding to history. At every new moon, he eats one of the thirteen sacred yams selected from new yam offerings made by every adult male after the yam harvest, and then offers a sacrifice to Ulu. This is a calendar system through which the clan regulates its collectivised life. The yam offering itself ensures an accurate annual census, since each man offers just one yam to Ulu. Through this ritual, Achebe employs the symbolism of numbering and measuring to develop an argument about the clan's development of a civilisation without any help from Europe's civilising mission. An interesting sidelight is thrown on this by Daniel J. Boorstin's comment that 'the word "moon" in English and its cognate in other languages are rooted in the base *me* meaning measure'.[13] One is also reminded of Aeschylus' *Prometheus Bound*, in which the Greek hero proudly claims the invention of 'number .... outstanding among clever devices' as one of his greatest contributions to civilisation. The New Yam festival additionally symbolises the clan's consciousness of historical change and the need for continual self-regeneration and self-contemporisation. This emerges from the fates of the minor gods who make their sole annual outings during the festival:

Some of them would be very old, nearing the time when their power would be transferred to new carvings and they would be cast aside: and some would have been made only the other day. The very old ones carried face marks like the men who made them, in the days before Ezeulu's grandfather proscribed the custom. At last year's festival only three of these ancients were left. Perhaps this year one or two more would disappear, following the men who made them in their own image and departed long ago.[14]

Ezeulu's personal tragedy becomes inevitable when intellectual curiosity about the nature of his power combines with a desire to gain political dominance by disrupting the New Yam festival at a time when the colonial regime's military 'pacification' of the territory has rendered Ulu and his priest redundant. Ogbuefi Nwaka points this out[15] and Ezeulu himself receives an intimation of the truth in his dream-vision at Okperi in which Umuaro people scorn Ulu and Ezeulu as anachronisms.[16] Imprisoned for thirty-two days by the District Officer, Ezeulu misses eating two sacred yams and, upon his release, refuses to rectify the dislocation of order by eating up the excess yams. The entire series of conflicts – between Ezeulu and Umuaro, Ezeulu and the District Officer, indigenous and alien colonial order – is presented by Achebe and his characters in metaphors of wrestlers challenging chaos, so that Ezeulu's refusal to eat the yams becomes an act of double abdication of duty. The ensuing famine constitutes a dissolution of order, the clan's descent into hell in its rite of passage. The transition into the new dispensation is eased by the discardment of Ulu and his priest, wrestlers who have become carriers of chaos.

Achebe is able to transform Umuaro's collapse into a rite of passage because of a crucial detail often ignored by his readers and critics, namely, that despite the prominence of Ezeulu and Ulu, the real protagonist-deity of Umuaro in the central conflict is not the human-made deity Ulu but the eternal and autochthonous-deity Idemili, Umuaro's counterpart to the white man's sky god. This explains many curious details in the plot, like Ulu's being consecrated through Idemili's myth and rituals[17] and the impact of the alien religion being measured in relation to Idemili's sacred python.[18] It is the python whose routing by children's taunts signals the imminent collapse of the old order,[19] exposes Ulu's shrine to assault from the Christian church bell,[20] and forebodes Ezeulu's own destruction and the 'ruin of the world'.[21] Contemporising this deity in his Christian counterpart enables Achebe to rationalise the colonial defeat as a rite of passage.

III   THE WRESTLER, ORDER AND THE NATION-STATE

As Roderick Wilson has observed, 'the new culturally-diverse society of late and post-colonial Nigeria is a paradigm of the "mere anarchy" which began in the world of *Things Fall Apart*.'[22] Yet it also represents a new form of order coalescing out of chaos. Indeed, *No Longer at Ease*, the first of the national novels, deals with the nation's birth crises and throes of becoming. Confronted with tribalism, corruption among public officials, and the progressive decay of the country's social institutions, Achebe traces their origins beyond the facts of human failings or corruptibility to the circumstances of the creation of the new nation-state out of numerous competing ethnic groups, and the plague of leaders bereft of vision and commonsense.

Unlike Umuofia which traced its origins to a common ancestry, and Umuaro which was forged out of common necessity and consensus among the federating clans, the nation-state of Nigeria comprises a host of competing ethnic groups forcibly amalgamated by imperial Britain to serve its own needs. Achebe's national novels have been preoccupied with the issue of how to create a genuine national and moral order out of the anarchy of inward-looking ethnic orders and the predatory legacy of colonialism. Set in the inter-dispensation period just before 'independence', *No Longer at Ease* introduces the incipient problem of leadership failures as well as the conflict between the demands of nationhood and the persistence of ethnic loyalties, while *A Man of the People* emphasises the anarchy, violence and immorality of independence politics. The situation is given a close-up treatment in *Anthills of the Savannah*, whose focus is on evils of power isolated from the citizenry. The monster is no less than the head of state himself, a military dictator with a pathological fear of contact with the people.

To comment on the new developments, new dimensions of the ritual-passage archetypes are brought to bear on the new phenomenon. For instance, whereas the Yeatsian gyre is employed in a primarily anecdotal sense in *Things Fall Apart* to define the pattern of Umuofia's collapse to the forces of chaos, it is only in the post-independence disillusionment novels that the full gyral dialectic is explored. In *No Longer at Ease* and *A Man of the People* the ritual-passage paradigms acquire the extra dimension of the heroic quest or 'sacred journey'. Joseph Campbell explains the basic motif: 'A hero ventures forth from the world of common day into a region of supernatural wonder: fabulous forces are there encountered and a decisive victory is won; the hero comes back from this mysterious adventure with the power to bestow boons on his fellow men.'[23] The nation-state is symbolically transformed into pre-cosmos, the spiritland of Igbo folktales.

In itself, the paradigm is morally neutral, a basic human desire for self-fulfilment. However, it is also liable to anti-social expression, as in the pillage of colonial territories by the colonisers, and later the plunder of the national wealth in the post-independence era by the indigenous elite. While a true hero or wrestler translates the boon into a promethean benefit for the people, a false one basely conceives the heroic boon as material loot and thus degrades independence or decolonisation into a mere change of despoilers rather than a radical transformation of social relations to ensure social justice. The pattern is clarified through integration with the eschatological cyclicism of 'The Second Coming' and 'The Journey of the Magi', which encompass the post-independence dialectic of betrayed promises and frustration at the point of escape, represented in the collision between the apex of one cone and the hypothetical base of the opposing cone in Yeats's gyre. The birth/child witnessed by Eliot's Magi, indistinguishable from death, is therefore the Yeatsian beast in the cradle, the ruler of the post-independence state. With disillusionment, the phrase 'second coming' rings ominously from novel to novel, and the underlying concept of apocalypse begins to strike the reader with its proper meaning as revelation.

Considerable narrative economy is achieved by Achebe through this integration of different paradigms, for social evils could then be explored both as manifestations of the moment and as part of a larger historical pattern of contradictions. Diagnosis of social ills simultaneously becomes prefiguration of worse to come unless chaos is tamed permanently. The figure of the Champion or Wrestler who carries a taint of anarchy within himself, seen in Okonkwo of *Things Fall Apart* and Ezeulu in *Arrow of God*, becomes fully developed into the leader as villain, the Messiah as Beast boldly striding into the promised land of the new-born state in the persons of Chief Nanga in *A Man of the People* and His

Excellency Sam, life President of Kangan in *Anthills of the Savannah*.

Action in the national novels accordingly unfolds in three zones: the nation-state, the ethnic group, and a reincarnation of the latter in the former. The ethnic world is home or cosmos, and is governed by certain moral principles whose contravention would provoke spontaneous moral outrage. The national zone is 'beyond', the equivalent of spiritland or chaos, where the moral principles governing 'home' lose their sanctions. Movement from 'home' to 'beyond' becomes a transition in that second sense of 'rites of passage' described by Arnold van Gennep, for 'whoever passes from one [territory] to the other finds himself physically and magico-religiously in a special situation for a certain length of time: he wavers between two worlds'.[24] In *A Man of the People*, Odili's father who is notoriously corrupt when operating outside the clan, and expresses the general view that 'the mainspring of political action was personal gain',[25] reveals exemplary probity within the clan. But the clan's moral borders are shrinking under pressure from the national arena. A village shopkeeper, Josiah, ostracised for fraud[26] in his village, is nevertheless acceptable as part of Chief Nanga's campaign team. The pervasive 'eating' imagery identified in *A Man of the People* and similar disillusionment novels by Obiechina[27] is consistent with the perception of the territory as booty. This gives a dangerous new meaning to the figure of 'a man of the people': he is not only their champion but also their mirror. Often, the name of the ethnic group is involved to rationalise a purely selfish enterprise. In *A Man of the People*, Chief Nanga urges Odili to come to the capital to help in securing the clan's share of the 'national cake', lest too much of it be appropriated by the 'highland tribes'.

The exploration of this phenomenon in *No Longer at Ease* uncovers the threats posed to national authenticity by an unfortunate interplay of individual drives, ethnic loyalties and competition, and economic contradictions within the new Nigeria. Uneven development and opportunities between the rising urban areas (typified by the national capital, Lagos) and the rural areas draw to the urban areas people to whom the nation-state is a nebulous entity, the national government an alien institution. The adventurers therefore try to enhance their competitiveness through kith-and-kin solidarity, symbolically re-creating the ethnic cosmos (and loyalties) in the national chaos, to the detriment of the nation. Such negative tendencies receive reinforcement from the adversary relationship between coloniser and colonised. By its very nature, a colonial government epitomises institutionalised illegitimacy and plunder, with questions of morality being strictly subordinated to economic interest. In dealing with it, therefore, its victims simply adopt its own amoral logic. Considerable linguistic evidence for this exists in the retention of concepts and vocabulary which distance speakers from national institutions. The civil service is the 'white man's establishment'; work done there is the 'white man's work' and a civil service job is itself a 'European post'.

A close-up view is given in the Lagos branch of the Umuofia Progressive Union in *No Longer at Ease*. Though not portrayed as plundering adventurers, the members certainly see no convergence between their interests and those of the nation; they have no stake in the well-being of the nation and would plunder it if they could. Formed six years earlier, the Union symbolically reconsecrates a portion of the alien chaos into a cosmos for Umuofia people:

> Those .... who leave their home town to find work in towns all over Nigeria regard themselves as sojourners .... When they have saved up enough money they ask their relations at home to find them a wife, or they build a 'zinc' house on their family land. No matter where they are in Nigeria, they start a local branch of the Umuofia Progressive Union.[28]

The main plot echoes the people's quest in the story of the protagonist, Obi Okonkwo. The plot is typical of that of the first-generation African novel of disillusionment, which often explores a variation upon the Promethean theme. The protagonist travels, literally or figuratively, to the West for higher education, and returns with grand visions of transforming the society. However, the society whose collective psyche has also been deformed by colonialism, rejects him.[29]

In this particular case, Obi Okonkwo returns to Nigeria after university studies in Britain to confront the ambiguities of an inchoate nation in the process of becoming. For Umuofia people, the correspondence between his career and that of the quest hero of folk tales is self-evident: 'In our folk stories a man gets to the land of spirits when he has passed seven rivers, seven forests and seven hills. Without doubt you have visited the land of spirits.'[30] To another, Obi is 'a little child returned from wrestling in the spirit world',[31] a reincarnation of previous clan heroes, especially his famous grandfather Okonkwo now legendized as a champion 'who faced the white man single-handed and died in the fight'.[32] Such perception is justified by the fact that they financially sponsored his sacred journey to bring back knowledge, a potent aid for wrestling in the new spiritland. The wrestling metaphor is obliquely sustained in the fact that they wanted him to become a 'lawyer' so as to champion their causes in litigation combats. The humane values behind the community's action are irreproachable, and the goal is a legitimate response to historical imperatives. Consequently, the plot presents such ventures as part of the dilemma of the nations coming-into-being, rather than as conflict between hero and community over a boon. This is quite different from the situation developed in the next novel, *A Man of the People*.

With Achebe's and his characters' unerring ability to identify equivalencies and contemporise roles, national politics becomes a new form of combat and the politician a new form of wrestler in *A Man of the People*. In a parody of the concept of representative government, people see their parliamentarian as their 'champion' and the representative regularly exploits this perception to dupe them. Achebe's emphasis on institutions and processes of governance in the two ethnic novels shows that the issue here is not that of unfamiliarity with the political system itself, but of discontinuity between local and national identities. In his fiction, criticism and political writings, he has constantly challenged Western claims to exclusive development of democratic institutions, and Western rationalisation of neocolonialism as an attempt to nurture democratic ideals in Africa.[33] It is the world of those novels rather than any Western ideals that provides the moral frame of reference; hence the national novels indict both the leaders and the citizenry for apostasy to indigenous ideals.

On the whole, it is the leaders who are cast as villains for betraying their inherently promethean responsibilities. This is a departure from the predominant treatment of this issue in African disillusionment literature, where the protagonist's promethean instinct clashes with the Olympian amorality of the leaders. Famous examples are Ayi Kwei Armah's *Fragments* and *Why Are We So Blest?* and the Sekoni story-strand in Soyinka's *The Interpreters*.[34] In Armah's terms, the hero starts as 'a crossover. One of those who rise from the plains to live on Olympus. A hero, Part man, part god.'[35] 'Promethean crossing' involves renouncing the privileges accruing to his new rank, and casting his lot with the down-trodden. Each

hero also has a definite boon of light: Baako in *Fragments* brings
film-making skills to interpret his people's historical experiences,
while Sekoni brings electrical engineering skills.

By contrast, Achebe's heroes bring no boons, and are indeed the
recipients of boons from the people. The circumstances of Obi's
departure evoke a 'Promethean crossing', especially in the imagery
of Ikedi's valedictory prayer:

> In times past, Umuofia would have required of you to fight in her
> wars and bring home human heads. But these were days of darkness
> from which we have been delivered by the blood of the Lamb of
> God. Today we send you to bring knowledge. ... We are sending you
> to learn book.[36]

Obi returns with nothing but Prufrockian bits and rags of poetry
through which he tries to tame his own internal chaos, but which
are useless to the society. It is no accident that his quarrel with his
people does not arise over material demands but over an issue (mar-
rying a girl branded as ritually impure in Umuofia several hundred
miles away from Lagos) which is extremely marginal to national
questions. Generations of critics have therefore erred in interpreting
it as conflict between Western idealism and corrupt indigenous
African cultures, or 'a paradigm of a man caught between the irreconcilable values of different ways of life'.[37] The quarrel has a special
significance as a test of Obi's adequacy for his role of wrestler in the
new socio-historical context. Having refused earlier to become the
people's courtroom champion, he now reveals an anarchic individualism by abdicating his promethean role of enlightenment.

In *Anthills of the Savannah*, the three foreign-educated joint-
protagonists and first-person narrators – Chris Oriko the
Commissioner for Information and Ikem Osodi the journalist and
poet, and Beatrice Okoh, Senior Assistant Secretary in the Ministry
of Finance – are variations upon the same model. While Ikem intuitively gropes towards the role, as shown in his courageous advocacy of the cause of the masses, Chris initially negates it because of
the nature of his office. Being basically honest and capable of self-
knowledge, however, all symbolically attain the role eventually (the
men doing so shortly before their deaths), and this attainment
comes through their contact with the masses, represented by the
urban proletariat and students.

Anthills of the Savannah fulfils the chilling scenario raised at
the end of *A Man of the People* of a vicious cycle of coups and

counter-coups. Both novels therefore strongly imply that part of the problem with the leadership springs from their path to power. None can lay a genuine claim to a popular mandate, a genuine vision, or a special equipment for leadership. Ultimately, this raises the question of the legitimacy of the political power exercised by leaders who come to power through such means. Though each coup d'état terminates an evil regime, it provides no assurance of a better leader or era succeeding the present. It is in this new spiritland, for instance, that Odili appropriates his political party's car and funds in *A Man of the People* while in *Anthills of the Savannah* a police sergeant, custodian of law and order, plunders a brewery truck and attempts to rape a girl. The scene evokes the final scenes of Armah's *The Beautyful Ones Are Not Yet Born*, juxtaposing the overthrow of a corrupt regime with the image of policemen and soldiers, the new messiahs, erecting road-blocks to despoil travellers. Ironically, Achebe himself had attacked Armah's novel as 'a sick book. Sick, not with the sickness of Ghana but with the sickness of the human condition ... in the best manner of [Western] existential writing.'[38]

Even the idealistic ending of *Anthills of the Savannah* must be balanced against the icon of the bus on the borders of hell, the furious police sergeant-as-beast rushing to his lair, and the absurdist model of struggle un-ironically enunciated in Ikem's university lecture (Chapter 9: 'Views of Struggle'), based on a folk tale in which a doomed tortoise frenziedly plants false evidence of heroic struggle before being killed by the leopard. Back in Beatrice's flat, Ikem's girl friend Elewa gives birth to a female child. In a significant departure from tradition, the child is collectively named by Beatrice and her circle of fellow survivors, a cross-section of the society, representing different social classes, professions, ethnic origins and religious affiliations. Obviously the nucleus of a new nation, this gathering is the grand resolution towards which Achebe's fiction has been moving: a national community harmonising the various ethnic cultures created by colonial masters all over Africa. 'Amaechina', the name of Elewa's baby, rendered in English as 'may the path never close', is both a prayer and a resolve that the new order should not again disintegrate in chaos, that the champion of the era in the throes of birth may overthrow the forces of chaos and break the apocalyptic cycle of the gyre.

With this, one also notices a final fusion of wrestler, champion and writer, in a culmination of a transformative process which hindsight now establishes being initiated at the end of *Things Fall*

Apart with the District Commissioner proposing to write a book on his empire-building adventures in Africa. Each of Achebe's novels shows at least one protagonist who is proposing to write a book, historical or fictive, as a means of creating harmony out of the chaos of experience. Obi in *No Longer at Ease* proposes to write a novel, while his father regards writing as symbolising the white man's power and timelessness attested in Pontius Pilate's 'What is written is written'.[39] In *Arrow of God* Ezeulu painfully recognises the birth of an era in which the wrestler-against-chaos is not the warrior or the priest but the hero equipped with the magic of education or 'writing'. He therefore sends Oduche his son to acquire this magic, as his (Ezeulu's) own vanguard and champion.[40] The process climaxes in *A Man of the People* and *Anthills of the Savannah*, both of which are attributed to writer-protagonists.

One suspects that Ikem's theory of struggle in *Anthills of the Savannah* signals the author's final concession to the historical reality of the failure of military and political processes to break Africa's cycle of futility and anarchy. Literature makes experience available to future generations in their own combat with chaos. Its creation constitutes the one combat the forces of chaos cannot win, and the writer or storyteller is the champion combating those forces. There is neither authorial irony nor self-parody in Chris's claim that he retained his ministerial post because he 'couldn't be writing this if [he] didn't hang around to observe it all'.[41] Romantic or idealistic as this may sound, it is consistent with Achebe's long-held view of the artist,[42] allusively embodied in the novel's last lines beginning with the English Romantic poet John Keats ('Truth is beauty'), followed by Yeats whose line ('A terrible beauty is born') is adapted and linked to the image of Kunene's Emperor Chaka in which it finds a grim echo. Consequently, in his remarkable synthesis of Aristotelian, Shakespearean and Igbo traditional concepts of the creative writer, the Abazon orator clearly examines various forms of resistance and finally endorses creative literature:

> It is only the story that can continue beyond the war and the warrior. It is the story that outlives the sound of war-drums and the exploits of bravefighters. It is the story ... that saves our progeny from blundering like blind beggars into the spikes of the cactus fence.[43]

This explains certain incongruities in Achebe's portrayal of his writer-protagonists. A distinction seems to exist between protagonists as writers or storytellers, in which role they are the author's

raisonneurs, and as characters in the story who are open to authorial satire. It is a difficult distinction to sustain, and Achebe's occa-
sional slips result in confusion over whether to interpret the
narrator ironically or literally. This dualism is ignored by critics
such as C. L. Innes who excuse even the most glaring contradiction
as ironical, and Adewale Maja-Pearce who sneeringly insists on a
literal intepretation when every textual evidence points to irony.[44]

With *Anthills of the Savannah*, Achebe's moralist approach to the
problem of order and chaos converges with the socialist practices of
such writers as Ngugi wa Thiong'o and the conservatism of Ayi
Kwei Armah. The convergence is largely compelled by their
exploitation of basically the same eschatological paradigms, including those of W. B. Yeats and T. S. Eliot, whose inherently cyclical
models of history generate tensions that cannot easily be reconciled
with the anecdotal or discursive aspects of the fiction. A famous
illustration is Ngugi's *Petals of Blood* (1977), in which the Yeatsian
gyre is so central to the Marxist structuring of themes as to provide
the epigraphs to the four parts of the novel: 'Walking ... Towards
Bethlehem ... To Be Born ... Again, La Luta Continua.' The grim
cyclicism is not relieved either by the Marxist slogan appended by
Ngugi to Yeats, or by the pervasive Marxist rhetoric of his raison-
neur, Karega, asserting the historical inevitability of victory for the
oppressed. Ten years and an ideology separate *Petals of Blood* from
Anthills of the Savannah, but the kinship has only grown closer.
Such inevitable affinities are often ignored as a result of critics'
search for an imaginary saving ideal called 'optimism'. Yet when all
forms of self-assertion unravel in conquest, and neocolonialism
receives a new dimension in religious, ethnic and class contradictions within individual African states, fashionable 'optimism' is not
the answer. What is required is a confrontation with the reality of
Messiah-Beasts whose perennial rebirths have ensured the triumph
of chaos.

This is the first appearance of the above essay which has been
specifically written for inclusion in this New Casebook.

NOTES

[Chidi Okonkwo's essay encompasses much of Achebe's major fiction. The
essay reflects formalist approaches to narrative in tracing motifs. Like much
postcolonial criticism, however, this essay has affinities with poststructural-

ist emphases upon the socio-cultural contexts of narrative creation – whilst it reveals the purposive nature of Achebe's development of mythical motifs drawn from African and Europen traditions. The author as significant to a textual analysis implicitly challenges the western Barthesian idea of the 'death of the author'. References to the novels are included in the following Endnotes, not in the essay itself. Eds]

1. Chinua Achebe, 'African Literature as Restoration of Celebration', provides even greater elaboration. See Okike: *An African Journal of New Writing*, 30 (November 1990), 11–13, passim. Achebe himself has explained that he started writing 'to help my society regain its belief in itself and put away the complex of years of denigration and self-denigration' by demonstrating through art that precolonial African societies 'were not mindless but frequently had a philosophy ..., poetry [and] dignity'. See Chinua Achebe, 'The Novelist as Teacher', 1974 essay reprinted in Achebe's *Morning Yet on Creation Day* (London, 1977), p. 44; also 'The Role of a Writer in a New Nation', *Nigeria Magazine*, 81 (June 1964), 160. The origins of Achebe's writing thus illustrate one of the more popular definitions of postcolonial literatures as those that 'emerged from the experience of colonisation and asserted themselves by foregrounding the tension with the imperial power, and emphasising their differences from the assumptions of the imperial centre'. See Bill Ashcroft, Gareth Griffiths, and Helen Tiffin, *The Empire Writes Back: Theory and Practice in Post-Colonial Literatures* (London and New York, 1989), p. 2.

2. Wole Soyinka, *Myth, Literature and the African World* (Cambridge, 1976), pp. 2–3.

3. Jurgen D. Moltmann, 'Eschatology', *New Encyclopaedia Britannica*, vol. 6 (1980), p. 959.

4. Chinua Achebe, *Things Fall Apart* (1958; rpt.London, 1976), p. 3.

5. As Mircea Eliade has demonstrated in *The Myth of the Eternal Return*, such a combat is a ritual archetype of man's conquest of chaos. See Mircea Eliade, *The Myth of the Eternal Return, or Cosmos and History*, trans. Willard R. Trask (Princeton, NJ, 1971), pp. 19 and 37 passim.

6. See 'Chinua Achebe: Nigerian Novelist', interview with Bill Moyers in Betty Sue Flowers (ed.), *A World of Ideas* (New York, 1989), p. 340.

7. Chinua Achebe, *Arrow of God* (1964; rpt. London, 1974), p. 14.

8. Ibid., p. 15.

9. Ibid., p. 7.

10. Ibid., p. 229.

11. Achebe in Interview with Robert Serumaga, *African Writers Talking*, ed. Dennis Duerden and Cosmo Pieterse (London, 1972), pp. 16–17.

12. *Arrow of God*, p. 189.

13. Danuiel J. Boorstin, *The Discoverers* (New York, 1985), p. 4.

14. *Arrow of God*, p. 202.

15. Ibid., pp. 39–40.

16. Ibid., p. 159.

17. Ibid., pp. 70–2.

18. Ibid., pp. 43–52.

19. Ibid., pp. 204–5.

20. Ibid., p. 210.

21. Ibid., pp. 220 and 222.

22. Roderick Wilson, 'Eliot and Achebe: An Analysis of Some Formal and Philosophical Qualities in *No Longer at Ease*', in *Critical Perspectives on Chinua Achebe*, ed. C. L. Innes and Bernth Lindfors (London, 1978), p. 161.

23. Joseph Campbell, *The Hero with a Thousand Faces* (1949; rpt. London, 1988), p. 30.

24. Arnold Van Gennep, *The Rites of Passage*, trans. Monika B. Vizedom and Gabrielle L. Caffee (London, 1960), p. 18.

25. Chinua Achebe, *A Man of the People* (London, 1966), pp. 114–15.

26. Ibid., pp. 84–6.

27. E. N. Obiechina, 'Post-independence Disillusionment in Three African Novels', *Nsukka Studies in African Literature*, 1: 1 (March, 1978), 54–78.

28. *No Longer at Ease*, p. 4.

29. The pattern is also found in the Sekoni subplot in Wole Soyinka's *The Interpreters* (London, 1965) and Ayi Kwei Armah's *Fragments* (1970) and *Why Are We So Blest?* (New York, 1972).

30. Ibid., p. 46.

31. Ibid., p. 47.

32. Ibid., p. 48.

33. 'There was democracy in many parts of Africa before colonial rule came,' Achebe argued in 1989. 'The colonial system in itself was the

very antithesis of democracy. So, no matter how long you stayed under it, you would not learn democracy.' See 'Chinua Achebe: Nigerian Novelist', interview with Bill Moyers in Betty Sue Flowers (ed.), *A World of Ideas*, p. 340.

34. Wole Soyinka's *The Interpreters* and Ayi Kwei Armah's *Fragments* and *Why Are We So Blest?* [details in note 29 above; but see note 35 below for text used for quotation].

35. Ayi Kwei Armah, *Why Are We So Blest?* (London, 1974), p. 101.

36. *No Longer at Ease*, p. 9.

37. Arthur Ravenscroft, *Chinua Achebe* (London, 1969), p. 20.

38. Chinua Achebe, 'Africa and Her Writers', *Morning Yet On Creation Day*, p. 25.

39. *No Longer at Ease*, p. 115.

40. *Arrow of God*, pp. 189–90.

41. *Anthills of the Savannah*, p. 2.

42. As Chinua Achebe's literature student in 1977, the present writer clearly remembers Achebe employing a version of Chris's argument, in teaching Ferdinand Oyono's *Houseboy*, to interpret Oyono's suffering hero Toundi as an artist figure, Toundi's notorious greed as the artist's greed for experience, and Toundi's failure to run away from his French tormentors as the artist's insistence on witnessing all so as to be able to record it for posterity. The operative noun and verb in characterising Toundi were the same: 'witness'. Though it is tempting to think that Achebe's views might have changed in the intervening years, this is evidently not so, for his current writing up to the 1990s has been more forcefully contemporising the same arguments which inaugurated his cultural-nationalistic writing, such as the attacks on Joseph Conrad, Joyce Cary and Albert Schweitzer. See for instance notes 1 and 33. See also Achebe's 'The Education of a "British Protected Child"', text of the Ashby Lecture given at Clare Hall, Cambridge University, January 1993, published in *The Cambridge Review*, 114 (June 1993), 51–7.

43. *Anthills of the Savannah*, p. 124.

44. C. L. Innes expresses surprise that 'early reviewers and critics of this novel could ever have identified Achebe with Odili' (*Chinua Achebe* [Cambridge, 1990], p. 84). For his part, Adewale Maja-Pearce, who begins by wrongly denying the ideological validity of Achebe's writing, proceeds by so determinedly ignoring Achebe's ironies that he undermines even his most revealing insights. The criticism is helped neither by the ill-conceived chattiness of the language which tends to under-

mine the seriousness of the argument, nor by the author's tendency to raise issues that are too complex to be adequately and fairly explored in the kind of general survey he has undertaken. See Adewale Maja-Pearce, *A Mask Dancing: Nigerian Novelists of the Eighties* (London, 1992).

5

The Politics of the Signifier: Ngugi wa Thiong'o's *Petals of Blood*

STEWART CREHAN

Critics have on the whole been fairly kind to *Petals of Blood*, a novel of epic ambitions that took its author six years to complete ... [M]ost critics of the novel seem noticeably bashful about honestly confronting it as a work of imaginative literature ... Could it be that the moralistic urgency of *Petals of Blood* is so infectious that the resultant spiritual heat has led otherwise level-headed critics to throw certain critical criteria out of the window? Or could it be that Ngugi's revolutionary status, confirmed by the banning of *Ngaahika Ndeenda*, his subsequent detention, and now his political exile, has prevented these critics – especially those with a residual sense of guilt – from voicing strong criticisms of his creative work for fear of being labelled agents of neo-colonialism? Whatever the reason, the 'complex web'[1] of *Petals of Blood* has been draped with another texture: a bland veil of praise that mystifies where it ought to clarify, and keeps silent where it ought to speak out. If one said that reading *Petals of Blood* is an unsatisfying, frustrating and painful labour that would, of course, be a subjective judgement requiring more 'objective' corroboration. Yet there is something insidiously dishonest – even puritanically self-denying – about a critical practice that represses the reader's own aesthetic response for the sake of some 'higher truth' – a practice that some African writers have possibly encouraged.[2] The 'higher truth', if it is anywhere, is encountered in the reading experience, which is, in the first instance, an encounter with language. If a novel a has a 'political message', that message is the entire text, not something to be abstracted or dug out, like coal from the surrounding rock.

... No one, for example, can doubt that *Petals of Blood* points its finger in the right direction: the ravages of drought, the cynical attitude of the comprador bourgeoisie towards the rural areas and the catastrophic results of capitalist 'development' are all urgently topical themes. This should not tempt us, however, to allow purely external criteria to take the place of the politico-aesthetic criteria which are clearly applicable in the light of the text's inherent strategies. Hence, what I have called 'the politics of the signifier', as opposed to a 'politics of the signified'.[3] With the latter, the 'content' or 'message' is extracted from the novel like a nut from its shell, where the nut is the message and the shell is its formal or stylistic presentation. With the former, textual strategies are analyzed, not merely as a means to a higher end (where the 'means' are value free and the 'end' is value laden), but as independent signifiers carrying their own signifieds. These signifiers function both within the text, interacting with each other to produce its textuality, and through and beyond it as part of a larger web, so that the novel seems less an autonomous entity than a local configuration of strands forever suspended 'between texts' – in other words, an 'intertext', for which no single author can be held responsible.

Intertextuality constantly refers us to other sets of strategies, other texts and genres:

> a text is not a line of words releasing a single 'theological' meaning (the 'message' of the Author-God) but a multi-dimensional space in which a variety of writings, none of them original, blend and clash. The text is a tissue of quotations drawn from the innumerable centres of culture.[4]

Some would maintain that in this blending and clashing of 'writings', all signifieds are ultimately deferred, but by deferring meaning in this way we neutralize writing as a political act: by avoiding judgement in the face of a 'plurality' of meanings, we let every writer of every hue off the hook. And there is a difference between naïve or unconscious 'quotations' and those that are made self-consciously, ironically or critically. The text may not be the emanation of an Author-God, but neither is it an arbitrary happening: textuality implies intentionality. The approach I am advocating here, however, must be set against those that posit total authorial control,[5] or reduce the text to a set of purely communicative strategies intended by an author for a sociologically defined group of readers as his or her own special addresses.[6] ...

The first and most obvious textual element in *Petals of Blood* is the story. Despite the multiple narration and complicated time-shifts, sequential patterns are of key importance; the novel not only sets out to explain the present in terms of the past, but tries to interpret the meaning of historical change ... At one level, the story is like a religious parable: a few chosen souls, mysteriously brought together, are drawn towards a spiritual goodness they can feel but do not understand, as Wanja is drawn back to Ilmorog; they are then made to see into Kenya's past, and the meaning of their individual pasts, in a series of induced confessions and verbal memoirs some revolutionary providence must have linked, and whose true import places a great strain on those afraid of the light. Since much of the story is told through intradiegetic narrators,[7] story and narration become closely intertwined. Yet one of the few long speeches that is also a significant speech event, i.e. one that advances the story, is Kareg's confession concerning Mukami, which leads to a violent change in Munira's attitude towards Karega. More often, 'action-in-the-present' is brought to a halt for the sake of sombre reminiscences; movement of the mind thus replaces 'dramatic' progression, creating the effect of mental wandering and physical stasis.

The function of these narratives is to provide the opportunity for buried secrets to be painfully brought to light, hearts opened, pasts shared, guilt unburdened and the mysterious 'meaning of it all' earnestly and soberly pondered – a meaning whose weighty seriousness the reader is never allowed to miss or forget.[8] Perhaps the heavy, soul-in-torment, humourless quality of the novel also derives from the fact that so much of it (most of part one, for example) is filtered through the ruminating, agonized consciousness of Munira, for whom 'Life ... had always been a strain.'[9] (Some of that strain rubs off onto the reader.) His multiple sense of guilt (echoing Njoroge in *Weep Not Child* and Mugo in *A Grain of Wheat*) is further complicated by unresolved tensions with his conventionally pious father and his unconventionally pious wife, with her 'silent prayers before and after making love' (p. 91). Munira's adolescent sexual complexes, which result from this puritan middle-class upbringing, take the form of a battle between flesh and spirit somewhat reminiscent of early Lawrence – except that in Munira's case spirit wins.

Interweaving 'the threads of social and personal events' is intrinsic to the epic mode. What we have in *Petals of Blood*, however, is the complicated unravelling and interweaving of four alienated lives, whose connection with 'social events' is often verbal or potential rather than real, illustrative rather than organic. All four at various times seek some kind of union with the 'other' – whether this be the past, the future, 'the struggle', the ancestors, peasants, workers or God. Munira strikes the keynote: 'Wanja! give me another night of the big moon in a hut and through you, buried in you, I will be reborn into history, a player, an action, a creator, not this, this disconnection' (p. 212). (For Abdulla, momentarily dazzled by Wanja, a woman is 'truly the other world' until he re-awakens to the 'world of chaos and injustice about him' [p. 315].) The subjective, purely verbal link between the personal and the historical is exemplifed when Nyakinyua 'talked as if she had been everywhere, as if she had actually participated in the war against the Germans, as if the rhythm of the historic rise and fall of Ilmorog flowed in her veins' (p. 123). So we are told, and indeed, Karega cannot sleep after the narrative: 'He took a walk in the plains, thinking about the woman's story. He lived it ...' (p. 124). This report of an agitated mind re-living past events (in this case, the 'event' is Nyakinyua's own story about the past) is obviously meant to deepen our awareness of historical perspectives. But we are unable to 'live' Nuakinyua's story, since it is no more than a bare, generalized account. There is no imaginative space for us to enter. Later we are told how, after Abdulla's story, 'the essence of black struggle apprehended in the imagination at the level of mere possibilities, had tonight acquired immediate flesh and blood' (p. 228). To be told that the word was made flesh for Karega after hearing a narrative we ourselves have just read is like making a simulated flight on automatic pilot: though we seem to be at several removes from the reality, the text continues to do all our responding for us.

An important episode in the main story is the rapid transformation of Old Ilmorog into New Ilmorog, but a sense of reality is lost when its effect on individual lives is sentimentalized or melodramatized. Technological change, it is implied, brings cultural and moral decline: where once there was the magic spirit-releasing Theng'eta, made by loving hands and drunk at 'beautiful' circumcision cere-

monies, now there is only a mass-produced product whose consequences are drunkenness, degradation, and industrial disputes.
Urban growth is even connected, at one point, with Munira's 'three
years of shameless enslavement to naked passion':

> It was as if the completion and the opening of the new Ilmorog shop-
> ping centre also saw the complete unmaking of Munira, the hitherto
> respected teacher of their children.
>
> (p. 274)

Shopping centres, like gin palaces, have a lot to answer for. Wanja's
own somewhat melodramatic transformation into a miniskirt-
wearing whorehousekeeper, high-class prostitute and business lady,
who even charges Munira for his night of pleasure so that she can
tell him (and the reader) that 'This is New Kenya' (p. 279), is
clearly intended to show us how corrupt, cynical and mercenary
city life is.[10] The predictable contrast is a nostalgic, idealized vision
of the authentic culture and simple virtues of traditional agricultural life, represented by Nyakinyua, Mother Africa's 'mother of
men', whose death – from which the last drop of pathos is wrung in
true Victorian fashion ('I shall never forget her words of pride and
joy ... "I am coming to join you, my warrior ..." and she closed her
eyes' [p. 325]) – is of course the end of an epoch.

Moments in the story where a positive fusion occurs between the
individual and the collective will are the acceptance of Munira in
Ilmorog, the journey to Nairobi (echoing the women's march to
Dakar in *God's Bits of Wood*) and the formation of the Theng'eta
Breweries Workers Union, followed by the strike. An interesting
pattern emerges. The old men quickly assess Munira: 'he's all right,
they said, and looked at one another with knowing eyes.' The collective voice is then made to say: 'He became one of us' (p. 10). Yet
the reader knows this is very far from the truth. The delegation to
Nairobi is not a militant social force like the women's march to
Dakar, but a kind of community project, whose aim, apart from
saving a donkey, is to petition for help. Karega first broaches the
plan to Munira, his fellow teacher, then to Wanja and Abdulla,
before the villagers, swung by Nyakinyua's powers of oratory
('They were all affected by her words'), collectively agree to it. On
page 116 we read: 'From that moment, they forged a community
spirit, fragile at first, but becoming stronger as they strove and
made preparations for the journey.' (Note the insertion of 'strove':
though it loosens the syntax and causes some semantic redundancy,

it at least throws in a general idea of struggle, and slows down preparations that might otherwise have seemed too light and easy.) The trek to the city, we are told, 'had awoken a feeling that the crisis was a community crisis needing a communal response' (p. 123). Karega's individual initiative has injected into the villagers a new sense of community that was presumably not there before. ... The formation of the union follows a similar pattern. Having learned the 'true lesson of history' (p. 303), Karega allows his thoughts to mature for six months while working as a counting clerk in the brewery. In due course anonymous pamphlets start appearing, in which 'Every dispute was put in the context of the exploitation of labour by capital, itself stolen from other workers' (p. 304). Then: 'Suddenly, after six months, people realized that something was happening in the factory. ... The directors and management were taken by surprise: whence this whizzing noise from those who only the other day were docile and obedient?' (p. 303). Readers might also be surprised that docile workers are so quickly unionized by a serialized treatise on exploitation.

Following A. J. Greimas, we might say that the actantial role of the masses in *Petals of Blood* is a recipient of the Good brought to them by the protagonist-hero.[11] The collective voice of the peasants is made to speak in humble gratitude, though there is clearly intended irony in the light of Ilmorog's fate:

> we shall not forget Munira and Karega and Abdulla and Wanja and the donkey – yes, Abdulla's donkey. They saved us. Their knowledge of the city, their contacts in the city, their unselfish involvement in our lives: all this saved us ...
>
> (p. 242)

It is the active few who, through their original ideas, leadership and guidance, transform the masses into active agents, rather than the masses who, through their independent actions, transform the few into active leaders. Only individuals, as outsiders, can rouse the masses from their slumber.[12] This leader-led ideology, so characteristic of populist nationalism, is not only a feature of the story; it is also one of the tacit 'signifieds' of the implied author–implied reader relationship inscribed in the text: the novel's didactic explicitness and what Robson calls the 'intrusive authorial presence' (p. 101) can thus be evaluated in political as well as aesthetic terms.

Yet the novel's didacticism can only be justified in its own terms if clear moral choices are validated, and if the middle-class habit of complicated retrospection, typified in Munira, is somehow resolved (or dissolved) in the uncomplicated simplicity of the peasants' collective voice and the unambiguous line of Karega's socialism. Translating the complex into the simple, according to William Empson, is the structural mode peculiar to pastoral, a mode he found operating in many 'proletarian' novels.[13] It is certainly operating in *Petals of Blood*, though the translation itself is a laborious process, an ordeal (hence the pattern of a spiritual quest or re-birth) which the novel's characters, and its readers, must undergo. Translating moral complexities into certainties entails a melodramatized, simplified scheme. Between the damned (vile seducers such as Kimeria) and the redeemed (heroes who have gained Eternal Life in the hearts of the masses, or strong, simple, noble-hearted peasants such as Nyakinyua) are those whose hearts are a battleground of opposing moral forces (Munira, Karega, Abdulla, Wanja).[14] Such a scheme invokes a set of easy reflexes: moral denunciation of wicked and depraved exploiters on the one hand, a sentimental idealization of the exploited masses on the other. From a political standpoint, this can be a very dangerous attitude, since it oversimplifies and distorts the nature of the struggle by turning it into a mere contest between good and evil. Far from raising consciousness, this can actually disarm the masses. Sentimentality and melodrama thus work against any attempt at an objective analysis of class formation and historical change – an analysis which the story line of *Petals of Blood* tries to illustrate – by confusing economic relations with moral ones.

One of the most important strands in *Petals of Blood* is the detective genre or 'whodunit'. ...The detective mystery is a 'closed' genre, for the solution to the puzzle must leave no 'loose ends'. Successful detection provides its own satisfaction; social and political problems that lie outside a criminological solution are held in check or edited out. *Petals of Blood* opens sensationally with 'murder in Ilmorog'. The reader responds to the word 'murder' like a Pavlovian dog. No sooner is the conditioned reflex aroused than the narrative proceeds to de-mystify the legalistic interpretation and the detective framework with: 'Murder of the workers' movement!' A much broader political theme is introduced. *Petals of Blood* thus adopts the detective genre in order to 'explode' it, yet this too is one of Barthes' 'quotations'. An expository summary or newspaper report, followed by an 'analeptic'[15] narrative that investigates deeper issues and causes rather than simply agents and motives, is a strategy well established in modern fiction. In such narratives the role of the detective is often subsidiary or redundant, for we soon realize that police work, detection and the law are themselves part of the system ultimately responsible for the kind of crime committed. ... Nevertheless, while exploring broader and deeper issues – examining not only the history behind the crime, but the history behind the history behind the crime – *Petals of Blood* keeps to the conventions of the mystery genre by laying false clues,[16] testing us with questions (the 'hermeneutic code'[17]), and withholding vital pieces of information until the end of the book, thereby allowing Inspector Godfrey's interrogation to proceed to its conclusion and the detective interest to return after the narrative of events over the twelve-year period has been completed. (Perhaps it is indicative of the genre's vitality that the most dramatically sustained dialogue in the book occurs in the interrogation scenes.) The detective genre – in spite of its 'closed' nature – is thus partly legitimated, although the written statement Munira gives to the police, which may or may not be the same document as the one referred to as 'a mixture of an autobiographic confessional and some kind of prison notes' (p. 190), and which, if it is, represents a 'tissue' of at least four 'quotations' (statement, autobiography, confession, prison notes), seems intended not only for Inspector Godfrey, who uses the document as evidence against Karega, but for God, Munira's soul, history, posterity, the novel's readers (Munira is at times like a novelist),[18] and Munira's friends and parents.[19] It is, of course, Mzigo, Chui and Kimeria who are the real criminals – by betraying Kenya's anti-colonial heritage and 'selling out' to imperialism. The smaller crime dwindles to a mere chink in the social edifice, through which we are made to perceive a vast epic canvas of struggle and change, a historical 'background' that tries to become the novel's 'foreground' (a problematic we shall return to later). Expectations are raised, not just of a 'whodunit', nor even of a 'whydunit', but of a politico-historical epic.

As we follow, or try to follow, the bewildering threads of this 'epic' narrative, however, it becomes increasingly clear that the novel cannot satisfy these expectations. Particularly weakening from a stylistic point of view is the fact that with each 'new horizon', each new perspective, an expected sharpening of focus does not materialize. With its lists of proper names, summaries and constant use of the habitual or iterative aspect of the verb, the text never rests, pinpoints or focuses attention – it is always 'moving on', rather than 'back'. It has a kind of fugitive, alienated, almost neurotically anxious quality, like a guilty man forever looking over his shoulder and hurriedly counting beads.[20]

'What makes the epic kind,' says E. M. Tillyard, 'is a communal or choric quality. The epic writer must express the feelings of a large group of people living in or near his own time.'[21] The 'communal or choric quality' in *Petals of Blood*, as I shall try to show, belongs to a pastoral rather than epic mode. Tillyard adds that in order to qualify as the 'mouthpiece of many', the writer 'must cause himself to be trusted in a special and profound way. And that way will be only through a union of abundant content and masterly control' (p. 15). The journey to Nairobi is given a full-blown epic treatment,[22] yet 'abundant content' is lacking; instead of 'masterly control', there is only artificial enhancement. The association of the journey with the Mau Mau freedom struggle through Abdulla's memories and reflections is particularly implausible: 'images on images crowded in his mind ... strange that it should be happening again in Ilmorog ... happening again ... an illusion?' (Not so, apparently, for ...) 'Aaa! New horizons ... again ... like that time in the forest ...' (pp. 136–7). There is something slightly odd too, we feel, about characterizing the recurrence of past events ('happening again') as 'New horizons' – unless we are meant to interpret 'New horizons ... again' as the recurrence of old and familiar 'new horizons'. (The suspension marks, which become a noticeable stylistic feature, are here almost parodies of those Iserian 'gaps' the reader fills in order to concretize the imagined world of the novel[23] – presumably using, in this case, some of those 'images on images' in Abdulla's mind. But none is described, so the gap remains empty, leaving only dots before our eyes.)

Stilted aggrandizement of mundane subject-matter always produces a mock-epic effect. Munira's schoolboy reminiscences, prosaic in themselves, are accompanied by such portentous, tragic seriousness that some readers may be tempted to laugh. Chapter 4 begins with a historical ramble in which, after the Arabs, Lord Freeze-Kilby, the battle of Ilmorog, and the heroic expulsion of the Asian shopkeeper (which brings: 'May the Lord bless Ole Masai' from the omniscient narrator), we finally reach the long-awaited climax of African pride: Abdulla's shop, re-organized by Wanja: 'The tea packets, bundles of salt and sugar and the curry powder tins [sic] were tidily arranged on the shelves' (p. 70). ... Elsewhere, the banality of the subject matter is such that not even this kind of artificial enhancement is possible. Munira's habit of making up advertising slogans, for example, gives us no added insight into Munira's character. Nor does it acquire any wider thematic significance. It remains a trivial motif whose sole purpose seems to be an ironic point: i.e. the fact that the Theng'eta slogan, of which Munira is the unacknowledged originator, is taken up and used by the brewery company. ... At such times, the triviality of the content becomes embarrassing. For this reason alone, one would have to disqualify *Petals of Blood* as an epic narrative. In novels truly conceived within the epic mode, the individual and the historical, personal events and social events, the microcosmic and the macrocosmic, are inextricably bound together as part of a total philosophical scheme or view of the world. 'Trivial' details take on a heightened significance through their relation to larger events. In *Petals of Blood* such details, whatever we may be told to think or feel about them, remain trivial. The result is usually bathos, as in the following passage, whose last sentence is an absurd non sequitur: 'Abdulla became the hero of the journey. He seemed to continue revealing newer and richer aspects of his personality. For a start people were now grateful for his donkey' (p. 134).

Part of the reason, then, for the novel's failure to achieve a true epic dimension lies in the gulf, which the text is unable to bridge, between large and small events, the personal and the social or historical, the 'trivial' and the heroic. The novel's explicit orientation towards the masses – the workers and peasants – as a heroic force for change is not imaginatively realized. Indeed, the implied attitude towards the peasants, as I have already suggested, is that they are a repository of virtue who are merely useful as a stagey chorus. (One could argue that one of the main reasons for the 'epic' journey to Nairobi is manipulative: i.e. 'using' the peasants in order to expose traitors and villains such as Chui and Kimeria, and hypocrites such as the Rev. Jerrod Brown and Nderi, the Ilmorog MP...Apart from Nyakinyua, Ilmorog's peasant farmers have little function other than to be proper names, talk about the weather and shake their heads on cue: on page 73 we are told it was 'a poor harvest and the peasant farmers looked at one another and shook their heads'; on page 263 'They shake their heads from side to side', and page 276 'They looked at her and they shook their heads'. We never see what goes on inside the peasants' huts, while planting and harvesting are cursorily reported:

Everybody was busy about the fields. Muturi, Njuguna, Ruoro,
Njogu: even these, for a time would not come by Abdulla's shop for
they were tired out after the day's involvement with planting or
walking their cows and goats in muddy fields ... So during the period
of planting, Munira drank alone or with only Abdulla and Joseph for
company ... The women only threw him hurried greetings as they
rushed to the fields between bouts of heavy downpour ... But he tried
to understand and he even made a lesson out of it all: 'There is
dignity in labour,' he told the children.

(pp. 20–1)

We have returned again to the psychological viewpoint of Munira,
the alienated intellectual tormented by class guilt. Formally, we
return to this viewpoint at: 'he tried to understand', but it is
arguably present in the superadded: 'involvement with' in: 'after the
day's involvement with planting'. Planting is a physical task;
'involvement with planting' suggests something else; not preoccupation merely, but commitment, an emotional or mental involvement
which the lonely Munira imagines and tries to 'understand'. If the
narrative fails to bring the reader close to the real world of the
Ilmorog peasant farmers, then this failure is mirrored in Munira's
own alienation from that world.

... One might well wonder how a writer with Ngugi's reputation
could have perpetrated such a string of arid clichés ('days of glory',
'thriving villages', 'sturdy peasants', etc.). The answer surely lies in
a moribund pastoral ideology. The author's attempt, in Florence
Stratton's words, 'to disguise his voice as that of the collective consciousness'[24] is equally unconvincing. Yet the desire embodies a
twofold strategy: first pastoralism (creating a mythical sense of
unity through condescending nostalgia), and second, populism,
where the sympathetic, monologic voice tries to 'merge with the
masses'. Stratton argues that in 'making the people a character' in
his later novels, Ngugi makes us 'feel that the voice of the people
embraces his own'.[25] Nowhere in *Petals of Blood* is this true – not
even if we accept an identity of interests between the patron and the
patronized, which from the reader's point of view is a relationship
between the teacher and the taught, the preacher and the preached-
at. It is here that the 'politics of the signifier' in *Petals of Blood* is
most vividly illustrated.

The text's implied author is a God whose power over his creations is unlimited, which means that the implied reader is able to

absorb each didactic point as it is made, regardless of the context. The Author-God can make his creatures 'spill the beans', as Chui is made to provide unsolicited self-incriminating evidence of his corrupt practices (p. 153); he can make them think thoughts of astounding ideological clarity, like Inspector Godfrey (p. 333) and Wanja (pp. 335–6); or, if he chooses, he can make them suddenly go blank, like Karega, who on page 289 is hammering home 'unity in labour ... unity of sweat ... sweat power,' and five pages later is racking his brains for an answer to Wanja's eat-or-be-eaten philosophy – before 'remembering in a flash [sic] all the places he had been to', after which he is 'clear about the force for which he had been searching' (thus doubly ensuring that the reader is also clear).

Sometimes a character or figure is introduced for no other reason than to serve as an illustrative example, underlining a point in the general thesis, or to make that point in a set speech after the appropriate episode or scene. On page 129 Wanja begins the long, almost unparagraphed narrative of her experiences as a barmaid and then prostitute in Nairobi. She decides to go for 'Europeans only', and meets a not-too-old, Swahili-speaking German at the Starlight Night Club, who tells her the story of his search for 'a girl from Kabete', and would 'I like to be his companion in the search?' (p. 132). Wanja, though clearly no innocent, was now, she tells us, of the opinion that 'Europeans were not bad, not bad at all ...'. (Thus from the reader's standpoint, this German now represents The European.) But she is taken into a bedroom with mirrors; a symbolic dog 'with huge green eyes' is around; so the experienced whore suddenly becomes a terrified little girl while the German is transmogrified, in fairytale fashion, into a nasty, lecherous pervert who lets out 'a nasty smell'. The white man's sexual urge now terrifies the hooker-turned-innocent, who tells her listeners – and there is nothing in the text to warn us not to take her words at face value – that

> Strength was ebbing out of me, it was if the green-red glow of the dog's eyes was sapping my energy and strength to resist. I was hanging in space ... nothing. But behind the terror, behind this inexplicable thing that was affecting my nerves to a tingling something and the slow deathness, was another feeling of watchfulness. And the man was now fumbling with my clothes and the animal was growling and wagging its tail and the man was trembling. The watchful feeling became stronger and stronger, struggling with the deathness, and the animal was about to lick my fingers when somewhere inside me I heard my own voice exclaim: 'Oh, but you know I left my

handbag in your car.' The moment I heard my voice I knew that the deathness was defeated and I was returning to life.

(p. 133)

By investing Wanja with new sensitivity and a remarkable poetic eloquence, the monologic voice instils into the impressionable reader another message: a message of Life against Death, and the revolt of a purer, deeply African sensibility against the exploitative grip of a decadent and corrupting European sexuality. The German has served his purpose, like the disgusting Joe Golder, the homosexual in Soyinka's *The Interpreters*. Life wins, and Wanja, like a Little Red Riding Hood escaping from the Big Bad Wolf, makes her getaway – into a car driven by a black Samaritan: 'I have never been so grateful for the sight of another black skin,' she says. Unlike the scores, perhaps even hundreds of other fellow-blacks who have used and admired Wanja's body, this (presumably single) man allows her to sleep in his house for two nights entirely unmolested: 'I felt like crying now with gratitude because he had not so much as tried anything on me' (p. 134). The man's parting words, which make the correct didactic points in set-speech fashion, are gems of sanctimonious self-righteousness and superior wisdom which Wanja's perfect memory reproduces exactly: 'This is what happens when you turn tourism into a national religion and build it shrines of worship all over the country', he says, adding: 'This city is no place for you ... well ... it is not a place for any of us ... yet!' For those who know Nairobi, it is impossible not to share such a view; but there is something of a 'slow deathness', even something slightly sinister, about the way in which the narrative has manipulated the unsophisticated reader into accepting it.

Many other examples could be found in *Petals of Blood* of this kind of manipulation and authorial 'telling' through the mouths of characters. ... Phraseological viewpoints are barely distinguished,[26] dialectical conflict and interaction are minimal, and there is only one – or the beginning of one – proper debate in the whole novel, between Munira and Karega (pp. 245–7). It was Bakhtin who castigated the essential monologism of Tolstoy's epic fiction as representative of 'limited official discourse',[27] as against the subversive anti-authoritarianism of the dialogic, the heteroglossic and the polyphonic.[28] Monologic discourse does not spring from the people, since it is always the voice of an Author-God we hear, whether as omniscient narrator, or 'disguised' as the represented speech and inner speech of intradiegetic narrators and characters. The voice is always talking down to the people or speaking for them – however much it may strive to be 'one' of them. ...

For all its monologism, *Petals of Blood* is actually riven by contradictory strategies. We noted above that its didacticism can only be justified in its own terms if the complex is translated into the simple, and that translation is itself an arduous process. This perhaps is only evident after one has read the novel. The impression on first reading is more likely to be a bewildering juxtaposition of strategies rather than a progressive resolution. Pastoral sentimentalism parable and melodrama ... are combined with a 'modernist', complexly anachronic narrative; the manoeuvres of an elementary instruction manual work alongside those of an involved mystery story, only a few of whose hermeneutic riddles are specifically tied to the detective genre. This implies two ways of reading the novel, if not two kinds of reader. The first is naïve and slow, and needs to be told the most basic points and conclusions about the content of the story; the second is nimble and alert, and is capable of negotiating frequent elliptical gaps,[29] time shifts, shifts of perspective and changes of narrator while holding in the mind numerous unsolved enigmas and puzzles. Although this seems to refute the notion of an intended reader, it might indicate an authorial dilemma as to who the novel's intended readers really are, a dilemma that may be bound up with the novel form itself. (It may also be connected with the language problem: the 'we' narrator speaks in English and uses phrases such as 'enigmatic smile' [p. 31], yet the sensibility is supposed to be that of a Gikuyu peasant.) The monologic voice cannot criticize itself for allowing such contradictions, for to do so would be to challenge its control, which in any case is largely illusory. Genuine self-criticism would be impossible without replacing monologic discourse with something else.

Bakhtin associates monologism specifically with the epic. ... Authorial intervention was also common in European fiction before Flaubert, when many writers felt they had a moral and social duty towards their readers. ... The writer's function as teacher and spiritual guide was, of course, also expected: the author's moral and spiritual authority in the text was reassuring in a world of rapid and bewildering changes, conflicting values and competing ideological systems.[30] The parallel with the modern African writer's situation is striking, and is surely not accidental.

One of the most prominent features of *Petals of Blood* is the pre-dominance of summary over scene, and of the habitual or iterative aspect of the verb over the singulative. A summary is a bare report, either of a single event ... or of a succession of events occurring over a considerable period of time. ... A summary 'speeds up' the narrative by giving a brief space to a substantial amount of narrative information or a substantial period of story-time. ... It does not allow for direct speech (e.g. dialogue) or detailed description. A fictional scene, on the other hand, is the detailed representation of a unique event occurring at a particular place and time, and consists in the main either of dialogue or description, depending on the nature of the event. It invites a more leisurely concentration. ... In *Petals of Blood* the scenes are few and usually of short narrative duration; those 'scenes' in which an audience listens to a set speech are hardly scenes at all, for what begins as a unique event is soon dissolved in the summaries, iterative narrative and reported speech that usually make up the monologue itself.

The novel begins with four arrests for murder. The victims' identities and manner of death are revealed at the end of the first chapter in a brief newspaper report. The arrest of Karega brings a workers' march to the police station (an event summarized in one sentence) and a series of slogans textually foregrounded by the use of direct speech ('Murder of the workers' movement!', 'Out with foreign rule policed by colonised black-skins!' etc.). These slogans are not ideologically distanced from the reader in the way the news-paper report is (by the use of the dismissive 'etc.' in: 'Kimeria and Chui were prominent and founding fathers of the KCO ... etc. ... etc. ...'), but are, in fact, legitimized by the style of the omniscient narrative itself, in the short summary a few lines later: 'Workers were waking to their own strength.' This partisan, interpretative summary is preceded by a narrative summary whose tone suggests that the narrator's point of view is not consistently with the workers, for it reads: 'One or two workers sustained serious injuries and were taken to hospital.' The verb phrase 'sustained serious injuries' is in a 'neutral', official register, while the vagueness of 'One or two' shows neither intimate knowledge nor concern to find out how many were injured; indeed, the implication is that workers are an anonymous mass, and that 'serious injuries' are not impor-tant details, but a common occurrence. It is just possible, given the context, that the viewpoint here has shifted to that of the police officer and his 'lieutenants'; whatever the reason, the effect of this kind of summary is to distance us from the workers, and hence from a working-class perspective. ...

Sembne Ousmane's *God's Bits of Wood* follows the principles of classic realism by keeping narrative summaries to a minumum, either as background illustration or as diegetic links between scenes. What we remember, therefore, are particular scenes, scenes that convey a strong visual impression and stay in the mind long after one has read the novel. *Petals of Blood* denies the scene its traditional function by attempting to foreground what, in most novels, provides the background to the 'main story': i.e. exposition, generalized reports and summaries. It is also remarkably Proustian in remembering the way things used to be, what used to happen, what somebody always felt or did, and what people would habitually do. This consistent use of the habitual or iterative aspect of the verb is called 'iterative narrative'.

By narrating once 'what happened *n* times',[31] iterative narrative merges and makes identical two moments: 'this strange equation', says Genette, 'is itself the law of the iterative.'[32] Although, like summary, iterative is a 'synthetic form of narration', it is 'a synthesis not by acceleration, but by assimilation and abstraction'.[33] Since habit is the recurrence of identical actions and feelings, iterative emphasizes the repetitive, customary and routine aspects of life. It is, of course, perfectly appropriate for regular seasonal occupations such as planting and harvesting, impressing upon us the rhythmic certainties of human existence within a cyclic cosmic order.[34] Yet in *Petals of Blood*, iterative narrative assimilates even the most uncustomary and dramatic of events. On page 66 we leave Munira as he follows Wanja into the hut. After some condensed historical narrative and iterative exposition on Munira's psychology, Christian upbringing and sexual inhibitions, we return on page 72 to his lovemaking with Wanja, as a scene he later remembers: 'And Wanja's pained face under the moonlit beam issuing from the window...' Iterative is then used within the scene. This Genette calls 'internal or synthesizing iteration':[35]

> Her scream calling out to her mother or sisters for help, *would give* him an even greater sense of power and strength until he sank into a void ... But he *would wake* to a terrified consciousness that somehow he had been led-on, and he did not feel any victory.
>
> [emphasis added]

By implying an oft-repeated, if already routinized act, the iterative both testifies to Munira's powers and destroys the sense of dramatic climax – which, by all accounts, he feared he had not aroused in Wanja either. ...

By suppressing uniqueness and singularity in favour of the synthetic, the habitual, the generalized and the stereotyped, *Petals of Blood* does not overturn a traditional hierarchy, for what we are left with is not a 'foregrounded background', but simply less foreground, a paradoxically prolix and repetitive condensation. Whereas summary and the report tend to distance us and at times alienate us from the novel's purported epic 'hero', those 'masses' who had 'always struggled' to 'end their oppression and exploitation' (p. 303), iterative narrative stresses the 'always', the frequently or endlesssly repeated act. One is left with a feeling not so much of optimism in the possibilities of change, but of monotony and dull uniformity – even a sense of futility. Munira, we are told on page 249, 'had always' been frightened by the 'repetition of past events', and had 'always' tried to escape 'the tyranny of the past'. For someone who is haunted by guilt and impelled by the need to forge a career, different from that of his plantation-owning father and his conventionally successful brothers, Munira's anxiety is understandable. Yet even Karega's final 'Tomorrow ... tomorrow ...' will be a repetition of past events, for the girl reports not only the 'movement of Ilmorog workers', but rumours of 'Stanley Mathenge returned from Ethiopia' and a 'return to the forests'. The spectre is finally raised of another – this time real rerun of history, a history to which the retrospective narrative has constantly returned. Like Abdulla's 'new horizons ... again', it is difficult to imagine the new as a repetition of past events. However, one can say in the novel's defence that if it is obsessed with the past, it is so for a very good reason, for that past is one the ruling Kenyan elite would no doubt prefer to forget.

Coming in more detail to the novel's prose style, we find, not surprisingly, a preponderance of abstract over concrete nouns. ... The majority of these abstract nouns pertain either to the affections (personal, religious, sympathetic and moral, in that order), intellect and ideas, or volition.[36] Terms such as power, people, struggle, history and growth take on a subjective tint through association with heart, dream, memory, spirit, faith, expectation, mind, desire, beauty, soul, wish and vision. If a lack of concrete description and a paucity of concrete adjectives prevent us from seeing the world afresh, then neither is the jaded reader buoyed up by Ngugi's heavy reliance on stock words and phrases such as 'strange', 'fatal', 'new horizons', and 'images on images'. ... One is tempted to catalogue the infelicities: over-use of and; weak synthetic rhythms and loss of balance: a monotonous use of pronominal substitution for obtaining linear cohesion, yet a lack of coherent focus in passages of densely packed information; an abundance of connectives such as then, but, for and so ...; over-reliance on commonplace words such as 'sad', 'happy', 'beautiful' and 'thrilled'; casual conversation 'fillers' such as 'or something' and 'anyway', which rob the narrative of seriousness; and a large number of clichés.

The novel's sentences are mostly short, while complex sentences are usually of the loose, trailing-constituent type. This, combined with the verbless sentence (frequently used in *Petals of Blood*) conveys the straightforward simplicity and directness of improvised oral discourse. Heightened effects are usually achieved through parataxis (juxtaposition of clauses), such as Karega's declamatory speech on pp. 240–1, with its anaphoric 'in a world ... in a world', and the description of Karega and Wanja's lovemaking (p. 230), with its succession of participial phrases ('groping ... working ... exploring' etc.). However, when abstract noun phrase is joined to abstract noun phrase in breathless succession, with repeated ofs and ands, the effect is a loss in rhythm and proportion rather than a gain in rhetorical intensity:

> Well, well ... we are all of the road now, part of the beauty of the partial achievement of the vision which gave rise to it and also of the hollowness and failed promises of which the road is a monument.
>
> (p. 262)

In the following example, the final nominalizations are ugly excrescences on what is already a syntactically weak sentence (note the characteristic participial phrases):

> Tomorrow it would be the workers and the peasants leading the struggle and seizing power to overturn the system and all its prying bloodthirsty gods and gnomic angels, bringing to an end the reign of the few over the many and the era of drinking blood and feasting on human flesh.
>
> (p. 344)

The author at such moments strikes one as having lost his temper, not only with the 'system', but with the English language itself –

which Ngugi symbolically abandoned in the stylistically richer, and satirically much more forceful *Caithani Muharaba-ini*, later translated as *Devil on the Cross*. (The term 'satire' is hardly applicable to *Petals of Blood*: specifically satiric techniques are not employed, apart from names such as 'Sir Swallow Bloodall'. Humourless anger precludes the ironic distance necessary for effective satire, suggesting a certain weakness or lack of confidence in the face of the enemy.) The effect in the last sentence quoted is of somebody declaiming, piling phrase onto phrase not in order to convince, but in order to prevent the listener (as a potential opponent) from answering back. This criticism should not be seen as a way of denying the importance of literature as a didactic or educative tool. In many cultures, and particularly in socialist countries, writers are often expected to teach through their work.[37] There is, however, a difference between teaching through concrete example and 'teaching' through the rhetorical transmission of pre-judged and pre-digested conclusions. In *Petals of Blood* the parabolic story and the destiny of a character such as Wanja do provide exemplary lessons, but there is on the whole too much 'telling' and not enough 'showing'.[38] The Author-God's dictatorial powers have to be acknowledged in at least one respect here, since none of the characters succeeds in taking on an independent life: ideas, not people, are what determine the novel's explicit content.

No sooner have we said this, however, than a major qualification needs to be made, a qualification that has, in fact, constituted the main argument of this essay. The 'obvious' theme of *Petals of Blood* is the rottenness of the 'New Kenya', the resurgence of the militant spirit of anti-colonialism and a new socialist awakening. Yet certain modes, strategies and stereotypes are adopted whose 'signifieds' clash not only with materialist or dialectical principles, but with the novel's explicit political 'message'.[39] If the novel fails aesthetically to renew or transcend these intertextual elements, then it also fails to overcome the ideological and political limits which these elements predicate.

I have concentrated almost entirely on *Petals of Blood* as a literary text. Yet every text has a context, which in this case could be briefly characterized as follows. Constitutional independence in Kenya was a defeat for the workers and peasants who, after a decade of armed struggle, saw the betrayal of those fundamental social and economic changes for which they had fought. The Kenyan economy remained subservient to multinational capital, while the ruling elite had entrenched itself on the basis of provisions made by the colonial regime in the 1950s, when a land consolidation and registration program made possible the emergence of a land-owning (and collaborating) African middle class. The economic recession that began in the mid-1970s exacerbated the gulf that had already opened between rich and poor, the landed and the landless. A groundswell of popular discontent, which was manifested in the democratic collectivism and anti-ruling-class feeling of the Kamiriithu Community project of 1976–77, and was to erupt in a violent, insurrectionary form on 1 August 1982, prompted intellectuals such as Ngugi to abandon a reformist position and adopt a more clearly revolutionary stance. *Petals of Blood* is thus a transitional book. If its sense of urgency is subjective;[40] if its mixture of populism and introspection, outspoken didacticism and involuted complexity is Janus-faced; and if the movement of the masses is subordinated to the movement of individual minds, then this reflects the process of ideological re-orientation that those intellectuals were compelled to undergo in order to become effectively involved in the movement for real social change at the practical level, and so find that 'connection' for which Munira yearns. The Kamiriithu experience was decisive: it showed a writer such as Ngugi that collective initiatives and the self-movement of workers and peasants were a reality. No longer were they merely a slogan, a memory or a possibility. The Kenyan ruling class, Ngugi wrote,

> were mortally scared of peasants and workers who showed no fear in their eyes; workers and peasants who showed no submissiveness in their bearing; workers and peasants who proclaimed their history with unashamed pride and who denounced its betrayal with courage.[41]

And in Ngaahika Ndeenda the monologic voice had to make way for the voices of the workers and peasants themselves. If the word was made flesh in Kamiriithu, it was also shown that it is not the word that sets the masses in motion, but the movement of the masses that gives power to the word, and that the fictional world is not so much a prophecy of what is to come, but a distorted reflection of what is already happening. The rich – and later, the bitter – lessons of Kamiriithu suddenly brought into focus those 'new horizons and possibilities' which *Petals of Blood*, as an example of 'bourgeois' literature trying to dissolve itself in the people's struggle, could only articulate in an abstract, condensed and rhetorical manner. The consciously theorizing mind is thus able to grasp at an abstract level a political program which, at the imaginative level, is muffled and distorted by the 'politics' of the text's intertextual 'signifiers' – coded elements whose medium (as Ngugi's subsequent works remind us) is that most notorious of minefields, the English language itself.

From *World Literature Written in English*, 26: 1 (1986), 3–24.

NOTES

[Stewart Crehan's essay, which has been shortened for the present volume, has initiated further reappraisals of *Petals of Blood* and reflects continuing discussion about the artistic form and politico-aesthetic function of revolutionary postcolonial writing. Structuralist notions of the text as a signifier are reinforced by formalist studies of sentence- and word-structure to deconstruct socio-political readings of *Petals of Blood* as a revolutionary novel. It is a useful example of a structuralist methodology applied to a poststructuralist reading of the novel's political aesthetic. Eds]

1. C. B. Robson, *Ngugi wa Thiong'o* (London, 1979), p. 96.

2. In his famous essay, 'Novelist as Teacher', reprinted in *Morning Yet on Creation Day* (London, 1975), Chinua Achebe speaks of his art as applied rather than pure, and asks: 'Who cares?' Public nonchalance on this issue was, however, belied in Achebe's authorial methods and craftsmanship: the second edition of *Arrow of God* shows that Achebe certainly cared about his art – as art, and not simply as a vehicle for various 'messages'.

3. The terms 'signifer' and 'signifed', which originate with Ferdinand de Saussure, are lynch-pins of modern semiotic analysis.

4. Roland Barthes, 'The Death of the Author', in *Image–Music–Text* (New York, 1977), p. 146.

5. Cook and Okenimkpe, for example, inform us that 'there is no doubt at all' that Ngugi 'knew exactly what he was doing in making this shift towards outspokenness. As a novelist Ngugi was taking a calculated risk. He was prepared to jeopardize the "suspension of disbelief" in order to ensure that his ideas stood out absolutely plainly. He deliberately sidestepped certain conventions of the well-made novel ...' (David Cook and Michael Okenimkpe, *Ngugi wa Thiong'o: An Exploration of His Writings* [London, 1983], p. 235). The main

reason for attributing complete foresight and a wholly conscious intention to an author in this way seems to be to justify the literary work of art, not according to its received effect, but by arguing back from the effect of its intended cause.

6. Abiola Irle comes very close to this position in *The African Experience in Literature and Ideology* (London, 1981) when he says: 'Literature takes place within a cultural setting, and no meaningful criticism is possible without a community of values shared by the writer and the critic which the latter can, in turn, make meaningful to the writer's larger audience' (p. 30). If this is true, then a fascist is the best critic of a fascist novel.

7. 'Intradiegetic' means 'inside the story'; 'homodiegetic' is an example where, as in *Petals of Blood*, the intradiegetic narrator appears as a character in his/her own story.

8. There is the portentous build-up: 'Wanga and Munira were quiet, very quiet ... Shadows passed over the walls: shadows passed over the faces' – and in case we miss the reference: 'Maybe also over their lives, Abdulla thought' (p. 27); the tantalizing build-up: 'At long last he was going to tell the story he had once refused to tell. Silence gripped the whole group, hanging on Abdulla's lips' (p. 140) – only to be served with a strangely anticlimatic non-story and much conspicuous signposting in order to extract the correct response from the reader: 'His voice had become more and more faint with the progress of the narrative' (p. 29), and: 'She had lowered her voice a little as she said the last words and Munira could somehow imagine a tortured soul's journey through valleys of guilt and humiliation ...' (p. 40). [See note 9 for details of the text of *Petals of Blood*.]

9. *Petals of Blood* (London, 1977), p. 91. Further references are incorporated in the text.

10. On page 295 the ominiscient narrator draws an almost Dickensian picture of the Fallen Woman: 'her head was bowed slightly and it was as if, under the bluish light of her creation, the wealth she had so accumulated weighed on her heavily, as if the jewelled, rubied cord around her neck was now pulling her very shadow to the ground. ...' On page 327 the fallen puppet is made to speak with her master's voice: 'This wealth feels so heavy on my head', she says.

11. See A. J. Greimas, *Semantique structurale* (Paris, 1966) and *Du sens* (Paris, 1970) and Etienne Souriau, *Les Deux Cent Mille Situations dramatiques* (Paris, 1950).

12. This is at the level of the story ('showing') but at the level of explicit statement ('telling') the text denies such a view: 'The true lesson of history was this: that the so-called victims, the poor, the downtrodden, the masses, had always struggled with spears and arrows, with their

hands and songs of courage and hope, to end their oppression and exploitation ...' (p. 303).

13. See William Empson, *Some Versions of Pastoral* (London, 1935).

14. The moral schema implicit in *Petals of Blood* is given explicit elaboration by one of Ngugi's remarkably eloquent workers, Muturi, in *Devil on the Cross* (London, 1981): 'Our lives are a battlefield on which is fought a continuous war between the forces that are pledged to confirm our humanity and those determined to dismantle it ... Each of the two forces builds a heart that reflects the nature of its clan. Therefore there are two hearts: the heart built by the clan of parasites, the evil heart; and the good heart built by the clan of producers, the good heart' (pp. 53–4).

15. 'Analepsis', like flashback, is 'a narration of a story-event at a point in the text after later events have been told' (Shlomith Rimmon-Kenan, *Narrative Fiction: Contemporary Poetics* [London, 1983], p. 46).

16. The newspaper report on pp. 4–5 leads us to believe that the murders are a direct result of the strike. But if this is so, there is no more mystery, and hence no story – certainly no need for the kind of story that follows. We therefore dismiss as a false clue what is also a false allegation made for political reasons (the newspaper wants to smash the union and wreak political vengeance). By following the hermeneutic code of the mystery story we also reject a report in a bourgeois newspaper with dismissive scepticism – which is what, politically speaking, the text wants us to do. This is a good example of the perfect fit that can sometimes be achieved between narrative technique and 'message', signifier and the overall, thematic signified (i.e. the explicit 'thesis').

17. 'Under the hermeneutic code, we list the various (formal) terms by which an enigma can be distinguished, suggested, formulated, held in suspense, and finally disclosed', Roland Barthes, *S/Z* (New York, 1974), p. 19.

18. E.g. 'For years, Munira was to remember that night of Theng'eta drinking. Later, years later, in Ilmorog Police Station, Munira was to try to recreate the feel of this period in Ilmorog ...' (p. 243).

19. One of Munira's more eccentric aims is to 'convert' Inspector Godfrey: 'he realized how difficult the task before him was: how was it possible to impress on a man administering the corrupt laws of a corrupt world, the overwhelming need and necessity for higher laws, pure, eternal, absolute, unchanging?' (p. 296).

20. 'I have read about the people's revolutions in China, Cuba, Vietnam, Cambodia, Laos, Angola, Guinea, Mozambique ... Oh yes, and the works of Lenin and Mao' (p. 340), says Joseph; 'He had fought and he

had defeated generals like Lt.-General Sir Erskine, General Hinde, General Ladbury and their armies brought from England: the Buffs, Lancashire Fusiliers, the Devons, the Royal Air Force, the K.A.R. and other forces that had seen action in the Canal Zone, Palestine, Hong Kong, Malaya ... There was also Mathenge, Karari wa Njama, Kimbo, Kago, Waruingi, Kimemia and others' (p. 141), says Abdulla. These tedious roll-calls may have more than a tenuous connection with the indigenous African tradition of praise song and epic eulogies and catalogues. If so, the poetry has been lost.

21. E. M. W. Tillyard, *The Epic Strain in the English Novel* (London, 1967), p. 15.

22. It is built up as 'The exodus toward the kingdom of knowledge' (p. 118); its hero, if not its Moses, Abdulla, shows 'stoic endurance' and infuses 'strength and purpose into the enterprise' (p. 34), and reference is made to 'the peak of their epic journey across the plains' (p. 143).

23. See Wolfgang Iser, *The Act of Reading: A Theory of Aesthetic Response* (London, 1978), pp. 165–79.

24. Florence Stratton, 'Narrative Method in the Novels of Ngugi', *African Literature Today*, 13 (1983), 128.

25. Ibid., p. 134.

26. Boris Uspensky distinguished between ideological, spatio-temporal, psychological and phraseological viewpoints in *A Poetics of Composition*, trans. V. Zavarin (Berkeley, CA, 1973).

27. David Hayman, 'Towards a Mechanics of Mode: Beyond Bakhtin', in *Novel*, 16 (1983), 174.

28. In her commentary on Bakhtin, Julia Kristeva writes: 'In the epic the addressee is an extratextual, absolute entity (God or community) that relativizes dialogue to the point where it is cancelled out and reduced to monologue. With this in mind, it is easy to understand why not only the so-called "traditional" novel of the nineteenth century, but also any novel with any ideological thesis whatsoever, tends towards an epic, thus constituting a deviation in the very structure of the novel; this is why Tolstoy's monologism is epic and Dostoevsky's dialogism is novelistic.' *Desire in Language: A Semiotic Approach to Literature and Art* (Oxford, 1980), p. 87.

29. Some ellipses are deliberately intended to create a feeling of confusion or strangeness, as when the old woman (Nyakinyua) waylays Munira: 'She waited for Munira outside the school kei-apple hedge' (p. 6). We are not told here who this 'she' is. But the authorial intention is spelled out in capital letters when she vanishes: 'Strange, mysterious, he muttered to himself' (p. 7). The whole style of the novel is one of com-

pressed brevity, and so tends towards the elliptical. But some omissions are simply structural faults: the school children are mostly unseen and unheard, and no explanation is ever given as to why Wanja did not leave Ilmorog with Karega.

30. See Iser, *The Act of Reading*, pp. 6–7.

31. Gérard Genette, *Narrative Discourse* (Oxford, 1980) p. 116.

32. Ibid., p. 143.

33. Ibid.

34. E.g.: '... and when the rain subsided they would wander about Ilmorog, would go to the shamba to break the clods of earth and of course plant together ... The older folk told stories of how Rain, Sun and Wind went a-wooing Earth, sister of Moon, and it was Rain who carried the day, and that was why Earth grew a swollen belly after being touched by Rain. ...' (p. 196).

35. Genette, *Narrative Discourse*, p. 119.

36. The classificatory categories are based on those in *Roget's Thesaurus*.

37. Ngugi completed *Petals of Blood* in the Soviet Union in a house made available by the Union of Soviet Writers. It is therefore not surprising that the novel should strive to fulfil the didactic aims enshrined in the doctrine of socialist realism even if much of the 'realism' is missing.

38. The distinction is elaborated in Wayne C. Booth, *The Rhetoric of Fiction* (Chicago, 1961).

39. This would apply to other stylistic features and organizational methods which for reasons of space I have not touched on. Segmentation is one example. The division into four parts (whose titles are all segments of one 'progressive' utterance) is fairly clear, but the chapter divisions and sections within chapters – some numbered, some not – can be very confusing and disorienting, especially when there seems to be no rational correspondence beweeen the subject matter and its formal organization. Add to this the sudden time shifts, shifts in narration, and the extreme condensation we have already noted, and the result is one of dislocation, even incoherence. Bwendo Mulengela, in a University of Zambia seminar paper entitled: 'Writing in English: A Study of Nabokov, Conrad, Ngugi and Achebe', has suggested the disorienting narration and plot structure in Ngugi's novel convey 'a sense of chaos in Kenya and in the mind particularly of Munira: the chaos of a failed revolution' (pp. 20–1). It also shows that Ngugi's populist didacticism will to some extent have been cancelled out by the impenetrability (for some) of the novel's style and organization.

40. This is illustrated, for example, in the use of deixis, one linguistic means whereby a particular viewpoint is established, action is fixed in

time and place ('now', 'here', etc.) and the environment is indicated ('this', 'that', etc.). Deixis in *Petals of Blood* is usually associated with an individual and subjective viewpoint. For example, Munira: 'But all *that* was twelve years after Godfrey Munira ...' (p. 5); 'And suddenly he was seized with an irresistible urge to tell that story of a school ...' (p. 26); Karega: 'Yes, he could see it all *now*' (p. 124); 'He is scared of *this* total silence ... He cries against *this* total isolation' (p. 235); and Abdulla: 'Yes, he could do *that* ... He went back to the streets, now that he had regained his strength ... He saw himself arrive in a donkey-cart twelve years ago' (p. 316). By way of contrast, in Achebe's *Things Fall Apart* and *Arrow of God*, deixis often conveys the here-and-now of a communal and cultural rather than individual and subjective viewpoint. For example, in *Things Fall Apart*: 'But this particular night was dark and silent. And in all the nine villages of Umuofia a town-crier with his *ogene* asked every man to be present tomorrow morning' (p. 10).

41. 'Education for a National Culture', paper presented to a seminar of Education and Culture, Harare, September 1981. Ross Kidd, in 'Popular Theatre and Popular Struggle in Kenya: The Story of Kamiriithu', in *Race and Class*, 24: 3 (1983), writes: 'the peasants and workers were in control rather than government bureaucrats or the middle class) and it [i.e. the KCECC program] was run in a highly collective fashion ... Even academic writing on the Kamiriithu experience (by the two Ngugis) had to be cleared first with the executive committee' (p. 293). No longer was it the case of an author 'telling the masses' – the masses were now the ones doing the 'telling'.

6

Ngugi's *Devil on the Cross*: the Novel as Hagiography of a Marxist

F. ODUN BALOGUN

INTRODUCTION

Depending on a reader's ideological orientation, *Devil on the Cross*[1] can elicit one of two diametrically opposed responses. The anti-communist Christian is likely to hate it not only for its marxist ideology but even more for the stylistic strategy adopted as a vehicle for this ideology. For precisely the same reasons, the reader with a marxist outlook will be doubly happy with the novel. *Devil on the Cross*, however, is not just another proletarian novel as it might at first appear, but one most carefully crafted to achieve the author's ideological objectives, one of which is making the Christian religion undermine its believers while at the same time it serves the interest of non-believers.

The popular identification of Christianity with capitalism and atheism with marxism[2] usually ignores the fact that there are capitalists who are atheists and marxists who are Christians. While the former situation is less publicized, the latter has recently become the subject of debate because of the development of the phenomenon called 'liberation theology' in South American countries. In the specific case of Africa, however, the identification of Christianity and Islam with imperialist exploitation has historical foundation in the roles these religions have wittingly or unwittingly played in

African development from the time of slavery to the colonial period and to the present stage of neo-colonialism. Opinions on this matter, of course, differ among African intellectuals but the literary response on the part of African writers has largely been critical. Reactions have varied from the mild criticism evident in Achebe's *Things Fall Apart* and Ngugi's *The River Between* to the biting satire characterizing Beti's *Poor Christ of Bomba* and Ousmane's *Xala* and to the vicious attack in Armah's *Two Thousand Seasons*.

On his part, Ngugi has shown in successive novels a growing impatience with the socio-political role of Christianity in Kenyan history. As a bourgeois intellectual in the fifties and sixties, Ngugi's criticism of the role of Christianity was understandably mild, even if unequivocal, in his novels published at that time – *Weep Not, Child*, *The River Between* and *A Grain of Wheat*. However, by the time of writing *Petals of Blood* in the seventies, Ngugi was already a marxist and, predictably, organized religion was subjected to a 'savage satire'.[3] By the time of writing the present novel, *Devil on the Cross*, Ngugi still regarded religion as an instrument of bourgeois exploitation,[4] but he was not as interested in satire as in depicting Christianity in the ironic situation of undermining capitalism and of actively promoting marxism. In fact, the anti-capitalist pro-marxist message that emerges from the totality of the novel – from its title, subject matter and setting to its plot, characterization, language and narrative device – is encoded in a composite religious idiom derived from Christian religious beliefs, symbols, church liturgy, biblical parables, allusions and motifs.

CHRISTIAN SYMBOLISM

The paradoxically symbolic title of the novel immediately announces the author's mischievous intention of forcing the Christian religion into a non-traditional role: instead of Christ on the Cross it is *Devil on the Cross*. The comfort that the right-wing Christian mind might derive from the illusion that the devil has at last received the punishment he deserves is ultimately destroyed by the gradual revelation of the true identity of this particular devil on the cross. The first hint about the identity of the devil is given in the note tossed to the heroine, Wariinga, by one of the thugs hired by her landlord to evict her from a rented room:

We are the Devil's Angels: *Private Businessmen*. Make the slightest move to take this matter to the authorities, and we shall issue you with a single ticket to God's kingdom or Satan's – a one-way ticket to Heaven or Hell.

(p.10)

More revelations concerning the devil's identity come as the narrator recalls the recurrent nightmare that plagues Wariinga:

And now Wariinga was revisited by a nightmare that she used to have when, as a student at Nakuru Day Secondary, she attended the *Church of the Holy Rosary*.

She saw first the darkness, carved open at one side to reveal a Cross, which hung in the air. Then she saw a crowd of people dressed in rags walking in the light, propelling the devil towards the Cross. The Devil was clad in a silk suit, and he carried a walking stick shaped like a folded umbrella. ... His belly sagged, as if it were about to give birth to all the evils of the world. His skin was red, like that of a pig. Near the Cross he began to tremble and turned his eyes towards the darkness, as if his eyes were being seared by the light. He moaned, beseeching the people not to crucify him, swearing that he and all his followers would never again build Hell for the people on Earth.

But the people cried in unison: 'Now we know the secrets of all the robes that disguise your cunning. You commit murder, then you don your robes of pity and you go to wipe the tears from the faces of orphans and widows.'...

And there and then the people crucified the Devil on the Cross, and they went away singing songs of victory.

After three days, there came others dressed in suits and ties, who, keeping close to the wall of darkness, lifted the Devil down from the Cross. And they knelt before him, and they prayed to him in loud voices, beseeching him to give them a portion of his robes of cunning. And their bellies began to swell, and they stood up, and they walked towards Wariinga, laughing at her, stroking their large bellies, which had now inherited all the evils of this world. ...

(pp. 13–14)

The details to be noted are that (1) Wariinga's nightmare used to take place when she attended church, (2) the devil has an enormous sagging belly, (3) the devil's skin is red like a pig's, (4) the devil is crucified by a crowd of people in rags, and (5) after the crucifixion the devil, in fact, becomes multiplied as his disciples take on his personality including the bulging stomach.

Soon after these details of the dream are provided, the reader meets the first of two variants of an invitation card to a feast in Ilmorog. The first card bearing the heading 'The Devil's Feast!' (pp. 28, 68) is fake and is printed by those who oppose the feast, while the genuine card is headed 'A Big Feast!' (p. 76). The objective of the feast as explained by Mwireri wa Mukiraai, a sympathizer, is this:

> 'First things first. This feast is not a Devil's feast, and it has not been organized by Satan. This feast has been arranged by the Organization for Modern Theft and Robbery in Ilmorog to commemorate a visit by foreign guests from an organization for the thieves and robbers of the Western world, particularly from America, England, Germany, France, Italy, Sweden and Japan, called the *International Organization of Thieves and Robbers*.
> 'Secondly, our university students have become very conceited. They have now devised ways of discrediting theft and robbery even before they know what modern theft and robbery really is. These students are spreading the kind of talk I have just heard from Wangari and Muturi, namely, that theft and robbery should end.
> 'So I would like to say this: I am very sure that people can never be equal like teeth. Human nature has rejected equality. Even universal nature herself has rejected any absurd nonsense about equality. Just look at God's Heaven. God sits on the throne. On his right stands his only Son. On his left side stands the Holy Spirit. At his feet the angels sit. At the feet of the angels sit the saints. At the feet of the saints sit all the Disciples, and so on, one rank standing below another, until we come to the class of believers here on Earth. Hell is structured in the same way. The king of Hell is not the one who makes the fire, fetches the firewood and turns over the burning bodies. No, he leaves those chores to his angels, overseers, disciples and servants.'
>
> (p. 78)

If the conflicting names of the feast are meant to reflect a divergence in moral assessment, ironically the sympathizer's explanation confirms its immorality even more strongly than the opponent's falsified title. The conscience of Mr Mukiraai is so totally dead that he not only fails to see the immorality of theft and robbery but actually defends them with such righteousness that the reader cannot but identify him with the world of the devils in Wariinga's nightmare. It is significant that, among other reasons, Mr. Mukiraai should justify theft and robbery as the means to maintaining social inequality in terms of the biblical hierarchical representation of heaven.

Events of the feast as it takes place inside a cave in Ilmorog reveal that Mr Mukiraai is in fact a benevolent devil compared to the generality of the delegates attending the feast. All the details of Wariinga's nightmare are represented in the setting, characters and episodes of the feast. Firstly, the feast takes place on Sunday. It commences in a solemn atmosphere reminiscent of church services as the Master of Ceremonies, like a priest, recounts his own version of the biblical parable of the talents: '... For the Kingdom of Earthly Wiles can be likened unto a ruler who ...' (pp. 82–6).

After the parable and the opening speech by the leader of the foreign delegation, the 'Hell's Angels band' in attendance 'struck up a tune' which 'was more like a psalm or a hymn'. After a few minutes, everyone turned towards the band, and they all started to sing, as if they were in church:

> Good news has come
> To our country!
> Good news has come
> About our Saviour!
> (p. 90)

Throughout the ceremony of the feast (church service), the delegates' speeches which are described in religious language as 'testimonies', but which might equally be termed 'sermons', are frequently punctuated with phrases from the Catholic Mass liturgy such as 'Kyrie, kyrie eleison' (p. 126), '*Per omnia saecula saeculorum. Amen*' (p. 171), '*Agnus Dei, qui tollis peccata mundi; Miserere nobis. ... Ecce Agnus Dei; Ecce qui tollis peccata mundi. ...* Take, eat, this is my body; Do this until I return. *Corpus Christi. Amen ... Dominus vobiscum*' (p. 190). Significantly, as always happened inside the church in her past, Wariinga once again experiences a nightmare during the feast (pp. 184–94). With all these details no reader can possibly fail to see the link between the setting of Wariinga's nightmare and that of the feast since the church and the cave have in essence been merged.

Secondly, the delegates at the feast exhibit the physical traits characteristic of the devil in Wariinga's nightmare. The black men invariably have the protruding stomach: ' "Here, in this cave, we are interested only in people who steal because their bellies are full," the master of ceremonies said, patting his stomach' (p. 95). Thereafter, those who mount the platform to explain why they should be crowned the king of thieves are almost uniformly alike. One has 'a belly that protruded so far that it would have touched the ground had it not been supported by the braces that held up his trousers' (p. 99) while another carries a belly that 'was so huge that it almost bulged over his knees' (p. 122). The White men, on the other hand, have the red skin: 'Wariinga noted that their skins were indeed red, like that of pigs or like the skin of a black person who has been scalded with boiling water or who has burned himself with acid creams' (p. 91). Thus, the aggregate of the delegates at the cave's feast is the devil in Wariinga's church nightmare.

Thirdly, in the novel's action, just as the devil in Wariinga's nightmare is chased and crucified by the crowd of people in rags, so are the delegates at the feast chased out of the cave by a procession of people, many of whom 'had rags for clothes. Many more had no shoes' (p. 202). The routing of the delegates in a battle for the cave actually equates with the crucifixion of the devil in Wariinga's dream. In fact, in their song, the ragged crowd identifies the delegates as the Devil and his disciples: 'Come one and all, / And behold the wonderful sight / Of us chasing away the Devil / And all of his disciples! / Come one and all!' (p. 207). Similarly, the initially victorious ragged crowd is ultimately defeated by the devil in both instances. In the nightmare, the devil after his crucifixion by the crowd is multiplied and transformed into his disciples; at the cave, the routing (crucifixion) of the delegates (the Devil) is avenged by the soldiers (Devil's disciples) who kill five and wound many more of the righteous crowd.

The clue to the symbolic meaning of the cave feast is contained in the following parable which features as a consistent religious motif throughout the novel:

> ... For the Kingdom of the Earthly Wiles can be likened unto a ruler who foresaw that the day would come when he would be thrown out of a certain country by the masses and their guerrilla freedom fighters. He was much troubled in his heart, trying to determine ways of protecting all the property he had accumulated in that country and also ways of maintaining his rule over the natives by other means. He asked himself: What shall I do ....
>
> And it came to pass that as the ruler was about to return to his home abroad, he again called together all his servants and gave them the key to the land, telling them: 'The patriotic guerrillas and the masses of this country will now be deceived because you are all black, as they are, and they will chant: "See, now our own black people have the key to our country; see, now our own black people hold the steering wheel. What were we fighting for if not this? Let us now put down our arms and sing hymns of praise to our black lords." '

Then he gave them his property and goods to look after and even to increase and multiply. To one he gave capital amounting to 500,000 shillings, to another 200,000 shillings, and to another 100,000 shillings, to every servant according to how loyally he had served his master, followed his faith, and shared his outlook. And so the lord went away, leaving by the front door. ...

And it came to pass that before many days had elapsed, the lord came back to that country through the back door, to check on the property he had left behind. He called his servants to account for the property and the money that he had given to each. ...

(pp. 82–6)

Thus, the feast at the cave is the reunion of the former colonial masters represented by people of the multinational companies and the Kenyan ruling elites represented by their businessmen. The 'testimonies' are the rendering of account by the latter to the former in respect of the talents which were to be looked after.

The way the Master of Ceremonies has recast the biblical parable shows that he is speaking about the nature of the political independence granted to African countries and the relationship existing between the former colonial masters and the African governing elites. The Master of Ceremonies says: '*The flag of Independence can be likened unto a man travelling unto a far country, who called his own servants, and delivered unto them his goods. ...*' (p. 174).

The testimonials reveal a gallery of the types of businessmen in Kenya today. They vary from the intellectuals like Mwirer wa Mukiraai to stark illiterates like Ndutika wa Nguunji. Mr Mukiraai is in fact the first person in the novel to use the parable of the talents (p. 81) and he identifies the system the businessmen operate as one 'based on the theft of the sweat and blood of workers and peasants – what in English we call capitalism' (p. 166). Mr Mukiraai also stands for the servant in the parable who buries his talents, his reason being that he prefers national capitalism and therefore resists the control of multinationals (pp. 170–1). Mr Nguunji, who like many of the delegates had been a saboteur of the fight for independence, dislikes Mr Mukiraai's 'nationalist' position and advocates international capitalism under the umbrella of multinationals. He tells his colleagues: 'Let's all forget the past. All that business of fighting for freedom was just a bad dream, a meaningless nightmare. Let's join hands to do three things: to grab, to extort money and to confiscate. The Holy Trinity of theft: Grabbing, Extortion, and Confiscation. If you find anything belonging to the masses, don't leave it behind, for if you don't look after yourself, who'll look after you?' (p. 177). Mr Mukiraai is also an exception in that he is sexually controlled while the majority are as promiscuous as Mr Gatheeca who prefers other peoples' wives as mistresses.

The delegates also vary from the recklessly avaricious ones like Mr Gataanguru, who wants to package and sell air to peasants and workers (p. 107), to the more cautious others like Mr Gatheeca who warns his colleagues, saying: 'Better meanness that is covert: better a system of theft that is disguised by lies, or why do you think that our imperialist friends brought us the Bible? Why do you think I go to all the church fund-raising Haraambe meetings?' (p. 123). While delegates like Gatheeca have no qualms about exploiting people of their own class, others like Gataanguru believe in the exploitation of only peasants and workers.

Not surprisingly, an old peasant woman, Wangari, is thoroughly incensed by the disclosures during the testimonies. She invites the police and denounces the delegates, saying:

> There are the men who have always oppressed us peasants, denying us clothes and food and sleep. These are the men who stole the heritage bequeathed to us by Waiyaki wa Hiinga and Kimaathi wa Waciuri, and by all the brave patriots who have shed their blood to liberate Kenya. These are the imperialist watchdogs, the children of the Devil. Chain their hands, chain their legs and throw them into the Eternal Jail, where there is an endless gnashing of teeth! For that's the fate of all those who sell foreigners the heritage of our founding patriarchs and patriots!
>
> (pp. 196–7)

Ironically, instead of arresting the delegates, the police end up bundling Wangari into prison! This is consistent with the novel's depiction of the police and the army as 'disciples' of the business tycoons – the devils, to use the metaphor of the novel.

Thus, the central action of *Devil on the Cross* is a parabolic rendering of how the revolt against Kenyan bourgeois elites by '[a]n army of workers ... peasants, and petty traders and students ...' (p. 203) is bloodily put down by government troops. However, while the conclusion at the level of action makes the capitalists the victors, the artistic rendering of the story stresses the moral victory of the revolting proletariat. The symbolic system of narration not only equates the bourgeois class with the devil but also makes the bourgeois themselves admit and boast of their devilish ways.

Therefore, being a band of religious hypocrites, thieves and robbers by their own admission, Kenyan capitalists are depicted as nothing but criminals at large, still awaiting arrest, judgement and punishment. But even more damning is the fact that these capitalists have no inkling whatsoever of the irreparable moral damage they have done to themselves as a class by the way they behave and speak. Being totally morally dead, they are depicted as caricatures.[5]

HAGIOGRAPHIC NARRATIVE DEVICE

The use of the Christian idioms to satirize capitalism in *Devil on the Cross* goes beyond symbolic exploitation of theme to include also the manipulation of narrative device, language, characterization and plot structure. The novel begins with the fervent, intimate testimony in the first person by a narrator who calls himself the 'Prophet of Justice'. This narrator further claims that the story he is about to relate is no ordinary story but a divine revelation granted to him after seven days of fasting, suffering and penance. The language of his narration shows close affinity to the language of the biblical prophets:

> And after seven days had passed, the Earth trembled and lightning scored the sky with its brightness, and I was lifted up, and I was borne up to the rooftop of the house, and I was shown many things, and I heard a voice, like a great clap of thunder, admonishing me: Who has told you that prophecy is yours alone, to keep to yourself? Why are you furnishing yourself with empty excuses? If you do that, you will never be free of tears and pleading cries.
>
> The moment the voice fell silent, I was seized, raised up and then cast down into the ashes of the fireplace. And I took the ashes and smeared my face and legs with them, and I cried out:
>
> > I accept!
> > I accept!
> > Silence the cries of the heart.
> > Wipe away the tears of the heart. ...
>
> This story is an account of what I, Prophet of Justice, saw with these eyes and heard with these ears when I was borne to the rooftop of the house. ...
>
> (p. 8)

The heroine of the revealed story, Jacinta Wariinga, is also a highly religious person. She is so devout in her belief that she prays constantly, and her prayers are often miraculously answered. She, in fact, seems to be a special elect of God. She is several times miraculously saved from death and, like Saint Joan in Shaw's play by the same title, she hears heavenly voices, and future events are revealed to her in prophetic dreams. Indeed, the whole of the introductory part of the novel which consists of the identification of the narrator, the appearance of Wariinga and her journey to Ilmorog reads like the introduction to a hagiography. It seems we are being prepared to witness the wonders in the life of a saint – Saint Wariinga!

What the story ultimately reveals, however, is the process of Wariinga's gradual growth from a devout Christian to a devout marxist revolutionary. Even though her final act of vindictive murder might lead her to the executioner's noose as a criminal, there is still a sense in which Wariinga becomes a revolutionary heroine (a saint). Her murderous act of revenge is at the same time a heroic act of revolt against the oppressors of her class. Thus, what the hagiographic narrative style has done is to lend religious authenticity to a marxist heroine revolting against the capitalist systems carried out in Kenya by the likes of the character Hispaniora Greenway Ghitahy – the Rich Old Man from Ngorika.

One of the first steps in the Christian process of beatification is investigation of the life of the candidate for canonization. Ngugi's strategy in *Devil on the Cross* seems, therefore, to have created a paradoxical situation whereby the reader seems to be witnessing the unfolding of the Christian process of beatification for a marxist revolutionary. And the whole procedure seems to have God's blessing, hence Wariinga's story is revealed to a 'Prophet of Justice'. In fact, the narrative canonization extends beyond Wariinga to also include Muturi, Wangari, and the student leader, all of whom are called 'The Holy Trinity of the worker, the peasant, the patriot' (p. 230).

This idealization of the positive proletarian hero in contrast to the caricaturing of bourgeois characters, the optimism of the total depiction and the practical demonstration of the dialectical law of historical materialism are some of the obvious characteristics of *Devil on the Cross* as a proletarian novel. Characters like Muturi, Wariinga and Wangari are at different stages of marxist consciousness. While Muturi is fully formed, Wariinga and Wangari are rapidly growing in social consciousness as a result of deepening oppression and exploitation at the hands of Kenyan bourgeoisie. The direct result of the awakening consciousness is the forging of the unity of 'the holy trinity' of workers, peasants and students, a unity that has started challenging and, as the novel intimates, will ultimately defeat the bourgeois class. This is the source of the optimism of the narrative whose tone is of a person already savouring future victory in spite of present difficulties.

HAGIOGRAPHIC FABULOSITY AS GATEWAY TO REALISM

The distinguishing characteristic of the novel as a literary genre is its realism, its emphasis on verisimilitude in matters of theme, characterization, language, temporal and geographical setting. *Devil on the Cross*, however, stretches the norms of verisimilitude with the licence of a hagiography. In almost all of its aspects, the novel is by and large fabulous, based as it is on prophetic revelations, mysterious voices, dreams, miraculous escapes from death, coincidences, parables and the fairy-tale concept of the cave feast. The paradox, however, is that in spite of all these elements of the romantic, *Devil on the Cross* is a solidly realistic novel, with the fantastic aspects merely serving to heighten the novel's objective depiction of Kenyan contemporary reality. In other words, fantasy in this novel is only the gateway to realism.

Three factors explain Ngugi's ability to transform fantasy into realism. These include (1) his judicious balancing of the elements of romanticism throughout the novel's plot development, (2) his use of the style of psychological realism, and (3) his reliance on a narrative language heavily saturated with common folk patterns of speech. Although the story begins with the fantasy of a biblical prophet turned into a twentieth-century narrator, the fantastic nightmare of Wariinga, her mysterious voices, the recall of her miraculous escapes from suicidal death and the incredible coincidences that brought so many misfortunes on her at the same time, the center of narrative focus remains Wariinga's predicament of sudden joblessness, homelessness and her emotional reactions to these misfortunes. Her predicament is so vividly presented in concrete realistic details that the fabulous elements of the story unintrusively dwindle into insignificance. For instance, the scene of the attempted seduction of Wariinga, her refusal to cooperate, the predictable reaction of her boss (the seducer), the subsequent loss of her job, the unjustified eviction from the rented room and her emotional reactions are all convincingly depicted apart from being predictable and

realistic. Indeed, they are all part of the sordid immorality and corruption routinely witnessed today in most modern African cities.

The journey from Nairobi to Ilmorog which constitutes the com-
plication of the plot is almost entirely realistic with hardly a trace of
the fantastic apart from the cloak of mystery still surrounding the
yet-to-be-revealed new characters and the exaggerated comic
description of 'Mwaura's Matatu Matata Matamu Model T Ford,
registration number MMM 333' (pp. 31, 33).

The central action of the novel – the cave feast – returns us once
more to fantasy. In fact, this section threatens to become a farcically absurd fairy tale with its fabulous setting, the cave, and the
assembly of so many characters, all of whom are multi-millionaires,
and whose testimonies of unbelievable atrocities and exploitations
read like chapters in a book of nightmares. But even this fantastic-
ally unbelievable part of the novel is clearly transformed into a realistic affair. To begin with, in spite of some exaggeration, the
testimonies of exploitation and corruption depict the factual history
of how the typical African multi-millionaire is made in countries
like Kenya and Nigeria. The trade-mark bulging belly, the arrogance of power, the uncurbed ambition and the cynicism characterizing African imperialist stooges in their pursuit of wealth are all
sad facts of life in today's Africa. More than the realism of subject
matter, however, what transforms this romantic portion of the
novel into realistic depiction is the well-balanced alternation of the
fabulous and realistic details. The eerie feeling in the cave created
by the fantastic testimonies is judiciously interrupted and replaced
by a feeling of tangible reality achieved through a technical break in
the plot and an emphasis on the ordinary details of life. A lunch
break is called and during this interval the narrator takes us
through a topographic tour of Ilmorog's exclusive quarters and
slums and also provides the mundane biographical details of
Wariinga's earlier life.

The end of the lunch break and the return to the cave mark a
fresh flight into the fantasy of the testomonies of Wariinga's new
dream of an encounter with, and temptation by the Devil.
However, this return to fantasy is soon terminated by the brutal
interference of factual events. Gatuiria wakes Wariinga from her
dream and tells her about the arrest of Wangari. Soon after, they
witness the revolt of the proletariat and the subsequent bloody
intervention of the army, both of which actions constitute the
climax to this part of the novel. A major interlude in the plot

follows and when the narration resumes two years later, the final developments in the plot from Gatuiria's wooing of Wariinga to the climactic termination of the novel with Wariinga's murder of Gatuiria's father are all given in realistic details. That the plot ends on a tragic note for the heroine is itself a realistic detail in that it shows that there is no easy solution – as in real life – to the class problem.

Ngugi's use of psychological realism creates a situation whereby even the most fabulous episodes in the novel are realistically motivated. Wariinga's mystery voice, for instance, is nothing but the voice of her inner mind offering advice and suggesting solutions to the problems raised by her troubled emotions. Being a devout Christian and spiritually inclined person, she usually internalizes her experience and gives expression to them in religious terms. For instance, since her young religious mind cannot conceive of any being other than the devil to be capable of such heights of religious hypocrisy, social-political corruption and the brutal sexual and material exploitation suffered by the Kenyans at the hands of their bourgeoisie, she consequently equates the latter with the devil incarnate. Thus, during her moments of meditation in the church and at the cave these characters become transformed into the nightmare devils that haunt her thoughts. Indeed, it would seem she has subconsciously found a most appropriate metaphor to express her total abhorrence for the inhumanity characteristic of the bourgeoisie depicted in the novel.

Similarly, Wariinga's conversation with the devil during her daydream at the golf course while taking a short break away from the testimonies at the cave is nothing but the subconscious dramatization of the intellectual doubts, questions and answers prompted by the spiritual and emotional crises she was in at the time. Wariinga's problems would not only end but life would actually be transformed at least for a time into a continuous sea of luxury if she were to surrender her principles and become the mistress of any of those ageing multi-millionaires ready to pay any price to own 'sugar babies' (pp. 22, 192). The temptation is indeed a great one. Lured, on the one hand, by abundant wealth in the world of the 'sugar daddy' multi-millionaires, and repulsed, on the other hand, by the inhumanity associated with this wealth, Wariinga is forced into the critical position of making a final moral choice: to follow the easy life of loose morals and wealth or the difficult path of proletarian resistance! It is the psychological agony of resolving this issue that is dramatized in the novel as her day-dream encounter with, and temptation by, the Devil, whom – as we remember – she equates with the Kenyan bourgeoisie.

Finally, another source of the earthiness, the palpable realism of *Devil on the Cross*, in spite of all its fantasies, is the folkish nature of the novel's language. Hardly does any character make a statement that is not couched in some choice proverb or folk saying. The pages of the novel literally overflow with these traditional modes of Gikuyu common speech which, being a common property of the people, is generously used by both positive and negative characters alike, including the narrator. Apart from anchoring the novel in a familiar realistic world, the folk language is also a source of aesthetic pleasure to the reader because of its wisdom and the shared beauty of expression, as is evident in the following examples:

> The wise can also be taught wisdom,
> So let me tell you:
> Gikuyu said that talking is the way to loving.
> Today is tomorrow's treasury.
> Tomorrow is the harvest of what we plant today.
> So let us ask ourselves:
> Moaning and groaning – who has ever gained from it?
> Change seeds, for the gourd contains seeds of more
>   than one kind!
> Change steps, for the song has more than one rhythm!
> Today's *Muomboko* dance is two steps and a turn!
>
> (p. 16)

> ... Boss Kihara waits, hoping that Kareendi will eventually yield. Too much haste splits the yam. One month later, he again accosts Kareendi in the office. 'Miss Kareendi, this evening there's a cocktail party at the Paradise Club.' Once again Kareendi disguises her refusal with polite phrases.
>
> The day comes when Boss Kihara reasons with himself in this way: The hunter who stalks his prey too stealthily may frighten it off in the end. Begging calls for constantly changing tactics. Bathing involves removing all one's clothes. So he confronts Kareendi boldly. 'By the way, Miss Kareendi ...'
>
> (pp. 20–1)

Thus, *Devil on the Cross* is an exceptionally well written proletarian novel. It seems to me that in deploying the Christian religion to the task of undermining those who claim it but abuse it, like the hypocritical African imperialist stooges testifying at the cave, while supporting a proletarian idealist heroine like Wariinga, Ngugi is indicating a new positive direction to organized religion in today's Africa.

From *Ufahamu: Journal of the African Activist Association*, 16: 1 (Spring 1986), 1–24.

NOTES

[Balogun's essay provides an example of marxist-realist postcolonial criticism of an important novel by Ngugi. The essay draws on formalist notions of defamiliarisation and cultural intertextuality, studies of narrative structure and postcolonial marxist aesthetics of historical materialism. In acknowledging that the literary text is perceived to have a direct political purpose, this essay differs from critical views that the text, freed from its author, is reconstructed by the reader: rather Balogun's essay seeks to demonstrate the closeness of the relationship between political and literary exegesis and between author/text and reader, a strategy common in some postcolonial criticism. Eds]

1. Ngugi wa Thiong'o, *Devil on the Cross* (London: Heinemann, 1982). Page references are indicated in parentheses within the essay. The novel was originally published in Gikuyu as *Caitaani Mutharabaini* by the author in 1980 under the imprint of Heinemann (East Africa) Ltd. According to a report by Ngugi published in *World Literature Written in English*, 24: 1 (1984), 7, the novel in the original Gikuyu was enthusiastically received in Kenya where it had three reprints of five thousand copies each within the first year of its publication.

2. Beginning with Marx and Engels, marxist intellectuals have always regarded religion, which they call 'the opium of the people', as an instrument of bourgeois exploitation. Bourgeois intellectuals, on the other hand, have invariably used atheism as a pretext to attack Marxism. To cite an example, in an article titled 'Soviet Threat Is One of Ideas More Than Arms' published in *The Wall Street Journal* (Monday, 23 May 1983), David Satter made the following comments:

> For this reason, and others, it is at last possible to mount the ideological counter-offensive now 65 years overdue, which may offer the best hope of stopping communism without war. The only requirement, if the US is to enter seriously the competition to sway men's minds in every country of the world, including the Soviet Union, is that we understand not only what we are against but also what we are for. Whatever we may think of communism, we must recognize that it attempts to answer basic questions about the nature of

history and the source of values, questions that have plagued mankind since the beginning of recorded time.

It is therefore essential that we answer in kind. If our notion of an ideological counter-offensive is to try to generate the fervor on behalf of free enterprise that communists are able to inspire on behalf of socialism we will only succeed in making ourselves look ridiculous. Capitalism stands in need of values to restrain and guide it. It can never be the source of such values. If representatives of the US are able to clarify for the world, the difference between universal Judeo-Christian values and the 'class values' of Marxist-Leninism, the world role of the US will be seen as inherently honorable as it is.

3. For the treatment of the theme of religion in *Petals of Blood* see G. D. Killam (ed.), *Critical Perspectives on Ngugi wa Thiong'o* (Washington, DC, 1984), pp. 283, 269–99 and F. Odun Balogun, 'Petals of Blood: A Novel of the people', *Ba Shiru*, 10: 2 (1979), 49–57. The way Ngugi handled the theme of religion in earlier novels is also discussed in *Critical Perspectives*, pp. 146–60, 201–16.

4. Ngugi wa Thiong'o, *Writers in Politics* (London, 1981), p. 22. This book of essays appeared a year before the English translation *of Caitaani Mutharabaini* (*Devil on the Cross*).

5. There are indications that the negative characters bear self-demeaning Gikuyu names. One of the multi-millionaires bragging with the records of their inhumanity and exploitiveness is called Fathog Marura wa Kimmeengemeenge (p. 122). The first name is English – 'Fat hog' – and it alludes to the physical characteristics of the Devil in the novel: obesity and red skin. The promiscuous rich old man who lured Wariinga away from the path of virtue has these comically accultur-ated names: Hispaniora Greenway Ghitahy. The hotels frequented by the negative characters to engage in sexual immorality are ironically named Modern Love Bar and Lodging (p. 19), Paradise Club (p. 20). Unfortunately, my efforts to get the Gikuyu names translated were unsuccessful.

7

The Master's Dance to the Master's Voice: Revolutionary Nationalism and the Representation of Women in the Writing of Ngugi wa Thiong'o

ELLEKE BOEHMER

> A writer needs people around him. ... For me, in writing a novel, I
> love to hear the voices of the people ... I need the vibrant voices of
> beautiful women: their touch, their sighs, their tears, their laughter.[1]

With these affirmative words, the Kenyan writer Ngugi wa Thiong'o
explicitly points to the strong position that women characters have
held in his work over the years. It is a position virtually unique in
Anglophone African literature. Where efforts to resist the most overt
forms of colonial oppression have dominated the centre stage of
African history, African writers (the majority of whom are male)
have tended to concentrate on themes of national self-assertion and
struggle. Relative to the liberation of nations or of 'peoples', the
emancipation of women has been rated as of secondary importance.
For this reason, Ngugi's exertions to include women in his vision of
a Kenya liberated from neocolonial domination merit recognition.
Yet, at the same time, precisely because of the prominence of his
achievement, the enduring patriarchal cast of his ideas cannot be
ignored. For it is by singling out female voices, by fixing women
beneath the evaluative epithets 'vibrant' and 'beautiful', that Ngugi
gives way to that tendency to distance and objectify women which,
also in the most recent texts, qualifies his attempt to grant them a
leading role in the revolutionary struggle for Kenyan liberation.

This ambivalence in Ngugi's attitude towards women forms a significant part of a wider contradiction undercutting his populist nationalist programme for a new Kenya. Beginning with the writing of his epic-length *Petals of Blood*, a project that extended over the early and mid-seventies, Ngugi has come unequivocally to identify with the plight of the betrayed Kenyan peasantry. His nationalism of the sixties has thus turned revolutionary: whereas in the early novels the concept of the nation was identified with a leader figure, a Kenyatta type of patriarch, it is now seen in terms of 'the people', bound together by their shared history and cultural traditions.

To Ngugi, however, a revolutionary future is seen to involve a necessary subjection to the single overarching idea of the People's nation, and participation in an ostensibly homogeneous culture. What transpires is that his adherence to such concepts of national authority threatens to undermine his ideals for joyous populist expression. The 'harmony in polyphony'[2] of Kenyan cultures that Ngugi acclaims, in effect becomes a national unisonance that has negative implications for Ngugi's fondest aspirations – on the nationalist level his project to champion the indigenous languages of Kenya and, as far as his commitment to social emancipation is concerned, his endeavour to give pre-eminence to the role of women in the struggle. Despite his rhetoric to the contrary, Ngugi, in certain important areas, gives his backing to the monolithic as well as to the patriarchal supports of the neocolonial regime he seeks to overthrow.

This becomes especially clear in his diligent efforts to include women in the 'people's' struggle. Investing his leading women characters with the dignity of ages or with an almost bionic power, Ngugi has erected heroines of immense, if not impossible, stature: either great Mothers of a future Kenya, or aggressive gun-toting revolutionaries. As he does at the start of *Detained: A Writer's Prison Diary*, where he hails Wariinga,[3] 'heroine of toil', as his inspiration,[4] Ngugi tends, in his recent work especially, to set up his women characters as icons – allegorical figures representing all that is resilient and strong in the Kenyan people. He thus seeks to identify with the liberation of African women as a part of his resistance to all forms of oppression. Yet, by maintaining relations of dominance in his portrayal of revolutionary forces, he is forced either to enlist his women characters into the ranks of a male-ordered struggle, or to elevate women to the status of mascot at the head of the (male?) peasant and workers' march. Ngugi's neglect, of both the gendered and the structural nature of power, whether that power is held by national or by proletarian forces, ultimately works to inhibit his rousing call for a new dispensation in Kenya.

In accordance with the name he has made for himself as a revolutionary Kenyan writer, Ngugi has, in recent years, encouraged positive critical comment by coming out in favour of the liberation of women in his non-fictional statements.[5] As women are 'the most exploited and oppressed section of the entire working class', he will, he has maintained, seek to create in his fiction 'a picture of a strong determined woman with a will to resist and to struggle' as an example for his audience.[6] He also makes frequent references to the part played by women like Mary Nyanjiru and Me Kitilili in resistance to Kenyan colonial oppression,[7] and to the way in which women participated with men in the dramatic experiments which he helped to organise at Kamiirithu in Kenya in the later seventies.[8]

We cannot fail to notice, however, that Ngugi's gaze remains fixed on the 'most remarkable'[9] historical figures; not the colourful crowds of his novel *A Grain of Wheat* (1967) with their songs and ribald badinage, but single dominant personalities who stand as points of moral focus in his text. Significant, too, is the report 'Women in Cultural Work: the fate of Kamiirithu people's theatre in Kenya', in which the ostensible pro-woman stance is rather obviously grafted onto a fairly straightforward factual account of the experience.[10] Similar inconsistencies also fracture Ngugi's many indictments of the repressions and exclusions of colonial education. In *Decolonising the Mind* (1986), his study of colonial and national cultural practice, Ngugi does not make a single reference to the ways in which women have been silenced by colonial and traditional power structures. Despite his professed delight at hearing women's voices, he never mentions a woman writer, not in his numerous inventories of canonical literary names nor in the lists of respected figures which he himself suggests for university curricula.[11]

We are led to assume that, in Ngugi's view, women's emancipation once again takes a second place to the national struggle against neocolonialism. The struggles cannot be seen as mutually reinforcing: in order to ensure the liberation of Kenya from the grip of neocolonial powers, women must either wait in the sidelines for the new social order, as structured by men, to emerge, or must usefully contribute to the struggle by fighting alongside their men, without a thought for their own position once arms have been laid down. Yet, as histories of national liberation movements have shown, the establishment of a new order does not always bring extended opportunities for women.[12] Traditional attitudes and roles prove resistant to change: patriarchal laws may be relaxed, or, in a crisis situation, adapted, but once the desired social transformation has been secured, political leadership will reimpose old structures with more or less the same severity as their former capitalist and/or colonial foes. Considering his fervent commitment to liberation for all Kenya, we might expect Ngugi to have in some way countered the sobering evidence of history. Yet apart from the glib didactic statement in *I will marry when I want* regarding the equality of the sexes, an equality which is simply taken as understood by its spokesman, Gicaamba,[13] Ngugi's most direct reference to social arrangements after the revolution is his 1981 blueprint for 'an education for a national patriotic culture' to produce individuals who are 'masters of their natural and social environment', 'fully prepared in their twin struggle with nature and with other men' (my emphasis).[14] As the nation must be an association of producers who are also fighters, military training forms an important part of the programme. No provision is made for those who are the reproducers, the nurturers of the nation.

In an interview for *Marxism Today* Ngugi makes his hierarchical ordering of values clear: though 'factors' of caste and race may contribute to social divisions, he stresses that these must not be allowed to blur the 'basic' reality of class struggle (the 'gender factor' is completely omitted).[15] Ngugi could, it is true, justify his accentuating class in this way by contending that the imposition of colonial structures has aggravated existing patriarchal attitudes and, consequently, that the more immediate evil of neocolonialism must first be eradicated. Further, though he tends to see the coloniser as the chief oppressor, Ngugi has acknowledged the 'reactionary' nature of traditional social norms.[16]

And yet, though confidently setting class above gender distinctions while still putting in a claim for women's liberation, Ngugi never pauses to examine the premises of his economic arguments. He ceaselessly refers to the workers of Kenya, but he does not define precisely what he means by a worker. From his portrayal of those who work, however, it is clear that he views 'productive' labour as male-dominated; even in his utopian fiction, the workers, as opposed to the peasants, are male: Wariinga, of *Devil on the Cross,* in becoming an engineer, is immediately a special case, a 'professional'. These divisions can, perhaps, be defended on account of their correspondence to the African reality. In more general terms, too, women's work spaces lie outside the field of 'real' labour. Yet it is in his silence regarding the activity of the so-called marginal economic sector that Ngugi's disregard for the work of women becomes significant. For if mothers are assumed to be non-workers, and prostitutes, like Wanja of Petals of Blood (1977), part of a lumpen-proletariat, and if most of Ngugi's women can be slotted into either category, then both groups are automatically and conveniently marginalised. They are available either for over-valuation as the heroines of the national troops, or for enlistment as the literal reproducers of those troops – support-roles in an essentially male struggle.

Still, even with such strict gender polarisation, we should pause to acknowledge that Ngugi's women characters remain pioneers in the field of Anglophone African fiction written by men. In their strength of character, their spirit, and their self-reliance, they are undoubtedly unique. More often than not they demonstrate a firmer resolve and a deeper understanding than their male counter-parts; Wanja is motivated by an energy and a conviction in the exe-cution of her plans that even the revolutionary leader, Karega, in his commitment to the struggle, cannot match; Wariinga, blazing a trail of defiance through the final pages of *Devil on the Cross,* must leave her vacillating beloved Gatuiria behind her. Both in *A Grain of Wheat* and in *Petals of Blood* the group of central characters is dominated by one woman – linking them together, as in Mumbi's case, in *A Grain of Wheat,* or forcing them apart, as does Wanja in her affairs with Munira and Karega. Yet it becomes clear that Mumbi and Wanja stand at the position of epicentre primarily on the strength of their being women or, more precisely, biological females. Whether as lover, prostitute or potential childbearer, it is essentially as sexual partner that the male characters are drawn to them. Ngugi fits his women characters into the thoroughly well-worn stereotypes of mother and of whore. Considering the preva-lence of Biblical imagery in Ngugi, we thus see the woman defined either as Mother Mary, the long-suffering Mumbi, whose name is that of the mother of the Gikuyu, or as the prostitute Mary Magdalene, Wanja, who leads men, both the capitalists (Kimeria) and their opponents (Munira) into perdition. That remarkable mag-netic power of Ngugi's women to which Cook and Okenimkpe refer in such glowing terms is simply another manifestation of the potent, nameless forces with which women as 'nature' or as 'wild' have traditionally been associated.[17]

Though in the early work single heroes still predominate and the women characters are not as powerful, the same tendencies emerge. In particular, as the focus is more on the remote past and the pristine origins of Gikuyu people, the mother figures are important. In the *Secret Lives* (1975) stories, the mothers suffer and find fulfilment in so far as they can give expression to their maternal instincts and thus satisfy their husband's demands; Mwihaki of *Weep Not, Child* (1964), Muthoni and the younger Nyambura of *The River Between* (1965), in their courage and endurance, may be seen as potential Mumbis, and, like Mumbi, are consistently viewed only in their relation to men. Mwihaki, for example, gives Njoroge strength and support when he is wavering, yet the ideals which she upholds are based on what he has taught her; Nyambura and Muthoni for their part, passively represent the two sides of a conflict over female circumcision directed solely by men. Yet these stereotypes are predictable: at this stage Ngugi had not yet come out in support of sexual equality, let alone of class conflict. But it is for this very reason that the characterisation of women in the early novels provides a useful point of reference. Here Ngugi upholds the patriarchal order by establishing archetypal roles and patterns of relationships that will continue, albeit in transmuted form, into the later novels.

In the early novels, if woman is not silent super-heroine, she is doomed to be equally silent victim. In *The River Between*, Muthoni's circumcision wound proves fatal, yet she dies, almost literally, in a beatific state; she believes she has been 'made beautiful in the tribe', that is to say, she has been glorified as a woman by submitting to the ancient laws of the elders, the fathers of the village.[18] In *A Grain of Wheat*, not only do Njeri and Wambuku lay down their lives for the hero Kihika, but, as though to ram home the image of women as victim, Ngugi introduces the one account of a rape in all the fiction about 'Mau Mau'.[19]

In *Petals of Blood*, once again, a woman is used as victim. As a thriving madam, obviously equipped with an extremely durable vagina, Wanja becomes a ready symbol for the ravaged state of Kenya.[20] Yet her courage and resourcefulness in turning her exploitation as a woman and as a member of the oppressed classes to her advantage, is finally discredited. As Karega self-righteously makes explicit, thus laying down the male law, her struggle means very little because her method of resistance is simply to exploit in return. His final word is one of condemnation; no possibility of negotiation and certainly no expression of tenderness is permitted.[21] And yet, at times, the only way in which Wanja could survive was 'to sell (herself) over and over again'.[22] Indeed, Ngugi allows her this; her immense resilience is recognised, but, in the last pages of the novel, the priority is given to the workers' struggle: the representative of the a-political lumpen-proletariat is discarded. Such a ranking of social values, however, rests upon unquestioned assumptions regarding the submission of women to male demand. Here, as elsewhere, it would seem that female power is recognised only in those areas where it is ultimately subdued to male control. In the field of sexual relations, certainly, the willing submission of women is the order of the day. The texts are unabashedly frank: from *The River Between* to *Petals of Blood,* all descriptions of sexual encounters invariably and emphatically cast the man in the dominant position. The woman, whether she is the adoring Nyokabi, or the self-sufficient Wanja, is passive, openly subordinate, 'exhilaratingly weak',[23] and apart from the raped Dr Lynd, consistently transported by phallic power.

As if to make amends, Ngugi, in his most recent work, introduces heroines who have made a decisive break with a former life of mothering and/or whoring in their commitment to a revolutionary cause. The figure of the old seer, 'Mother of men',[24] the Wambui of *A Grain of Wheat,* the Nyakinyua of *Petals of Blood,* reappears as the ancient and noble Wangari who, like her predecessors, was involved in 'Mau Mau' as a messenger and carrier of arms, but, unlike them, plays a more prominent role in the present action of the novel, being finally proclaimed as 'heroine of our nation'.[25] As for the younger women, the Woman and the woman fighter in the play, *The Trial of Dedan Kimathi* (1976), and Wariinga in *Devil on the Cross,* if the heroines of the earlier novels were forceful, then these women characters, in their fortitude, the fierceness of their resolution, and their resourcefulness, are larger than life. As in the earlier novels, this stature is highlighted by their standing as the lone representatives of their sex in a field of male characters.

With Wariinga, certainly, Ngugi has pulled out all the stops. After her experience at the Devil's Feast, a competition to choose the most successful thieves and robbers in the world, Wariinga finds a new purpose in life, the struggle for a more equitable social system, and changes accordingly. The reader is not allowed to miss a detail.

Wariinga, we are told, new 'heroine of toil', simultaneously 'black beauty' and 'our engineering hero', has said 'goodbye to being secretary', the flower in Boss Kihara's life, and has '(stormed) a man's citadel'. She is not only a qualified engineer, a modest fourth in her all-male class, but a formidable practitioner of judo and karate who airily knocks down her opponents, and, if they still offer resistance, produces her gun.[26] Yet, though she is said to engage enthusiastically in the struggle with nature that Ngugi has previously cast in terms of the male generic pronoun, she is reclaimed for womanhood; despite her hard labour in the workshop, she remains sexually attractive. The point is repeatedly emphasised: Wariinga's clothes are said to fit her like a skin,[27] both her boyfriend and Rich Old Man are floored by her beauty. In this way Wariinga is confirmed in her heroic status. She is the exemplary female revolutionary, a fighter and 'still a woman', as perfect and untouchable as a holy image and made to order like her clothes.

Clearly, Wariinga is put in service of the didactic text. Just as the Woman's voice in *The Trial of Dedan Kimathi* sounds out, disembodied, enjoining the boy to 'become a man',[28] so Wariinga appears as inspiration in a struggle that is still defined and operated by men. She is aggressive, fearless and single-minded; she will contribute her energies to changing society; but, though she gives up all else, she does not sacrifice her femaleness, her soft hair and comely shape: in her bag she carries both a phase-tester and a hand mirror.[29] And further, in order that there may be no mistake as to their crusading roles, both Wariinga and the Woman are granted the possession of a gun. Women, we realise, are not to be left out of the military-preparedness programme. Yet, in this bestowing upon his revolutionary heroines the quintessential emblem of phallic power, Ngugi betrays his firm patriarchal affiliations. Instead of preparing the way towards liberation by dismantling those structures that marginalise and oppress women, he disguises the rigid distinctions that such structures enforce when his women come dressed as men. Instead of questioning processes of objectification, he places a male weapon in the hands of his women characters and sets them on pedestals as glorified revolutionaries, inspiriting symbols for a male struggle. Male values thus come encased in female shape, just as in *The Trial of Dedan Kimathi,* guns come disguised as loaves of bread.[30]

To Ngugi, then, all other interest must give way before the 'higher social system of democracy and socialism' within a free Kenya.[31] Yet the shells of the systems, the skeletons of old structures remain: a different statue is erected in the town square, perhaps even a '(monument) / To our women',[32] but it is no less a monolith. The difficulty does not, however, lie in the need for system as such. Harmonic polyphony could not thrive without linguistic structure. It is also not a matter restricted to Ngugi's work alone. Ngugi stands together with many others when he attacks the colossus of white Western maledom, yet hesitates to dislodge the ramparts of its patriarchy. Simply expressed, the problem would rather seem to be an identification of national freedom with male freedom and an inherited state structure. Thus a patriarchal order survives intact.

A significant part of this problem is the continued adherence to the concept of a single monolithic system: a centrally-based authority, an extensive apparatus of control administered from above and by men. Within such structures the people's culture, the vitality of which Ngugi has so often proclaimed, will not be allowed to flourish on its own. Culture, he stresses, 'must prepare (its) recipients to change the world'.[33] Yet, as Mikhail Bakhtin, an ardent proponent of multivoicedness or polyphony, has said, the 'consolidation' of any one dominant ideological system requires that:

> All ... creative acts are conceived and perceived as possible expressions of a single consciousness, a single spirit ... the spirit of a nation, the spirit of a people, the spirit of history. ...[34]

In effect, the people, the broad masses of Kenya, and also the 'liberated' women, must march in the forces and swell the one national chorus. The policies of the future remain official and bureaucratic, dominated by the interests of the patriarchal state before all else. Dissenting voices, decentring languages, are against the rules. Benedict Anderson's comment in his analysis of the failure of national liberation struggles, suggests the resilience of the monologic order, and of the patriarchal presence securely lodged with it:

> Like the complex electrical-system in any large mansion when the owner has fled, the state awaits the new owner's hand at the switch to be very much its own brilliant self again.[35]

The overlord of old remains in charge; it is still 'the master's dance to the master's voice'.[36]

From *Journal of Commonwealth Literature*, 26: 1 (1991), 188–97.

NOTES

[This essay adds an important feminist dimension to readings of the revolutionary writings of a male author like Ngugi. Boehmer's position has affinities with Western feminist poststructuralist and deconstructionist positions, developed by Kristeva and Showalter among others. In describing an underpinning patriarchal ideology, the essay, like many feminist critiques, leads to important questions about the credibility of the political radicalism advocated in the novel. Eds]

1. Ngugi wa Thiong'o, *Detained: A Writer's Prison Diary* (London, 1981), pp. 8–9.

2. Ngugi wa Thiong'o, *Devil on the Cross* (London, 1982), p. 60.

3. Wariinga is one of the central characters in *Devil on the Cross*, a novel that Ngugi began to write during his period of detention.

4. *Detained: A Writer's Prison Diary*, p. 3.

5. As early as 1971, Eddah Gachukia commended Ngugi for correcting the negative image of women in African fiction. (Gachukia, 'The role of women in Ngugi's novels', *Busara*, 3: 4 (1971), 30–1). More recently, Cook and Okenimkpe have emphasised the vital role of women in Ngugi's novels. David Cook and Michael Okenimkpe, *Ngugi wa Thiong'o* (London, 1983), pp. 135–6. Charles Nama and Tobe Levin also find inspirational value in Ngugi's vision of women in revolt. Charles A. Nama, 'Daughters of Moombi', *Ngambika: Studies of Women in African Literature*, ed. Carole Boyce Davies and Anne Adams Graves (Trenton, NJ, 1986), pp. 139–49, and Tobe Levin, 'Scapegoats of Culture and Cult', *Ngambika*, pp. 205–21.

6. *Detained: A Writer's Prison Diary*, p. 10.

7. Ibid., pp 10–11, 46–8; *Barrel of a Pen* (London, 1983), p. 41, pp. 55–6; *Decolonising the Mind: the Politics of Language in African Literature* (London, 1986), p. 102.

8. *Detained*, pp. 74, 74–8; *Barrel of a Pen*, pp. 39–51; *Decolonising the Mind*, pp. 45, 54–6.

9. *Detained*, p. 46.

10. *Barrel of a Pen*, pp. 39–51.

11. *Decolonising the Mind*, pp. 12, 18, 29, 70, 91, 99, 105.

12. See, for example, Miranda Davies (ed.), *Third World – Second Sex* (London, 1986); Sheila Rowbotham, *Women, Resistance and Revolution* (London, 1972).

13. Ngugi wa Thiong'o and Ngugi wa Mirii, *I Will Marry When I Want* (London, 1984), pp. 104–5.

14. *Barrel of a Pen,* pp. 98–9.

15. Interview with Ngugi, *Marxism Today* (September 1982), 34.

16. *Detained,* p. 106.

17. See, for example, Susan Griffin, *Woman and Nature* (London, 1975) and Shirley Ardener (ed.), *Perceiving Women* (London, 1975).

18. Ngugi wa Thiong'o, *The River Between* (London, 1978), p. 44.

19. The observation regarding the uniqueness of this rape is David Maughan-Brown's in his *Land, Freedom and Fiction: History and Ideology in Kenya* (London, 1985), pp. 252–5.

20. As does the younger Wariinga. For an explicit analogy, see *Detained,* p. 59.

21. Ngugi wa Thiong'o, *Petals of Blood* (Cape Town, 1982), pp. 326–7.

22. Ibid., p. 325.

23. Ngugi wa Thiong'o, *A Grain of Wheat* (London, 1982), p. 45.

24. Ibid., p. 70.

25. *Devil on the Cross,* p. 198.

26. All references are to *Devil on the Cross,* pp. 216–21.

27. Ibid., p. 217.

28. Ngugi wa Thiong'o, *The Trial of Dedan Kimathi* (London, 1985), pp. 22, 41, 43.

29. *Devil on the Cross,* p. 217.

30. *The Trial of Dedan Kimathi,* p. 43.

31. *Barrel of a Pen,* p. 99.

32. *The Trial of Dedan Kimathi,* p. 73.

33. *Barrel of a Pen,* p. 99.

34. Mikhail Bakhtin, *Problems of Dostoevsky's Poetics,* ed. and trans. Caryl Emerson (Minneapolis, 1984), p. 82.

35. Benedict Anderson, *Imagined Communities: Reflections on the Origin and Spread of Nationalisms* (London, 1983), p. 145.

36. *Petals of Blood,* p. 163.

8

'Going in the Opposite Direction': Feminine Recusancy in Anita Desai's *Voices in the City*

HARVEEN SACHDEVA MANN

> Monisha, standing in the doorway, suddenly called out her first independent sentence of the evening. 'Amla,' she cried in the sudden, harsh tone of a night jar, a wild bird flushed from some unexplored depth of jungle, 'Amla, always go in the opposite direction.'
>
> *(Voices in the City, p. 160)* [1]

Since its publication in 1965, Anita Desai's second novel, *Voices in the City,* has been variously described as an existentialist fiction about the meaninglessness of lives devoid of commitment to a cause, a study of the predicament of the artist torn between aesthetic and material values, a narrative about the deleterious effects of urban living, and a portrait of the dark, nocturnal side of Calcutta.[2] Whatever the disparity in their views regarding the primary subject matter of the book, critics like Darshan Singh Maini and Madhusudan Prasad are unanimous in declaring the bohemian male character, Nirode, to be its protagonist. Not only do most such critics thus pay scant attention to Desai's treatment of female characters in *Voices in the City,* but Maini goes so far as to posit that the novelist's portrayal of Nirode's two sisters, Monisha and Amla, is an artistic failure. He believes that '[seeing] no way of carrying [Nirode's] story forward except through a vicarious involvement in the lives of his sisters,' Desai simply mirrors his nihilism in Monisha's tragic life and final suicide, whereas Amla's more 'gay and provocative' existence '[do]es not quite fit into the pattern' established by her Hamletian brother.[3]

Opposing such supposedly apolitical and 'universalist' but essentially androcentric readings of *Voices in the City,* I contend that the novel can be regarded as a significant discourse on modern Indian feminism. As she portrays female characters who, even when they fall victim to the gendered social hierarchy, destabilize and subvert the patriarchal underpinnings of Indian society – in short, as she depicts women who 'go in the opposite direction' – Desai fashions in *Voices in the City* a culturally and historically specific text that participates in creating a new feminist ideology in Indian literature written in English.

An avowedly 'subjective' writer, Desai nonetheless displays an acute understanding of the social, cultural, and material impediments faced by her female characters in their search for self-fulfillment. And while she does not portray female exploitation and oppression across all classes and castes in her fiction, Desai does document the specificities of the victimization of educated, middle-class urban women. *Voices in the City,* in particular, can be effectively read as a political structure within a feminist context because it insistently questions and opposes the quintessential 'feminine' ideal (from a masculinist perspective) rooted in Hindu mythology. Whereas Monisha and Amla dismantle the old mythologies and iconic presentations of women as subservient, self-sacrificing, chaste, and devoted to family, their mother, Otima, and beyond her the city of Calcutta, personify two of Desai's strongest statements of female resistance to the traditional structures of patriarchy. Repeatedly likened in the narrative to Kali, the Hindu goddess of destruction, Otima and Calcutta respectively counter the idealized images of a tender, nurturing mother and motherland. By creating such oppositional female characters and by adopting Kali as the reigning goddess of her novel, Desai presents recusant images of Indian femininity that underscore her dissent from the still pervasive ideology of gender in modern India.

I first review the cultural background which engenders and perpetuates the marginalization of Indian women and against which Desai casts her female characters' narratives. Next, I briefly discuss the alternative image of Indian femininity embodied in Kali. And in the third and final section of my analysis, I examine the registers of women's resistance in *Voices in the City*, ranging from Monisha's suicide, through Amla's compromises, to Otima's iconoclasm. As she reverses the Hindu idealization of women and creates subversive portraits of Indian womanhood, Desai contributes to the abrogation of orthodox male authority in both the literary and social domains.

I

In a country in which the scriptures as well as the Hindu legal codes have historically circumscribed women, the latter have for centuries been forced into a servitude that, in historian Stanley Wolpert's words, 'border[s] on slavery'.[4] The *Bhagavad Gita*, for example, prescribing brahminical male domination, declares women, like the lower castes, to be baser forms of life with no right to transcendence and eternity. Sita, the heroine of *The Ramayana*, chaste, utterly devoted to her husband, the very personification of selfless sacrifice, is regarded as the feminine ideal even in contemporary times. And the influential *Manava Dharmashastra*, the Law Code of Manu, encodes the dependent and inferior status of women as men's property, arguing that rigid male control of female sexuality is necessitated by woman's inherently lascivious and adulterous nature.

Although Manu's code has long been replacd by more modern legal structures, the orthodox sentiments underlying it persist to this day, ensuring the continued sexual colonization of women. Even as twentieth-century India battled British colonialism, its nationalist revolution was not accompanied by a revolution in the sphere of male–female relations. In fact, as Ketu Katrak points out, the independence struggle proved in many ways to be detrimental to the women's struggle. The glorification of indigenous traditions – intended to bind the populace together and to counteract colonial, racist denigration of the culture – impacted negatively upon Indian women after independence[5] because, with few exceptions, Hindu tradition subordinates and denigrates women.

Psychologists Joanna Liddle and Rama Joshi further demonstrate in their studies of Indian women that the postindependence Indian class structure is no more egalitarian than the caste structure (which persists regardless of protestations to the contrary) with regard to gender and social hierarchy in the ideological and material realms.[6]

Whereas the caste system dictates women's subordination in terms of domestic seclusion, severe restrictions on education and employment, economic dependence, and rigid controls over female sexuality, the class system contains its own set of gender inequalities. Under the latter, women have only limited control over the type, quality, and purpose of their education and the kind and level of employment they can find; they are sexually harassed in the workplace; and they have to perform all the domestic along with paid work.[7]

Thus, although some modifications were made to accommodate women's resistance and they were granted constitutional equality following Indian independence in 1947, women continue to labor under religiously and socially sanctioned patriarchal oppression in modern India. Psychoanalyst Sudhir Kakar, quoting tellingly from the ancient Hindu texts, establishes that in spite of modernization, urbanization, and education, a 'formidable consensus on the ideal of womanhood ... still [in the mid 1970s] governs the inner imagery of individual men and women as well as the social relations between them in both the traditional and modern sectors of the Indian community'.[8]

As if in agreement with the social scientists and cultural critics quoted above, Desai underlines the continuing 'imprisonment' of the female sex in India in contemporary times, locating one of its primary causes in the Hindu deification of women. In a 1990 article entitled 'A Secret Connivance', she comments upon the 'one hundred thousand ... cults built around the Mother Goddess', the 'fecund figure from whom all good things flow – milk, food, warmth, comfort. Her ample bosom and loins, her exciting curves and buxom proportions make her not merely the ideal mother but the ideal woman – consort, lover, plaything.'[9] Citing as well the conterminous constraints of widespread illiteracy and material dependence that make Indian women themselves 'connive at' this mythological idealization, Desai concludes that they 'ha[ve] no alternative' but to be complicit in their servitude. 'The myth keeps [the Indian woman] ... bound hand and foot,' she points out; '[t]o rebel against it ... would mean that she is questioning the myth, attacking the legend, and that cannot be permitted: it is the cornerstone on which the Indian family and therefore Indian society are built.'[10]

Desai nonetheless challenges such an idealization of Indian women by portraying female characters who 'question the myth' in various ways. Not only do Monisha and Amla in *Voices in the City* serve as counterpoints to the middle-class ideology of the Indian

Hindu woman, but Otima and Calcutta as incarnations of Kali also present alternative, empowering images of Indian femininity.

II

Although Hindu mythology is replete with narratives extolling the virtues of ideal females like Sita, a considerable body of cultural imagery portrays women as powerful rather than weak, active rather than passive, autonomous rather than dependent, violent rather than quiescent. It is as such an oppositional figure that Kali stands out in Indian feminist historiography. The product of a pre-Aryan age given over to the predominantly female-centered beliefs, Kali presents the most potent counterpoint to the latter-day stereotypical image of Indian women as self-abnegating, passive, and dependent and thus offers Desai a highly effective tool for subversion and counter-discourse.[11]

Cast as the antagonist of all evil, Kali is more significant as the embodiment of the female power principle. As she annihilates the mighty demon Raktabija by drinking his blood, she epitomizes the destruction of the male principle and phallic power. In addition, the figure of Kali is an enabling one for women because of the goddess's legendary sexual dominance over Shiva. And as one of the numerous manifestations of Shakti, feminine divine power, she contributes to the constitution of a larger matriarchal culture that reverences woman in all her roles.

Most often portrayed iconographically as a black woman with a garland of human heads and girdle of human hands, her mouth dripping blood, Kali is not, however, the murderous cannibal of common perception. Rather, as Ajit Mookerjee demonstrates, the symbolism generally surrounding her is 'equivocal', and she dons different guises for different purposes.[12] The human heads, for instance, symbolize knowledge; and the human hands – instruments of work – remind one that *moksha*, ultimate freedom from the cycle of life–death–rebirth, is to be gained through laudatory actions. As the virgin-creator (virginity here affirming woman's autonomous freedom), she is depicted as white; as the sustaining mother as red; and as the absorber of all as black.[13] Thus, to her believers, Kali conveys the totality of existence – purna – that enables them to accept life's contradictories – good and evil, creation and destruction, birth and death – with equanimity.

III

In a 1983 symposium hosted by the Commonwealth Institute of London, Desai acknowledged that the sensibility of modern Indian women writers remains clearly distinguishable from that of their male counterparts. The former, Desai believes, 'tend to place their emphasis differently from men' because their experiences and 'values' are likely to differ. Living relatively confined lives, women writers are 'more concerned with thought, emotion and sensation', whereas men are preponderantly 'concerned with action, experience and achievement'.[14] Like Samuel Taylor Coleridge and Virginia Woolf, however, Desai holds that 'the great mind is androgynous ... undivided and therefore fully, wholly creative and powerful'.[15] To her, the literary ideal is one fashioned after the Hindu mythological figure of the Ardhanarishwara – the Hermaphrodite – which depicts the union of Shiva and Shakti, of male substance and female energy.[16] But while contemporary western literature is, in Desai's view, becoming increasingly androgynous – while such novelists as Doris Lessing, Muriel Spark, and Iris Murdoch display many of the same themes and styles as those modern-day male writers – Indian women writers are, in Desai's words, 'still exploring their feminine identity and trying to establish it as something worth possesssing'.[17] Although she rejects collective, militant feminism,[18] Desai's own 'explorations' of Indian femininity and gender politics readily reveal themselves in her fiction as she attempts to make her readers 'understand and feel what it is to be a woman, know how a woman thinks and feels and behaves'.[19]

Voices in the City is particularly concerned with the articulation of women's stories. Set primarily in postindependence Calcutta, the novel narrates the initiation into adulthood of the three siblings, Monisha, Amla, and Nirode Ray. Behind them looms the figure of their mother, Otima, and beyond the human mother lies the vengeful city-mother, Calcutta. Whereas Nirode grapples with existential questions regarding the meaninglessness of life, the nature of rebellion, and the value of suffering in the face of deadening bourgeois respectability in an ostensibly gender-neutral world, the female characters in *Voices in the City* are actively, sometimes tragically engaged in a search for self-fulfillment as women (and human beings) in an India still governed by a dominant patriarchal ideology.

Desai's strategy of dividing *Voices in the City* into four parts, each named for and given over to the narrative of one member of the Ray family, reflects her concern with the issue of communication as it is predicated upon gender relations. Written from Nirode's perspective, Part I almost exclusively recounts his life; his experiences as a petty journalist, his attempts to start a little magazine, his dealings with the Calcutta pseudoliterati, and his existential musings upon life and death. The near-total silencing of women in Part I, except when Otima imposes herself upon Nirode through two letters, is significant. Only once in his narrative does Nirode think of his sisters – to wonder what they thought of their father's funding of the education abroad of a second brother, Arun, and not their own. And then, in idle curiosity, he conjectures about what they might be 'thinking tonight', but he dismisses them a sentence later: 'Nirode did not know' (p. 8), and he does not care to find out.

Pursuing his own dreams singlemindedly and confining women to the periphery of the 'masculine' world of work, Nirode reflects the arrogative dominance of Indian men in the 1950s, the chronological setting of *Voices in the City*. Conflating India's servitude under colonial rule with the Indian woman's modern-day circumscription, he stereotypes the latter as 'one of those vast, soft, masses-of-rice Bengali [or, by extension, Indian] women', with 'nothing in her head but a reckoning of the stores in her pantry, and nothing in her heart but a stupid sense of injury and affront', a woman who, following the country's independence, went 'back to [her] old beauty sleep of neglect and delay and corruption' because of her 'slave' mentality (p. 81). Although in his nihilism Nirode does not hold much hope for the men he knows either – Sonny Ghosh, Jit Nair, and David Gunney – at least he tells their stories more fully and sympathetically than he does the women's. His accounts of the latter's lives are, by contrast, dismissive, parenthetical, or pejorative, his misogyny the result of the cultural marginalization of women as well as his own incestuous – and therefore forbidden and guilt-ridden – attraction to his mother (an emotion that perhaps also paradoxically accounts for his implied homosexuality).

It is, therefore, doubly ironic that, failing in his existentialist quest, Nirode finds meaning and completes his 'rebellion' against the absurdity of life via Monisha's suicide. Although he claims that in the face of cowardly compromise, it is 'better not to live' (p. 18), he makes no such grand gesture of revolt himself. Rather, it is through the 'excess of caring' which leads Monisha to her death that Nirode reconciles himself to others and to 'the whole fantastic design of life and death' and admits the 'deceit' of his earlier self-centered stance (pp. 248, 250). But even his epiphanic vision is negated at the novel's end, for, unable to shoulder the responsibility of true human 'communion' and to 'reverence' his mother, he sees her only as a castrating figure who has sentenced him to 'death' (pp. 250, 256).

In stark contrast to Nirode's solipsistic narrative in Part I, the remaining three parts of the novel – 'Monisha', 'Amla', and 'Mother' – transcend such a rigid dichotomizing of genders to draw in the stories of both women and men. Even in her diary – a highly personal text – Monisha refers frequently to Nirode, recording her concerns about his vulnerabilities, her nursing of him after his breakdown, her finding comfort in what she perceives to be a temperamental affinity with him. Amla too seeks out her brother's counsel as she struggles to come to terms with Calcutta and adulthood. In her heartache over her relationship with the married painter, Dharma, she turns to Nirode rather than to her sister, the more conventional choice of a confidante. Despite his jibes to her about the schoolgirlish nature of her infatuations, the philistinism of her work as a commercial artist, and her resemblance in her 'feminine' possessiveness to their mother, Amla retains a familial fondness for Nirode. And in the last, climactic segment, 'Mother', all the major characters come together for the first time in the novel, momentarily unified by Monisha's death as Otima reasserts her role as matriarch.

The issue of communication and its converse, silence, is particularly significant to Monisha's history as it is recorded not only in her own narrative in Part II of the novel but in Amla's and Otima's narratives in Parts III and IV as well. Intelligent, well-read, and self-aware, Monisha is, however, given no voice in determining her spouse and hence the course of her life after leaving her parents' home. Her marriage with Jiban appears, at first, to have been arranged for the sake of social expedience. Her mother, unhappy in her own incompatible marriage and aware that so educated and sensitive a young woman as her daughter would not appeal to scores of prospective husbands and in-laws, 'excuses' the match on the grounds that Jiban's family, 'stolid, unimaginative ... just sufficiently educated', would at least 'accept [Monisha] with tolerance' (p. 199); and her father approves of Jiban's 'respectable, middle-class Congress family' that is 'so unquestionably safe, sound and secure, so utterly predictable' (pp. 199, 198). But when Amla puzzles over her parents' choice of a husband for her sister, she reveals her father's proclivity to incest. Perhaps he selected Jiban because 'fathers did, unconsciously, spite their daughters who were unavailable to them', she reasons (p. 198). And to Amla's question, '[W]hy had Monisha ... never rebelled?' (p. 198), there are several potential answers, all predicated upon an oppressive sexual politics. Monisha conceivably maintained her silence because of her guilt at having provoked incestuous thoughts in her father; because she saw herself as a sacrifice to her parents' floundering marriage; because she felt compelled to play the part of a dutiful daughter conforming to the patriarchal practice of arranged marriage; or because she was overwhelmed by a sense of fatalism at the lot of Indian women.

Circumscribed both mentally and physically by gender, familial, and economic ideologies, Monisha serves as the type of countless Indian women. The opening entry of her diary, a record of her first meeting with Jiban's extended family, elucidates the actual and symbolic subjugation, imprisonment, and 'silencing' of the Indian daughter-in-law in an orthodox Hindu household. The passage bears quoting at length:

> The Bow Bazaar house ... the reception arranged by the heads of this many-headed family. In the small of my back, I feel a surreptitious push from Jiban and am propelled forward into the embrace of his mother who ... while placing her hand on my head in blessing, also pushes a little harder than I think is necessary, and still harder, till I realize what it means, and go down on my knees to touch her feet. ... Another pair of feet appears to receive my touch, then another. ... More – I lose count – but many more. Feet before faces here. ... Into the courtyard we go, in a procession, and the tiered balconies ... rise all around us, shutting out light and enclosing shadows like stagnant well water. The balconies have metal railings, intricately criss-crossed: one could not thrust one's head through them. ... Upstairs to our room ... a black, four-postered bed in the centre, and a gigantic black wardrobe against the wall. But it is not they that intimidate me – after only one night, I already feel familiar with them, their smells, their silence – but the bars at the windows. Through the thick iron bars I look out on other walls, other windows – other bars.
>
> (p. 109)

The symbols of enclosure and incarceration – the dark balconies, confining metal railings, and impregnable iron bars – underline the barriers not only to Monisha's but also to the Indian woman's articulation of an independent self.

Early on, Monisha attempts to make a success of her marriage, to 'be Jiban's wife' (pp. 111–12) within the strictures of a traditional Bengali family. But her initial efforts to adapt, to make the 'language' of her married family 'her own' (p. 113), come to naught, and a total breakdown of communication ensues as her mother-in-law accuses her of stealing money from Jiban. Neglecting to defend Monisha, Jiban contributes to her growing withdrawal from reality. Deprived of any confidantes, and increasingly alienated from her philistine, impassive husband, Monisha turns to keeping a diary, communing only with herself in Kafkaesque ruminations of darkness, enclosure, and madness.[20] Suffering as well from the larger absence of 'that vital element ... of love' (p. 135) in her childlessness and abandonment by her mother, she chooses suicide over a lingering death of the soul, ending her life in 'unimpeachable silence' (p. 246).

On one level, therefore, Monisha can be regarded as a victim of Hindu familial ideology and patriarchal oppression. Her unfulfilled sexuality, her metaphorically and literally barren marriage, her lack of privacy, her waiting upon men, her material dependence despite her education, and her violent death are all marks of her sexual colonization. On another level, however, she can be seen as a victor, transcending the reaches of patriarchy in her 'madness' and death. Measured against the teachings of the Hindu scriptures that equate women's mental health with domesticity and motherhood, Monisha appears abnormal. Intellectual, silent, and introverted, she is 'distrusted' by her in-laws and perceived as 'dangerous', 'an infidel who ought never to have been allowed into this stronghold of ... practicality and chatter' (p. 119). In some of her diary entries, Monisha reveals her internalization of others' beliefs regarding her irrationality and underscores the patriarchal pressures that have driven her to distraction. She imagines the incessant repetition of Sanskrit verses by a nephew to 'have been contrived solely to drive [her] mad' (p. 112); she is fearful that an unidentified 'they' will 'spring on [her], claw the flesh off [her] back and devour it'; and she imagines that 'there is no escape from them' (p. 118). But her 'madness' can also be interpreted as her protest against an intolerable situation. In her abnormality she not only questions the institutions of marriage and family but also puts herself beyond their confining reach. '[A]part' from others, and 'separate' (p. 239) from Jiban's family, she is aware that 'they cannot touch [her]' (p. 138).

In contrast to countless other women who endure endless suffering and lead meaningless lives, Monisha thus 'go[es] in the opposite direction' in her 'madness' as well as her death. Rather than keep 'waiting for nothing, waiting on men self-centred and indifferent and hungry and demanding and critical, waiting for death and dying misunderstood, always behind bars, those terrifying black bars that shut us in' (p. 120), she voluntarily chooses the freedom of death, thus also imparting meaning to her life.

Such an alternative interpretation of Monisha's end as heroic is additionally supported by the imagery of Kali that surrounds it. That Desai intends Monisha's suicide to be read against the mythology of Kali is evident. She not only describes the event in the last part of *Voices in the City*, 'Mother', in which Otima is repeatedly portrayed as Kali incarnate, but she also attributes Monisha's decision to end her life to her encounter with a street singer who is cast as another personification of the goddess. Positioning the narrative from Monisha's perspective, Desai contrasts the 'raw passion' of the itinerant street singer with the former's deadened emotional state as she stands 'unnaturally cool, too perfectly aloof, too inviolably whole and alone' (p. 238). Monisha sees the singer not only as a contrastive figure – in her apotheosis of a love, passion, and sensuality that Monisha herself has never known – but also as Kali come to life; and the symbolic parallels between the singer and the goddess proliferate.

As she fantasizes about the singer's history, Monisha imagines her, in the likeness of Kali, 'building the funeral pyres of her own children', 'slit[ting] throats and drain[ing] blood into her cupped hands', and 'bath[ing] and soak[ing] in the sweat of lust' (p. 237). Her face is that of the Eternal Mother, the Earth Mother,[21] 'ravaged by the most unbearable emotions of woman'; her 'terrible black eyes [hold] an eternally unfulfilled promise of vision, of understanding, of boundless love' (p. 237). Aware that she herself has 'not given birth ... not attended death' – in short, that she has not lived life fully – Monisha is impelled to partake of the 'primaeval truth' regarding life and death that the singer epitomizes (pp. 240, 238). In an effort to exchange her emotional barrenness for 'a passion that ravages the soul and body and being' (p. 239) and to participate in the physicality and undifferentiated wholeness of life that Kali deifies, Monisha goes bravely to her death.

In her choice, then, Monisha can be regarded as one of those heroic Desai characters who, 'driven into some extremity of despair', has 'turned against, or made a stand against, the general current'.[22] Resisting compromise and meek submission, she has cried out 'the great No'.[23] Yet, because in real terms Monisha's self-immolation fails to herald a new beginning for Indian women, the narrative in *Voices in the City* describes it as a 'cloistered tragedy', noting tellingly that '[n]o ashes of that fire drifted out over the city, no wind carried the smoke away to inform others' (pp. 242–3). However, the external fire which Monisha sets can be construed as symbolically positive, albeit on a limited scale: not only does the fire outside reflect the 'fire' inside Monisha as she experiences acute desire and feeling for the first time in her life, but her fiery death also enables Nirode to reconcile himself to human fate, and it points the way for Amla's less self-destructive approach to life. In this context, Monisha's dying words, ' "No! No! No!" ' (p. 242), can be read both as the articulation of the tragedy of Indian womanhood and of the oppositional intervention of women in the prevalent patriarchal sociolect.[24]

In Amla, whose story is told in Part III of *Voices in the City*, Desai investigates an alternate, perhaps less courageous but also less devastating mode of resistance to male hegemony. At first glance, the young, extroverted Amla appears to be a counterpoint to her detached, isolated sister. But beneath her vivacious exterior Amla shares with Monisha a 'terrible destructiveness', what an acquaintance of hers describes as a 'dark way of thinking and feeling through life towards death' (p. 175). This description also links Amla to the totality of life that Kali represents: aware of the 'inevitable decline' that follows 'the perfection of the moment' (p. 219), she is made even more acutely conscious of the inextricable design of life and death by Monisha's suicide.

Initially excited at being in Calcutta and savoring her economic independence as a commercial artist in an advertising firm, Amla soon feels the 'rot' creeping into her life (p. 173). She perceives the fraudulence underlying her work, the pettiness of her social round, and her lack of connectedness with family and friends. Even as she tries to '[proclaim] her youth, her aliveness, her courage', Calcutta – and the mortality that it stands for – '[lays] waste all that [is] fine and moral' (p. 150), until she starts to sink into a despair resembling Monisha's and muses repeatedly upon death.

Again like Monisha, Amla is sexually circumscribed and has no passionate relationships with a man. Coming upon a statue of Shiva and Parvati locked together in an embrace, the sisters quickly look away, the goddess's 'purpose' and 'delight' being especially 'inexplicable' to them (p. 147). Brought up in a culture that compels women to repress their sexuality, Amla and Monisha are further betrayed by passionless or manipulative men. Whereas Jiban quells Monisha's early ardour with his impassiveness, Dharma's treatment of Amla is even more reprehensible. Taking advantage of her vulnerability to his charms – she feels his 'magic' and 'hypnotism' come over her like 'anaesthesia' (pp. 187, 188, 193) – Dharma exploits Amla's candor and freshness as a model to draw him out of a stultifying surrealism into the palpable world of realism in his paintings. But his use for her over, he discards her in favor of other models, unmindful of her desires. Thus, Amla realizes that her pursuit of feminine selfhood, of 'something more rare, more responsible' than the 'security' of marriage can only end in disillusionment, a compromise with life, and an abiding isolation (p. 145).

Yet Amla displays a resilience and independence that enable her to live on her own terms. Declining the amorous attentions of several young men, she appears poised at the novel's end to pursue a career as an illustrator of children's stories, thus betokening hope for the future. Like Monisha, therefore, Amla defies the quintessential ideal of woman as dutiful wife and mother and 'goes in the opposite direction', but after her own fashion. Her sister's death having given her a glimpse of 'what lay on the other side of this stark, uncompromising margin', she resolves never to 'lose herself' but rather to 'go through life with her feet primly shod, involving herself with her drawings and safe people' (p. 248). An unyielding stance like Monisha's, though admirable in its dauntlessness, usually ends in self-destruction, Desai seems to argue; so a compromise like Amla's – one that does not jeopardize the self – is perhaps the best available alternative for Indian women at present. As Desai stated in a 1977 interview, '[I]f one is alive, in this world, one cannot survive without compromise. ... It is for heroes and martyrs to say "the great Yes" or "the great No" [as Monisha does] – most of us have not the courage to say either Yes or No. We say ... "All right then, if I must ... ".'[25]

Referring more specifically to Indian women's current situation, Desai observed in 1988 that 'they have a life presented to them and they have to make the best of it'; their rebellion can consist only of 'exercis[ing] whatever control they can within those parameters'.[26] The pragmatist in Desai thus acknowledges that the majority of Indian women fatalistically accept their lot, while those who do resist patriarchal hegemony do so within a confined space. Yet she portrays a strong female character like Otima in *Voices in the City* who subverts the established patriarchal code by shattering the myth of the ideal feminine.

In a culture that historically sanctioned and glorifed *sati* and that even today demands that a widow be self-abnegating, dependent, and passive, Otima proves iconoclastic in her widowhood. Long resentful of *mariage convenable* – her husband married her for her inheritance – Otima finds herself liberated by his death. Independent and sensual even in her middle age, she consorts with Major Chadha, thereby overturning the constrictive pattern of sexuality and behaviour culturally prescribed for widows. In addition, in a country that institutionalizes and paradoxically reveres motherhood – paradoxically, because it simultaneously marginalizes, disfranchises, and even derogates women – Otima reverses the paradigm by rejecting and symbolically destroying her children. Even though she rues the marriage of her older son, Arun, to an American woman because she feels she will lose him forever, and although she appears stricken by Monisha's suicide, Otima 'rejects' her remaining offspring, Nirode and Amla, 'pushing them away' so that 'she might stand alone and free' (pp. 255, 251). Having once raised her children affectionately, she now abandons them and lives alone in her childhood home in Kalimpong (a town appropriately linked to Kali), which she admits is a 'secluded paradise' with 'no channel of communication' with her children (p. 201). Having once given them life, she now deals her children death – a literal death in Monisha's case as she fails to come to her daughter's aid, and a metaphoric death in Nirode's case as she 'ensnares' him in maternal bonds even as she denies him.

Cast in the role of antagonist along with the city of Calcutta, Otima appears for the first time in *Voices in the City* following Monisha's death. Even more than the street singer, the narrative directly and indirectly equates her with Kali. Tellingly enough, the direct identification is made by Nirode, the chief male character in the novel and hence a representative of the masculine principle that Otima–Kali threatens. As he drives his mother through Calcutta, Nirode imagines the sky darkening and the people lighting *divas* or lamps in her honor; he hears them chant hymns to her and '[knows] at once then, that she is Kali' (p. 255).

Contrasting Hindu sexual mythology with that of other patriarchal societies, Sudhir Kakar underscores just such a male fear of the 'sexual mother' in India. While Hindus share the widespread patriarchal impulse to 'superimpose' the image of woman-as-mother and thereby to erase the picture of woman-as-sexual-being, they differ from other patriarchal communities in their conception of the 'composite image' of the sexual mother.[27] Describing the latter construct as 'the most salient feature of male fantasy in India', Kakar asserts that it is 'an overwhelming presence in the [Indian] men's perception of woman, a being to whom one is in danger of ceding both genitals and the self'.[28]

That Nirode experiences such sexual anxiety linked to the figure of the castrating mother is clear in his association of Otima with Kali and with death in general. It is only in Monisha's death that, according to Nirode, their mother is appeased. ' "She is Kali",' he cries to Amla; ' "[s]he has watched the sacrifice and she is satisfied" ' (p. 255). To Amla's remonstrances that she is 'Mother ... that is all,' he replies, '[S]he is the mother of us all ... once she has given birth to us, she must also deal us our deaths' (p. 256). Within her person Otima reconciles life's contraries, as Kali does, he believes: she is 'good and evil'; 'knowledge and ignorance'; 'everything to which we are attached' and 'everything from which we will always be detached'; she is, finally, in the image of Kali, the 'amalgamation of death and life' (p. 256). As if to confirm Nirode's assessment, the novel ends with a procession celebrating the goddess, as Otima, now in white – also potentially signifying the birth of a new order for women – stands silent watch over Nirode and Amla. In the contemporary Kali Yuga, the Age of Kali, of Hindu tradition,[29] Otima can thus be seen as an appropriate symbol of the resurgence, albeit limited, of feminine power.

Whereas Madhusudan Prasad criticizes Desai's representation of Otima as Kali, declaring it to be both 'unconvincing and inappropriate',[30] it is precisely through such associations that the novelist offers her most serious challenge to the patriarchal underpinnings of Indian society. The antithesis of the prototypical selfless and submissive mother and wife, Otima maintains her independence even in marriage, motherhood, and widowhood. Her association with the mountains – she writes repeatedly of the Kanchenjunga range in her letters – signifies her autonomy even as it confirms her in the role of the archetypal female. And at the end of *Voices in the City*, Otima evinces a desire to divest herself of all familial bonds and to seek self-fulfillment in unfettered solitude. Like Kali, she is herself whole and undifferentiated; like *Shakti*, or primal female energy, she is *svatantrya*, independent, her existence contingent upon nothing extraneous to herself. Having borne witness to both life and death, she has attained 'that consummate widom besides which all others were incomplete, aborted beings' (p. 254). And in defiance of Hindu masculinist tradition that reserves the right of *moksha*, release from the material world, for men alone, Otima appears at the novel's end to be preparing herself for this final stage of existence. Thus 'going in the opposite direction' in her manifestations as Kali, Otima reveals the latent power of women and offers her sex the potential for subversive action.

Desai employs the metaphor of Kali not only at the human level but also at the non-human, portraying Calcutta primarily as an expressionistic city devoted to the goddess after which it is named[31] and only secondarily as the recognizable east Indian megalopolis. Desai's Calcutta, which comes to function as a character in its own right in *Voices in the City*, is, significantly, a place of moral and physical turpitude, of poverty, disease, and death. The narrative, furthermore, repeatedly invokes Kali as the city's patron deity and foregrounds the tenebrosity of life there. The darkness of Calcutta can be variously interpreted. On one level, it can be seen as a metaphor for the 'darkness' of human existence in India at large. On another level, it can be regarded specifically as a symbol of women's subjugation and oppression. On a third, it can be read as a counter to the idealized image of a tender, nurturing 'Mother India' or *Bharat Mata*.[32] Finally, in its link with the imagery of blackness that surrounds Kali, it can be construed as an indicator of women's latent sexuality and strength.

Hardly recognizable as one of India's leading commercial centres, the home of great literature and music, and the site of incendiary politics, Desai's Calcutta is a 'monster city' that 'live[s] no normal, healthy, red-blooded life but one that [is] subterranean, underlit, stealthy and odorous of mortality' (p. 250). Images of blood, death, and cannibalism abound in the novel, linking the city unambiguously to Kali in her destructive aspect: a fallen racehorse is torn and devoured by birds of prey; Calcutta is a 'coagulated blaze of light and sound and odour' (p. 8), its streets lined with 'dark, gap-toothed houses where the half-dead and the half-alive live' (p. 92); and again, the 'beastly, blood-thirsty' (p. 96) city, with its reminders of a 'gory history ... slow mortality ... [and] corruption' (p. 150), covers everything with 'filth and blood and rot' (p. 182).

Yet in its very carnality, Calcutta also represents the potency of a specifically female sexuality that has ever threatened male dominance. Walking through the city streets, for instance, Nirode shudders to think of 'marriage, bodies, touch and torture'; he is 'almost afraid of the dark of Calcutta, its warmth that clung to one with a moist, perspiring embrace, rich with the odours of open gutters and tuberose garlands' (p. 35). Conversely, Monisha, caught in an emotionally and physically barren marriage, her 'calamitous pleasures and pains' neglected by Jiban, shuts herself off from palpable humanity, ignoring the 'shrieks', 'groans' (p. 135), and 'cries' emanating from the city (p. 138). But in her own death by fire – imaging the 'fire' within her to 'experience desire, to experience feeling' (p. 240) – she paradoxically reconnects herself with 'life' in Calcutta, with all those 'capable of responding to passion with passion, to sorrow with sorrow' (p. 238).

Commenting on the alternative perspective on reality that Kali affords her devotees, David Kinsley, a religious studies scholar, notes that '[t]o meditate on the dark goddess ... is to step out of the everyday world of predictable *dharmic* order and enter a world of reversals, opposites, and contrasts and in doing so to wake up to new possibilites and new frames of reference.'[33] As Desai depicts female characters who, in the image of Kali, 'go in the opposite direction' to subvert or abrogate orthodox male authority in *Voices in the City*, she too can be seen as contributing to the overturning of the patriarchal social dharma that circumscribes Indian women.[34]

From *Ariel: A Review of International English Literature*, 23: 4 (October 1992), 75–95.

NOTES

[This essay develops recent feminist reappraisals of Anita Desai who has been formerly presented as a 'subjective' writer. Mann's essay draws upon historicism as a means of destabilising orthodoxies of Indian patriarchies. It also reflects the important relationship that has been established between phenomenological approaches to the 'subjective' text and poststructuralist/feminist refusals to ignore the social/political functions and contexts of literature. Eds]

1. Anita Desai, *Voices in the City* (New Delhi, 1988). All page references to this edition of the novel are given in brackets within the essay.

2. See, for instance: Darshan Singh Maini, 'The Achievement of Anita Desai', *Indo-English Literature*, Ed. K. K. Sharma (Ghaziabad, India, 1977), pp. 221–2; Madhusudan Prasad, *Anita Desai: The Novelist* (Allahabad, India, 1981), pp. 22–46; Ramesh K. Srivastava, 'Voices of Artists in the City', *Journal of Indian Writing in English*, 9: 1 (1981), 47–57.

3. Darshan Singh Maini, 'The Achievement of Anita Desai' (cf. note 2 above), p. 222.

4. Stanley Wolpert, *A New History of India* (New York, 1989), p. 366.

5. Ketu Katrak, 'Indian Nationalism, Gandhian "*Satyagraha*", and Representations of Female Sexuality', *Nationalisms and Sexualities*, ed. Andrew Parker et al. (New York, 1992), p. 398.

6. Joanna Liddle and Rama Joshi, *Daughters of Independence: Gender, Caste and Class in India* (London and New Delhi, 1986), p. 236.

7. Ibid., p. 234.

8. Sudhir Kakar, *The Inner World* (Oxford, 1978), p. 68.

9. Anita Desai, 'A Secret Connivance', *Times Literary Supplement*, 14–20 Sept. 1990, p. 972.

10. Ibid., p. 972.

11. Desai is not alone in presenting the goddess as an empowering figure for women. Joanna Liddle and Rama Joshi believe that the matriarchal myth of Kali, despite its later circumscription by a patriarchal discourse, 'tells the story of [Indian] women's continuing power and their resistance to male control' over the ages (*Daughters of Independence*, p. 55). The latter is perhaps also the reason that the contemporary Indian women's movement has adopted Kali as a symbol to convey its goal of freedom from oppression and that India's first feminist publishing house, established in 1984, is called Kali for Women.

12. Ajit Mookerjee, *Kali: The Feminine Source* (New York, 1988), p. 62.

13. Ibid., p. 62.

14. Anita Desai, 'Indian Women Writers', *The Eye of the Beholder: Indian Writing in English*, ed. Maggie Butcher (London, 1983), p. 57.

15. Ibid., p. 58.

16. It is, however, ironic that even the androgynous Ardhanarishwara does not signify a true equality of the sexes. As Wendy O'Flaherty points out, the word is a masculine noun for a male hermaphrodite, and the puranic mythological figure is always regarded as a form of Shiva, not

a form of Shiva and Shakti/Parvati or of Shakti/Parvati alone (Wendy O'Flaherty and Wendy Doniger, *Hindu Myths: A Sourcebook*, trs. from the Sanskrit [Harmondsworth, 1975], p. 317).

17. Anita Desai, 'Indian Women Writers', p. 58.

18. In a 1979 interview, Desai declared, 'I find it impossible to whip up any interest in a mass of women marching forward under the banner of feminism. Only the individual, the solitary being, is of true interest' ('Anita Desai', interview with Yashodhara Dalmia, *Times of India* [Sunday Bulletin] 29 Apr. 1979, p. 13).

19. Anita Desai, 'Indian Women Writers', p. 58.

20. One of Monisha's diary entries specifically notes the parallel to Kafka: 'Kafka, a scene for you', it begins (p. 112).

21. Klaus Klostermaier points out that the hundreds of goddesses wor-shipped in India through the ages are 'but manifestations of an unman-ifest Supreme Goddess (Devi, the Great/Eternal Mother), appearing in various guises and exercising a variety of functions' (p. 156). Kali is but one dimension of this divine feminine. (Klaus K. Klosternaier, 'Sakti: Hindu Images and Concepts of the Goddess', *Goddesses in Religions and Modern Debate*, ed. Larry W. Hurtado, University of Manitoba Studies in Religion, vol. I [Atlanta, GA, 1990], pp. 143–61).

22. 'Anita Desai', interview with Yashodhara Dalmia, p. 13.

23. Ibid., p. 13. In *Where Shall We Go This Summer?* Desai quotes the following excerpt from the Greek poet Constantine Cavafy, which acknowledges the courage necessary to cope with life's demands but also underscores the heroism of rebellion:

> To certain people there comes a day
> When they must say the great Yes or the great No.
> He who has the Yes ready within him
> reveals himself at once, and saying it he crosses over
> to the path of honour and his own convictions.
> He who refuses does not repent. Should he be asked again,
> he would say No again. And yet that No –
> the right No – crushes him for the rest of his life.
> (*Where Shall We Go This Summer?* [1975; New Delhi, 1988],
> pp. 37, 139)

Desai also refers in interviews to this conflict between 'Yes' and 'No' to underline the choice between compromise and valorous, although finally ruinous revolt ('An Interview with Anita Desai', interview with Atma Ram, *World Literature Written in English*, 16: 1 [1977], 98; 'Anita Desai', interview with Yashodhara Dalmia, p. 13).

24. The ambivalent nature of Monisha's end is also indicated by its sym-bolic association with *sati*. As Julia Leslie notes, the practice of widow

immolation undeniably reveals the victim status of women, but *sati* can also be regarded as an empowerment, as 'a strategy for dignity in a demeaning world' that condemns a widow to a very difficult ascetic path (cf. *'Suttee* or *Sati*: Victim or Victor?' *Roles and Rituals for Hindu Women*, ed. Julia Leslie [London, 1991], pp.188–9). Similarly, Monisha's suicide can be interpreted as a demonstration of her ultimate power in an otherwise powerless situation.

25. 'An Interview with Anita Desai', interview with Atma Ram, pp. 98–9.

26. Anita Desai, 'Against the Current: A Conversation with Anita Desai', interview with Corinne Demas Bliss, *The Massachusetts Review*, 29: 3 (1988), 524.

27. Sudhir Kakar, *Intimate Relations: Exploring Indian Sexuality* (Chicago, 1989), p. 143.

28. Ibid., p. 143.

29. Whereas traditionally the Kali Yuga has been defined as the Age of Darkness in which there is a dearth of virtue and scripture carries no authority (O'Flaherty, *Hindu Myths*, pp. 43, 345), Ajit Mookerjee presents an alternative interpretation. As the ascendant deity of our times, Kali will in the Kali Yuga annihilate the patriarchal universe to reveal the truth of things and restore to us the divine feminine spirituality we have lost, he asserts (Agit Mookerjee, *Kali: The Feminine Source*, p. 9). In a kindred spirit, I read Desai's adoption of the Kali myth as contributing to the formation of a new feminist ideology in the literary and social domains.

30. Madhusudan Prasad, 'Imagery in the Novels of Anita Desai: A Critical Study', *World Literature Today*, 58: 3 (1984), 363–9.

31. Calcutta is the anglicized version of Kalikata, the name of the city built on Kalikshetra, the land of Kali. The city is also the home of several temples dedicated to Kali, the most famous of which is the Kali temple at Kalighat, which Desai specifically refers to in *Voices in the City* (p. 233).

32. A nationalistic discursive construct introduced by the nineteenth-century Bengali novelist Bankim Chandra Chatterji, the image of India as mother nevertheless continues to function as 'truth' in modern times. Whereas Chatterji's hymn 'Bande Mataram', 'Hail to Thee, Mother', described India as benevolent and protective as well as explosive and virile, contemporary patriarchal culture privileges the former characteristics and virtually excludes the latter. In her focus upon Kali, the dark goddess, in *Voices in the City*, however, Desai overturns such an ideal hegemonic reading of the sacrality of the land and of women more generally.

33. David Kinsley, *Hindu Goddesss: Visions of the Divine Feminine in the Hindu Religious Tradition* (Berkeley, CA, 1986), p. 130.

34. An early version of this article was presented at the 1992 Twentieth-Century Literature Conference held in Louisville, Kentucky.

9

Fire on the Mountain – a Rite of Exit

BETTINA L. KNAPP

Anita Desai's novel *Fire on the Mountain* (1977) dramatizes the ordeals of an initiatory experience: the rite of exit from life. The word 'initiation' comes from the Latin *in ire*, meaning 'to go within' or to reconstruct one's knowledge of life. Nanda Kaul, a great-grandmother and the protagonist of *Fire on the Mountain*, undertakes just such a discipline, which alters and amplifies her existential and religious outlook. She becomes another, fully prepared for the rite of exit.

Nanda Kaul, an earthly replica of certain Hindu deities, is archetypal in stature: a complex of opposites, both mortal and immortal, individual and universal. Like the Shiva/Parvati couple she is psychologically androgynous: feminine and masculine, passive and active. In the manner of *shakti*, that vital energy which moves throughout Nature, Nanda Kaul's inner currents course through her, in nuanced or violent tempos. Identifiable also with Kali, her destructive/dark side sometimes predominates, when circumstances require a balancing of irregularities.

Desai's archetypal Old Woman is sign and countersign – the repository of filled and unfilled needs and feelings which the reader discovers and slowly sorts out during the course of the narrative. At the outset of the novel, Nanda Kaul gives the impression of enjoying harmony of being. The prototypal Indian woman, she has been both wife and mother. Her formerly active empirical existence justifies her present withdrawal on a mountain top in the Punjab

region. She has chosen to live out her remaining years in this topos
– which is really an a-topos – a non-place – in serenity and repose.
Here, too, will her initiation be completed: and psychologically, an
ex-centering or de-centering of her ego will take place.

The impediments to the achievement of Nanda's goal, when
viewed symbolically, must be seen as obstacles purposefully set on
her path, forcing her to struggle with troublesome adversities. Her
combat will compel her to come to terms with factors she had
either rejected or overlooked during her active years as mother and
wife. The agonia she encounters in the process of gaining awareness
arouses content within her subliminal realm that might otherwise
have lain dormant. Once energized and brought to consciousness,
her view of life broadens. New orientations have expanded and
enriched her vision, allowing her to pass from one ego-centered
limited domain, to a supra-individual Cosmic sphere (the Absolute
or *atman*), to become multiple and also One.

That Nanda must go through an initiatory process in order to
reconstruct her knowledge of life is in keeping with Hindu dicta.
The real world, it is believed, is the inner one. The exterior realm –
Maya (Cosmic Illusion) – is a deception which remains
impenetrable until an individual's blindness gives way to sight.
Psychologically, Nanda's ordeal dramatizes a dispersion of the ego
(center of consciousness) into the Self (total psyche). ...

THE ARCHETYPAL OLD WOMAN

Nanda Kaul, tall, thin, and stately, is the archetypal Old Woman
par excellence. Representative of a structural dominant of the
psyche, she is a product of both her primordial past and of her own
individuality.[1] Her name alone takes us back to both a historical
and mythical past, to a powerful dynasty reigning in India at the
time of Alexander the Great: and to Nanda, Lord Krishna's foster
father. Like her great Vedic Aryan ancestors who inhabited the
mountain tops near the Himalayas, so Nanda also chose to live
close to nature, at the Carignano, near Kasauli, a hill station 1900
meters above the Punjab plains and accessible only by footpath.

Nanda is first glimpsed pausing under a pine tree near her small
hill-top house. Her eyes, looking down onto the valleys below and
up toward the jagged cliffs in the distance, seem to be ferreting out
the mysteries hidden amid and beyond the seemingly endless slopes,

ridges, and gorges. Nana's eye, like Shiva's organ of perception and intuition, takes in both the world of appearance and that which lies beyond the sensate domain. It grasps the multiple and the disparate, the articulated and the unarticulated, and transforms these into a single unified principle.

Conscious of the law of devolution – old age and a concomitant decrease in active participation in life's work – Nanda looks forward to the slowing down process. Virtually, alone among the pines (symbols of immortality since they remain green all year), she lives cut off from the outside world. Animals and insects are her only companions and she has made their languages her own. As for their vibrations – their music – they parallel her heartbeat, as though she has become one with *shakti*. Nevertheless, from the very outset, we note that not everything within her psyche is smooth-running: here and there, irregularities and smarting sensations surge.

The music emanating from animals and insects infiltrates Nanda's world: it speaks to her in several notes at times, or in but a single tone. The 'scented sibilance' of the cicadas, for example, replicates the stridulations of life's duality and her own, by extension. Nature's silences and sounds are a complementary couple: as presences that befriend or alienate her. The cuckoo as it flutters by or the eagle soaring toward the sun make their songs heard. The wind floating through the pines sends out its spiritual message in natural orchestrations. Such pure intensities become vehicles for subtle modal systems in Desai's text as well as adding a religious flavor to it. The wind, for the Hindu, ushers in the presence of Indra, the great Vedic atmospheric God responsible for rain and thunder, so vital to life in India. It is he as well who assures the crucial connection between heaven and earth. He, like Nanda, has made his home on a mountain top – the fabulous Mount Meru, purportedly the center of the earth, somewhere to the north of the Himalayas.

Nanda, in the manner of a goddess, stands tall and erect, her dark sari emphasizing the austerity and sparseness of her life, in tune with the stark rocks that surround her. She constitutes a law unto herself, living, as did Lord Shiva, the fashioner of the world, outside of linear space and time. Resembling Shiva's consort, Parvati, the 'Daughter of the Himalaya Mountain',[2] Nanda, too, embodies feminine creative energy. Let us recall that it was Parvati who provided Shiva with *shakti* power.

As Nanda stands rooted to the ground – stark against a sun-drenched sky – she seems withered, severed, unrealized. Although she feeds, spiritually and psychologically, on the world around her – trees, grass, mountains, gorges, and cliffs – the nourishment gained from these natural elements is insufficient to sustain her and to give her the force necessary to perform her exit ritual.

Like the traditional Indian Mother, who dedicates herself wholly to caring for husband and children, Nanda has fulfilled her obligations, but without joy or love. Disillusioned early in life, for reasons we discover only at the end of the narrative, Nanda's emotional universe has been relatively empty.

To gain the tranquility she so desperately yearns for, Nanda has learned to peer into nature, perhaps unconsciously, using her field of vision as a meditative device – a mandala, enabling her to transcend the phenomenal world. Flower, tree, and cliff permit her to indwell, to center her gaze on a point in real space, thereby escaping the world of human suffering, where she has neither loved nor been loved. The mysterious power that seems to be tearing at her soul/psyche may be likened to the bird that had ripped the flesh from the apricot in the image above. What force within her has remained unacceptable and unresolved is yet to be discovered.

Nanda withdraws into her house – her figurative and literal *temenos*. A sanctuary for meditation and for indwelling, it is a further protection from the medley of disturbances which the outer world thrusts upon her. Within its walls, she feels she can reach down into her center, stand firm without experiencing the pull and tug of the tension of opposites in the empirical world. When returning outside, however, and much to her dismay, she sees her cook and the mailman down the path chatting. The latter's appearance she considers to be an unmitigated intrusion. He must be carrying a letter for her, she reasons, and her annoyance mounts. Whether due to the play of the sun's rays or to her own inner readings of the scene, she sees both figures 'going up in flames with their arms outstretched, charred, too, about the trunks'.[3] The fire image, representative of psychic energy, acts as a catalyst for Nanda, evidently forcing into consciousness some unwanted level of being – something unwilled. Rather than bringing her the sought-for condition of quietude for which she longs, the mailman's presence – and the letter he is to deliver – paves the way for an ominous and eruptive condition.

Nanda sits down on her veranda to read the letter the mailman has just handed her, and here Desai halts the pace of her narrative, thus arousing tension. Descriptions follow, of geraniums, fuchsias, apricot trees, bul-buls, and birds of all types, vibrating, inhaling and exhaling the aromas of all living things. The musical tones of the bird songs, refined and dematerialized as they make their way to Nanda's ear, are received as carefully structured compositions. Like a *mantra* – the OM – an auditory perception which reaches various levels of a person's consciousness, so nature's noises, when concentrated upon, become carrier waves of universal tone, evoking feelings and relationships between sound and psyche in the process.[4]

Nanda is forced to cut off her mantra-like meditation, back to the letter, by a butterfly – a creature symbolizing flightiness, transience and inconstancy, and suggesting the illusory nature of human preoccupations. The butterfly puts an end to Nanda's rapturous vision as she would like to lead it. In the *Bhagavad Gita*, we read that 'humans rush to their end like [the] butterfly hovers around [a] brilliant flame'.[5] Nanda is likewise affected by the hustle and bustle of peripheral existence: by Maya/Illusion, the 'Mother of the World'. Despite the fact that she seeks to repulse duality, she is, nevertheless, continuously caught up in its complexities. She is unaware of the fact that only through existence in the concrete world (and not escape from it) will feelings of opposition within her surface; will antagonistic sensations be activated, confronted, coped with, and perhaps eventually integrated within her psyche.

The letter which Nanda finally opens is from her daughter, Asha. The least favored of her progeny, Asha has spent all of her days beautifying herself instead of devoting herself to her daughter, Tara. The result: Tara married a diplomat who drank and brutalized her. After several breakdowns, she decides to go to Switzerland with her husband to try once again to put her life with him in order. Raka, their daughter, who has just recovered from a serious bout with typhoid, is too thin and frail to stand such a journey. The mountain air at Carignano and her great-grandmother's good food would – they have decided – put flesh onto her bones.

As Nanda's yes 'floated' over her daughter's letter 'bloated with self-confidence', her anger flares (p. 16). She resents the making of such a decision without consulting her; she also takes umbrage at Raka's presence, which she regards as an unwanted intrusion. As she sits back on her chair and muses, a whole personal past infiltrates her present; she thinks back to her role as a model wife to her husband, Vice-Chancellor of a small university in the Punjab, and all the colleagues and friends she used to entertain. Everything she did for her family was always perfect. Everyone said so. The servants were well-trained and obedient; the children, brought up according to tradition, were a source of pride to the parents. How fortunate the Vice-Chancellor was to have her as a wife, people used to say. The perceptive individual, however, could detect a strange expression in Nanda's eyes, mirroring a distaste for her position and function: 'like a pair of black blades, wanting to cut them, despising them, crawling grey bugs about her fastidious feet' (p. 18). Nevertheless, she bore secretly all of her spiritual, physical, and emotional deprivation.

That Nanda reacted as she did to her condition as wife and mother is not unique in India. A basic conflict pervades Indian culture in general and the woman in particular: the ascetic versus the erotic. The Shiva Puranas teach the devout that Shiva was an ascetic, invulnerable to desire. Yet, because of his very detachment and remoteness, he caused his wife, Parvati, to want him all the more. While ruling out the call of the flesh, Shiva was, paradoxically, the householder and, therefore, a lover. Let us recall that Shiva was the one who destroyed *Kama*, the god of love. To do away with this deity served only, psychologically speaking, to increase love's power over the world.[6]

Nanda was an ascetic. In this regard, she was Shiva-like. Although the mother of many children, her sexuality had remained untouched, barren and cold. Never having developed any real sexual or feeling relationship with her husband, she viewed the whole birth process with distaste [i]n the 'small filthy missionary-run hospital', where the nurses were forever flitting around her but never helping her in any way. As for her children, they had always been a burden and an imposition – imposters of sorts. Drudgery, resentment, and despair stalked her at home, where she never really felt she belonged.

As readers follow Nanda in her repeated flashbacks, regressing further and further into a past that was anathema to her, they are exposed to increasingly turbulent vibrations and fiery innervations, as images of children at play emerge in her mind's eye: one falling from the swing, another stung by a wasp, a third wailing inconsolably. Clutter, noise, and toil mount in intensity. As pace heightens, sparks fly; signs and de-signs, like so many incendiary bombs, explode, sear and char an already troubled inner climate.

Nanda yearns to experience the *moksa* stage of life. As conveyed in the 'Four Ends of Man' of the Hindu tradition, *brachmacharia*, *artha, kama, moksa* they are four different periods in a person's earthly sojourn. Although conceived for men only, some women may also follow the pattern, if impelled by an inner necessity. *Brachmacharia* refers to the student years when one is initiated into Vedic studies and lives in an ashram: *artha*, to the period spent acquiring material wealth; *kama*, to the years when love and pleasure become important factors in life; *moksa* (the root, *muc*, 'to loose, set free, release, liberate') to old age, when energies are turned inward and spiritual matters become all encompassing, preparing the individual for his final release from the cycle of transmigrations. Of crucial importance in these four stages is the concept of *dharma*: from the root, *dhr*, 'to sustain'.[7]

Nanda seeks the quietest ideals to which the Hindu aspires: a withdrawal or renunciation of life's activities. *Moksa* is identified with the flowering of a successful and fulfilled existence: the last human adventure.[8]

Nanda's need for isolation on her mountain top retreat was, however, an escape from commitment and from the pain of life's dualities. Any intrusion, therefore, into her willed solitude, even the ring of the telephone, is considered offensive to her. The call from her friend, Ila Das, shortly after Nanda's receipt of the letter, sounds more shrill to her ear than normal and her friend's 'hideous' and 'screeching' voice grates on her nerves. No, she explains, she cannot visit her at this time since her great-grand-daughter is coming to stay with her and she will be too busy.

Society – in any way or form – is a vice for Nanda. The more she thinks of Raka's visit, the greater is her sense of frustration which Desai transmutes physically in hot, gluey and insect-filled images. The continuously moving, grinding, buzzing flies and insects, their clamminess and gumminess, and the heat enfolding her and its stickiness, create an unpleasant visceral condition mirroring Nanda's psychological attitude. She is glued to her flighty, insect-like world, not yet liberated. *Moksa* is not hers, despite her outwardly ascetic ways and her withdrawal into her hill-top *temenos*.

Still, she does her utmost to offset her involvement in earthly matters. In the afternoon, for example, when the sun rises in the heavens (considered symbolically a heightening of perception and cognition), Nanda closets herself in her room, psychologically shutting out the conscious sphere and allowing free access to her subliminal domain. There she lies on her bed, closes her eyes and withdraws into her darkness, visualizing in her mind's eye the sun's colorful circular orbs transforming themselves into mandalas. To this meditative device she adds the ritual of gesture (*mudra*).

Mudra, like *mantra* and *mandala*, is a meditative device which permits its practitioner to enter into communion with the collective sphere. Designed to harness disparate emotions, *mudra* is used as a kind of self-hypnosis provoked by physical means, to prolong concentration and to take an individual, psychologically speaking, from ego-consciousness to Self-consciousness.

Placing her hands in a very special position on her chest, Nanda lies immobile, like a 'charred tree trunk in the forest' or a 'broken pillar of marble in the desert' (p. 23). Both images depict energy being broken and cut off from her, leaving her listless and virtually lifeless on her bed of despair.

Would Raka distract her from the great serenity she feels is her due? Will she disturb her privacy? As Nanda makes her way out of her darkened room she bumps her knee on her bed post and bruises it: a physical indication of the pain which Raka's arrival holds in store.

RAKA – 'THE MOON'

That Raka's name means 'moon' indicates the role she will play in Desai's narrative. Unlike the celestial body, however, the young girl's face is neither round, calm, nor radiant. She looks like one of 'those dark crickets that leap up in fright but do not sing' (p. 39). Raka is thin; her head is shorn; and she shuffles as she walks up the hill. When greeting her great-grandmother, 'There was a sound of bones colliding' (p. 40).

The word 'collide' conveys both the psychological and physical impact Raka's presence is to have on Nanda. The contact between the bony bodies expresses the violence of clashing generations and conflicting life styles. Raka, the archetypal child, is emerging in all of her innocence as if from the collective womb of Nature, whereas the aged woman is preparing to return to the earth/tomb. The collision of these two forces and the hurt that is to ensue will prepare Nanda for the painful illumination preceding the completion of her intiation ritual.

Psychologically, Raka is a *shadow* figure. She represents the unlived aspects in Nanda's unconscious, elements the older woman has kept hidden in some dismal corner of her subliminal world.

Like the Moon, which shines only when the Sun's rays focus upon it, so Raka is a reflective force: she is consciousness illuminated by her unconscious. Deprived of her own light, we know Raka only through Nanda's perception of her. Indeed, we may even look upon her as her great-grandmother's creation, or an incarnation of Nanda as a little girl, before being forced to conform to India's social structure. Prior to Nanda's becoming a role model for Indian women, she had not been the disconnected, disoriented, deprived and identitiless human being she later became.

Like the Moon God, Chandra, who measures time, is the bearer of nectar (*soma*), and is said to foster Thought and Ideas, Raka represents a period in Nanda's life. Contained within her being is that all-vital nectar which nourishes the Gods; and because of the subdued light which encapsulates the moon on certain nights, she fosters indirect knowledge. As the moon is responsible for bringing water onto the parched earth and nourishing it, so Raka will fecundate Nanda's inner world, allowing her to articulate, to conceptualize those primordial waters which give birth to a fresh approach to life. With increasing consciousness, Nanda will be able to integrate the Raka factor – those chthonian forces – into her psyche, thereby helping her dilate her life experience – and enabling her to pass into death.

Raka, a reflection of Nanda as she used to be, is free, provocative, and essentially naïve. We see her in many stances: trudging up and down the path, rushing about the fields, climbing the cliffs, and descending into the gulleys and gorges. More and more she comes to stand for undisciplined nature – that irresponsible life force that seeks to participate in primitive substance. Raka, like Nanda, is silent and uncommunicative; yet, renewing herself continuously in accordance with Nature's rhythmic cycles, everything she feels, perceives, and intuits is lived inwardly. She shares nothing with other human beings; her libido is forever driven into that secret realm which, like the Moon's, remains enveloped in darkness. Raka is mystery; she is secret. So, too, is Nanda. She does not know herself *plain;* she will have to learn to see through that network of hidden matter [if] she wants to experience harmony.

As Raka enters Nanda's house, she palpates, touches, senses, *feels* every object. The visceral and not the rational is her approach. Everything she investigates within and outside of the house, as we shall see, she does with hands and feet – appendages which allow her to relate to the living world in silence, through body language.

When she 'sagged across the bed on her stomach', she feels its soft-
ness, hardness, and its contours (p. 41). Later, rather than walk out
of the house through the door, Raka slips one leg over the window
frame to freedom.

What part of Nature attracts Raka most? Not the garden and its
flowers. They are too tame. As representatives of society and social
consciousness, they are overly ordered. Structured ways have little
allure for her. Cliffs and gorges, Nature's dangerous features, hyp-
notize her. The wild, disheveled, frenetic powers beyond her reach
lure her on. 'The tip of the cliff and the sudden drop down the
red rock-spattered ravine to the plain', that whole segment of life
that she had not yet discovered and wanted to know, fascinated her
(p. 41)

Nanda has never delved into these primal segments of her psyche,
the very ones that 'collided' with what was expected of her as
mother and wife. To be a role model was the facade which had
imbricated itself upon her being. Raka, in opposition, stands
outside the pale, representing that whole unfulfilled universe which
has to be discovered to know *moksa* so as to go beyond.

What do *cliffs* represent, that Raka climbs their steep sides with
such unabated joy and reaching the top, bathes her body in the
fresh and healthful wind-swept climes? Because of their hardness,
cliffs represent durability and continuity. Unlike stones, however,
which may be smooth and round, cliffs can be dangerous – jagged,
sharp, and steep. One false move and Raka could fall to her death
in the ravine. Careful as she mounts toward vertiginous heights, she
is sure-footed, for her instincts guide her unhesitatingly every step
of the way. Magnetized by the beauty of the Himalayan hills,
nature, for Raka, is a sign of her rapturous love for all that sprouts,
grows, and generates life.

Although Nanda is concerned each time Raka climbs to the top
of a cliff, she cannot help but admire her fearlessness and openness.
Projecting herself onto Raka activates her whole feeling world for
the first time. She sees herself in this child, and feelings of tenderness and warmth replace those of coldness and austerity. Raka is
Nanda at that age: a living presence who has aroused something
within the older woman, which had remained dormant within her
for so many years.

The ravine, like the cliffs, also plays a role in Nanda's growing
awareness and understanding of her spiritual and psychological
condition. Raka, and Nanda through projection, is drawn to this

long, deep hollow in the earth's surface; she wants to investigate
this area worn down by the action of a body of water. Lower than
other regions in the district, it can be considered the earth's recepta-
cle for primordial vibrations – a cavelike uterine area. For the
Hindu, it may be likened to the 'womb house' or *yoni*, the female
counterpart to Shiva's 'sacred phallus' (*lingam*), symbol of the male
energetic factor inhabiting the world. Dating back to pre-Vedic
times (2000 BC), *lingams* were placed in the holiest of areas in
temples or caves. Combined with female energy or yoni, it stood for
the creative union that made for the procreation and sustenance of
life. Shiva (*lingam*) and Parvati (*yoni*) are humankind's archetypal
parents: Father and Mother of the World.[9] The ravine, then, is
yoni: female energy, where water, moisture, and earth become
active and the transformatory process goes on.

The ravine or gorge contains refuse and putrescent matter. For
the alchemist, this rejected stuff spelled *nigredo* (*necro* in old
French), charred and blackened primordial matter. Not necessarily
negative, within this rich rotting and decaying material exists the
very substance that gives birth to new elements. Likewise, the
unconscious – that dark shadow factor, that unformed, unlived substance – when investigated and palpated, can usher new and vaster
visions into the world.

In the Hindu religion, the deity Kali is featured in sculptures and
paintings as a black woman with two dead bodies for ear rings, a
necklace made of skulls and a girdle of dead men's hands. A grue-
some hag with bony fingers, protruding teeth, red eyes, and breasts
smeared with blood, she is always hungry and obsessively voracious.
Kali worship for the Westerner may seem surprising at first, particularly when contrasting it to the Christian ideal of the Immaculate
Virgin Mary. For the Hindu and the Gnostic, however, to be
'uncontaminated by the darker principle' in life is to reject the
shadow on a psychological level. Just as good is implicit in life and
deity, so, too, is evil for the Hindu, and for mystics in general
throughout the world. India's Mother Kali, then, is a 'caressing-mur-
dering symbolization of the totality of the world creating-destroying
eating-eaten one'.[10] She is the all-producing, all-annihilating factor
in the existing and non-existing process which is life.

Kali means time: the time it takes to grow and die, to give birth
and to take back into the womb/tomb. Her blackness may be
looked upon as a counter color, representative of undifferentiated
matter, the original tenebrous void, the chthonian, passive, virtually

inert, deathlike state. Like the Great Mother Goddesses, the black Aphrodite, for example, who make their homes in obscure areas, operating in subdued, virtually unseen darkness, transforming the inert into the active matter, charred into flaming fire, so the uncreated becomes incarnated.

Psychologically, black Kali stands for the primitive unconscious level within the psyche: the *prima materia*, the original chaos, the hermetic nigredo – initial obscurity before it has been brought to consciousness. Now that Raka has entered the physical domain and Nanda has pentrated it visually, the transformation ritual can commence: stasis give way to activity; the unlived to the lived.

That Raka saw a sleeping snake during one of her forays in the ravine is also of great significance. A personification of *naga*, the great serpent that directs terrestrial waters (lakes, ponds, rivers, and oceans), it is the keeper of life's energy, the guardian of the riches in the sea. That it made its presence known to Raka indicates, psychologically, that Nanda, through projection, is becoming aware of the immense power her shadow/Raka has encountered – a fecundating force in its own right. Although Raka has been warned not to explore the ravine and disregards the advice, [it] is an indication of her extreme need to see things through to the end, no matter what the dangers involved. And much to her joy, she even boasts that the snake she saw in the ravine did not bite her; that she welcomed its presence – a symbol of inner strength which rises from the earth and may some day, under proper circumstances, become sublimated and spiritualized.

The ravine, then, with its primal matter, its Kali blackness, its corpses, snakes, stray dogs and other detritus/riches is coupled with another image, that of fire: also aimed at enlightening Nanda.

As Raka stands staring out of the window into distant space, she sees a storm brewing: dust, clouds, fire. Trees have been set ablaze, perhaps by lightning or due to the sun's intensity. Outside of the house, disordered and disarranged powers are raging out of control; within the inner space, the *temenos*, a closure, action, both physical and verbal, is arrested. Raka is disappointed when she learns that the flames she saw were those of a small brush fire and not a full-fledged conflagration.

It must be noted that for the Hindu, the fire principle and the fire God, Agni, are of crucial importance. He represents the warmer of the unborn, the digestive fire within human beings, the household fire in the hearth, lightning in its atmospheric form, and the celestial fire in the sun's rays. As the swift messenger-god in his capacity as fire, Agni connects earth and heaven. Since he exists in two pieces of wood, but manifests himself only when these are rubbed together, he is considered a miracle worker.[11]

That Raka longs to see fire and flame indicates that she needs heat: psychologically, she has to be libidinized.[12] The moon or shadow qualities symbolized by Raka have to be given expression and have to be fluidified, vitalized, and electrified, in order for Nanda to experience them transferentially. Libido arouses fire and force; psychologically, it helps the ego develop gradually out of the unconscious and experience its identity in a space/time continuum. It is that power that encourages the ego to connect with the unconscious contents.[13]

The psychic energy Agni brings into things, which obsesses Raka and Nanda through projection, is that power that will help transform an undirected, unchanneled, and unredeemed force into an active, warm, loving, and creative power. No longer merely viewed as an external image, Agni/fire will have taken on an inner psychic meaning.

Not long after the first brush fire, a real forest fire breaks out. Raka remained transfixed by the sight. Agni was there, blazing in full glory, destroying, devouring, yet nourishing the earth while also filling the universe with his infinite energies.

In time the external fire is extinguished. Not, however, the inner blaze. Nanda tries to keep Raka within the *temenos*, to hold her attention by telling her tales about her childhood. She relates that her father had visited Tibet and brought back exotic animals, Buddha figures and other spectacular objects. Raka, however, 'could no longer bear to be confined to the old lady's fantasy when the reality outside appealed so strongly' (p. 100). She escapes outside. Nanda remains within, moving 'from one window to the other, mournfully looking' for Raka (p. 101), annoyed by her own solicitude. A new feeling, with which she is not yet comfortable and with which she cannot yet cope, has taken flame within her. Nanda has begun to love the little girl tenderly and is moved by her wistfulness. Psychologically, Nanda has begun loving that part of herself that Raka represents. She has warmed up to her own qualities – to her shadow forces. What had formerly been cast out is now returning, integrating itself into her life.

THE EXIT RITUAL

Raka/Moon/Shadow has made Nanda conscious of aspects of her nature which she had repressed for so many years. No longer does she look out on life through her eyes alone. A whole visceral, feeling, sensate dimension has awakened into being. Perception through the mind is now accompanied by understanding via the body. So that *moksa* may be experienced, plenitude and balance are necessary to prepare for the exit ritual: to die to life and be reborn in the cosmic sphere.

Ila Das, Nanda's girlhood friend, is in the vicinity. She telephones Nanda who, though she despises the idea, cannot not ask her to tea. Grotesque in appearance, Ila represents all that is awkward and old-fashioned in society. She is depicted as 'proceeding towards Carignano with her uneven, rushing step, in her ancient white court shoes, prodding the tip of her great brown umbrella into the dust with an air of faked determination' (p. 107). Young urchins jeer at her as she walks up the path, mocking 'her little grey top-knot that wobbled on top of her head' and her 'spectacles that slipped down to the tip of her nose and were only prevented from falling off by an ancient purple ribbon looped over her ears', and the 'grey rag of the petticoat that gaped dismally beneath the lace hem of the sari' (p. 108).

Ila is a spectacle. A remnant of a defunct way of life and a civilization that is no longer, she is not by any means passive. She answers the jeering boys back, threatening to tell their teacher, and, in desperation, opens up her umbrella and charges at them. Ila is out of harmony with the world; she is retrograde, stilted, static, and unevolved. Contention and strife are 'the motif of her life' (p. 111). Her life is 'contradiction' incarnate: disparate, fragmented, 'simply not all of a piece' (p. 110). Nanda now realizes that Ila 'was that last little broken bit of a crazy life, fluttering up over the gravel like a bit of crumpled paper' (p. 112). As for her voice, it was shrill, strained, jarring, crackling, screeching, and agitated. Even when Nanda and Ila were in school together, teachers and playmates had tried to soften that harsh grating voice of hers. To no avail.

When Ila takes Raka's hand in greeting, as abruptly and rashly as she does everything else, she says to her: 'My dear, you and I are simply bound to be friends, you know, bound to be' (p. 114), unaware of the fact that in Raka's domain, no binding or constraint is possible. Although she sits for a bit with the two old ladies as they reminisce, Raka 'wilted' and could not participate in 'that game of old-age – that reconstructing, block by gilded block, of the castle of childhood so ramshackle and precarious' (p. 16).

Ila's strident voice repulses Raka. Her insensitive manner annoys her, as do her tomboyish ways and her legs 'an inch or two above the ground [swinging] to and fro, happily, as if five years old and at a party once more' (p. 115). Then, amid the reminiscing, Ila begins singing 'Darling, I am growing o-o-old', her voice more repulsive than ever.

Ila was a *puella:* a girl who had remained an adolescent and never matured in any way. Added to her fundamental naïveté, are her staid and old fashioned traits, her hypocrisy, her lack of taste and refinement, and her insensitivity. True, her life had been a series of misfortunes: her father had died when she was young; her mother had remained an invalid for many years; and her brothers, in keeping with Indian tradition, had inherited the family's fortune and had squandered it on drink and horses. Nanda and her husband had rescued Ila many times from penury – finding teaching and government posts for her. She failed in these posts, as she did in the piano and French lessons she gave. She had no span of attention but thought she was 'doing her duty' by fighting against child marriage, and struggling for medical reform, but she alienated people at the same time.

When Ila finally leaves, walking down the hill 'as jerky and crazy as an old puppet', Nanda sees her 'doomed' and 'menaced' (p. 133). How has she survived all these years? she wonders. Hours pass. Suddenly, the telephone rings, shrilly. Nanda picks up the receiver: Ila has been found raped and strangled. She must go to the police station to identify the body. Nanda's shock is great: not that she loved Ila, but she did represent a segment of her past – even though it stood for all that was repugnant to her. Now it is dead and with it the sham and facade that had been Ila's life. A woman who had never learned to face herself and had never grown up, Ila was no longer there to concoct lies and to share her little stories with Nanda. Her death meant the end of illusion and of sharing of lies.

This last wrenching away, this cutting out of part of her own flesh, forces the truth out of Nanda. She cries out to Raka, perhaps in desperation, that everything she had told her about her happy childhood, her wonderful parents and her marvelous marriage, had been an untruth. All had been a fabrication – fantasies that helped her sleep at night and stories that dulled the pain of her life.

Nanda's father had been a traveling salesman; he had never been to Tibet. Her home as a child had never been filled with exotic animals, but merely overfed dogs. As for her husband, he had neither loved nor cherished her. He had carried on a lifelong affair with the mathematics teacher in the school. He would have married her had she not been Christian. As for Nanda's children, they were 'alien to her nature'. She neither understood nor loved them. Nor had she chosen to live out the rest of her life at Carignano. Her children had forced it upon her for lack of anything better. Because her life had been so painful to her, Nanda could not even mourn Ila's passing and the end of a world that had been so utterly barren and untenanted.

Strangely enough, Nanda's distress is such that Raka had left the house unnoticed and reappears some time later as if from nowhere. Happiness radiates from her face. Why? Unbeknown to Nanda, or the cook, Raka had taken a box of matches and had set fire to the grasses and trees. 'Look, Nani,' she says with extreme satisfaction. 'I have set the forest on fire. Look, Nani, look – the forest is on fire.' Nanda sits still on the stool. 'Down in the ravine, the flames spat and crackled around the dirty wood and through the dry grass, and black smoke spiralled up over the mountain' (p. 145).

Agni, the Purifier, had come to destroy Nanda's greatest illusion – that of life. With Ila's death, the last vestige of impurity and inauthenticity has been wrenched from Nanda, able to see behind the ordinary world and the little impurities which have helped her make life bearable. Love has now taken over. Her joy in Raka, the Moon, her shadow factor, has made it possible for Nanda, the observer, the remote rationalist, the perfect wife and mother – the role model – to reconnect with her world of instinct, to feel into things, to experience eros. Accepted by the little Raka whom she had feared and rejected in the beginning, Nanda has been awakened to a new feeling dimension.

The presence of the Fire God, Agni, paved the way for the great liberation. Having experienced the meaning of love in Raka, an aspect of herself, Nanda is prepared to fulfil her potential: to experience the exit ritual. A correspondence between spirit/body has come into being. Past and present, mortal and immortal fuse. Nanda Kaul is now one with herself and the Cosmos.

The primeval sacrifice which gave birth to the Cosmic Being, according to Vedic scriptures, required self-immolation. Likewise,

Nanda passes into living coals, thereby blending with Agni, deity's flame, and penetrating the 'essence of fire' – the substance of eternal life. As written in the *Bhagavad Gita*:

> Both he who thinks that this can kill
> And he who thinks that this is killed,
> have neither truly understood,
> this does not kill, is never killed.

> He never dies and never born is he,
> came not to being and never comes to be,
> primeval, in the body's death unslain,
> unborn, eternal, everlastingly.

> Eternal and indestructible,
> this is unborn and unchangeable,
> and when a man knows this how may
> he kill, whom will he cause to slay?...

> 'Tis never cut and never burnt
> not ever wet or ever dry,
> eternal, ever-present, firm,
> this primal one, immovable.[14]

Fire, the purifier and regenerator, the devourer and illuminator, terminates Nanda Kaul's life, thereby breaking down the barriers of flesh and illusion. No longer does obstruction lie in the way of enlightenment. Energized and liquefied, the different planes of her psyche and consciousness allow an immanent of Higher Self to be born. Like the Great God Shiva, who created the world as he danced the circular Nataraja – unifying space and time within evolution – and surrounding himself by flames incarnating eternal energy, so Nanda is divested of dross. Her adamantine essence sparkles in all of its purity, beauty and eternality.

From *Journal of Evolutionary Psychology*, 8: 3–4 (1987), 223–37.

NOTES

[Bettina Knapp's essay adopts a psychoanalytical and feminist approach in considering Anita Desai's characterisations, and draws upon Hindu mythology and traditions in order to provide contextualisation and interesting insights into Desai's naming of characters, and the novel's symbolism and imagery. Eds]

1. Mircea Eliade, *Rites and Symbols of Initiation* (New York, 1965), p. ix.

2. Mircea Eliade, *Yoga* (Princeton, NJ, 1973), p. 247.

3. Anita Desai, *Fire on the Mountain* (New York, 1981) p. 12. [All further page references to this edition are given in the text of the essay.]

4. Eliade, *Yoga*, p. 133.

5. *The Bhagavad Gita*, translated by Geoffry Parrinder (New York, 1975), II, p. 29.

6. Manisha Roy, *Bengali Woman* (Chicago, 1975), p. 41.

7. *Sources of Indian Tradition*, 10, ed. William Theodore de Bary and others (New York, 1958), pp. 211–19.

8. Heinrich Zimmer, *Philosophies of India* (Princeton, NJ, 1974), pp. 41, 44.

9. Heinrich Zimmer, *Myths and Symbols in Indian Art and Civilization* (Princeton, NJ, 1974), p. 127.

10. Ibid., p. 215.

11. W. J. Wilkins, *Hindu Mythology* (Bombay, 1981), pp. 21–9.

12. See C. G. Jung, 'On Psychic Energy', *Structures and Dynamics of the Psyche*, pp. 29–30.

13. Ann Belford Ulanov, *Receiving Woman* (Philadelphia, 1981), pp. 18–19.

14. *The Bhagavad Gita*, pp. 10–11.

10

History and Letters: Anita Desai's *Baumgartner's Bombay*

JUDIE NEWMAN

Anita Desai has always sidestepped any recognition of language as a social fact, disavowing political intent and describing her work in 'universalist' terms. In one interview she maintained that she had avoided many of the ideological problems created by the use of English, by not writing 'social document' novels.

> By writing novels that have been catalogued by critics as psychological, and that are purely subjective, I have been left free to employ, simply, the language of the interior.[1]

In *Baumgartner's Bombay*, however, Desai departs from her previous practice, in order to interrogate the relation of discourse to history, the language of the interior to that of the outer world. In this connection various intertextual devices are significant – letters, literary references, songs, nursery rhymes and travellers' tales.

The novel opens with the murder of Hugo Baumgartner, a Jew, by a young German, many years after Baumgartner's escape from Nazi Germany to India. As the recurrent image of the racetrack suggests ('the circular track that began in Berlin and ended here in Bombay')[2] Baumgartner's story comes full circle and his trajectory is strongly marked by repetition. After being dispossessed in Germany as a Jew, narrowly avoiding the Nazi camps, he is seized in India as a German, and imprisoned for six years as an enemy alien in a British internment camp. When world war gives way to Partition struggles, his Moslem business partner in Calcutta is dis-possessed in his turn by Hindus. After Baumgartner's return to Bombay, however, the death of his new Hindu partner sees him booted out once more, into an independent India which has little use for Europeans. The plot, therefore, seems to imply that history is only a meaningless series of re-enactments, a story which repeats itself. In Salman Rushdie's dictum: 'Europe repeats itself, in India, as farce.'[3]

Throughout the novel Baumgartner, shabby, smelly, shortsighted, his nose a warty, wobbling purplish lump (p. 5) is established as a clown, known to his neighbours as the madman of the cats for his habit of adopting strays. Even his death is presented in a mode of black comedy, combining the effects of Keystone Cops slapstick with a chase sequence and lashings of melodrama. Bloodstained footprints are sighted, and the wrong man promptly arrested by stereotypically plodding policemen, who subsequently unleash two Dobermanns. As cats fly in all directions, one of them, defenes-trated, narrowly misses the bald perspiring head of the landlord (p. 225); the appearance of the fire brigade only adds to the confu-sion and to the spectators' delight. The murder is presented as a fact in the public domain, presided over by assorted officials, in strong contrast to the opening scene in which Baumgartner's friend Lotte reads the letters found by his body.

As the novel opens, the initial impression is of entry into a tragic interior. The process of reading is highlighted by the presence of a fictional reader, mediating beween the reader and the letters. As Lotte's co-readers, we become equal partners in the enterprise of decipherment. Lotte is thus the point of entry to both the letters and Desai's text. Inner sanctum and text are equated as she fumbles with the door to her room, 'as though she had forgotten its grammar, her fingers numb, tongue-tied as it were' (p. 1). Initially, Lotte poses theatrically, clutching the letters to her breast in the manner which comes naturally to an ex-actress. Once alone, however, the public persona falls away. The dichotomy between private and public space typifies the tension created for the reader between the fictive and the historical. As Lotte weeps over the letters, public farce appears to conceal private tragedy, as if Desai were directing the reader back from Rushdie to Hegel: 'All acts and personages of great importance in world history occur, as it were, twice ... the first time as tragedy, the second as farce.'[4]

Baumgartner's Bombay comes full circle in its last sentence as Lotte spreads out the letters. Repetition is, therefore, embedded in the fictional structure, which encloses the story of Baumgartner's life (narrated in flashbacks) within the events of one day; itself framed as a flashback by the initial and final sequences. The effect is rather of a *mise en abyme* of infinite regress, in which the novel ends as Lotte, the surrogate reader, begins to read the letters which will initiate the novel. From an interior space of reading the reader moves to a public scene and thence back ad infinitum.

Repetition is also the mark of the letters, in the repeated phrases which reduce each to a quasi-facsimile of its predecessor:

> each line seemed like the other, each card alike: 'Are you well, my rabbit? Do not worry yourself. I am well. I have enough. But have you enough, my mouse, my darling? Do not worry...'
>
> (p. 3)

From these empty repetitions Lotte looks away towards the glass of her window, to see only 'A blank sky, as always, with neither colour nor form. Empty' (p. 4). The image extends the emptiness represented by European letters into the Indian scene. World and text appear to mirror each other as if interior language and material reality were one indissoluble entity. Meaninglessness, perpetual recurrence, and blankness are thus the initial impressions created by the letters. In addition, in their sugary endearments they offer a sickly-sweet language of childhood which is construed as destructive. As Lotte reads,

> All the marzipan, all the barley sugar, the chocolates and toffees of childhood descended on her with their soft, sticking, suffocating sweetness. Enough to embrace her, enough to stifle her, enough to obliterate her. ... Lotte wept and drowned.
>
> (p. 5)

As the novel continues the letters become emblematic of a stifling European textual world, linked to destructive illusions, and, also, the point of entry to a tragic history. Mirroring, copying and repeating are important motifs as the novel interrogates the moral relation of history to fictional discourse.

In this connection, Baumgartner's experiences as a Jew in Nazi Germany are all important. A long flashback presents Baumgartner's pre-war childhood in Berlin as a redolently textualised world which conjoins bitter-sweet imagery with a succession of intercalated German nursery rhymes and songs, set against the highly cultured background of Baumgartner's elegant Mutti, with her Goethe, Schiller and Heine. Because they are reproduced in German (largely without a gloss) these intertextual motifs create the impression of a thoroughly self-centred European society, an infantilised interior world which makes little concession to readers outside. They, therefore, function as a means of condemning the claustrophobic over-immersion in texts of that society, in order to reassert the importance of engagement with the sociohistorical world. Traditional criticism tends to see the Imperial power as the mother-country, the origin and nurturer of value.[5] In contrast, the colonised understand the Imperial refusal to recognise the autonomy of other worlds as a species of infantile blindness – just as babies think the world exists only for their own omnipotent selves. In *Baumgartner's Bombay* Desai takes the Imperial convention for representing the colonised (immaturity) and redefines it as a property of Europe. Thus, while Mutti's nursery song laments an absent mother (p. 28), Hugo's mind moves to a baby hedgehog, separated from its mother, which he had 'rescued', only to kill it by overfeeding, until its corpse oozed warm milk. The sentimental image of mother-love is undercut; the hedgehog died less because it was separated from its mother than from an excess of milky sweetness. Indeed, as the reader later learns, had Baumgartner remained with Mutti in the nursery world of Europe, he too would have died. Although his mother constantly attempts to shore up the illusion of a world of sweetness and light, Hugo comes to see the 'encirclement of her soft, sweet-smelling arms' (p. 33) as an imprisonment. His mother's attempt to play 'horsey' (p. 35) is no substitute for a longed-for excursion to the racetrack with his father. Desperate to accompany him, Hugo resorts to primitive linguistic magic, repeating 'Mick-muck-mo, Make-it-so' (p. 34) as he formulates his wish. In pre-war Berlin, however, word and world fail to coalesce. Originally, Hugo's mother had appeared to him as the entire universe. Her gilt-framed mirror 'held the whole room slightly tilted on its calm and shining surface' (p. 27). Downstairs, however, in his father's furniture show-room, the world is already more fragmentary and disquieting, reflecting the Fatherland's new definition of Jews as aliens. Here, Hugo is alarmed by the reflection in the three-piece looking-glass: 'turning you into a stranger before your own eyes as you slowly rotated to find the recognisable' (p. 26). Mutti's enclosed world contrasts with the showroom, where 'the opulence of the interior' (p. 26) is none the less on display to – and dependent upon – the public.

By now, the wealthy Jews who patronised Herr Baumgartner's furniture shop have begun to invest their money in more portable assets, and the business is failing. In Hugo's dreams 'the brilliant mirrors tipped out their highly coloured and illuminated reflections like pools of water from unsteady basins, then slipped out of their frames and crashed' (pp. 39–40). The song 'Es tanzt ein Bibabutzemann' (a bogeyman dances in our house) introduces the character of Herr Pfuehl, the merchant who will eventually appropriate the business to his Aryan ownership. Isolated in her textual world, Mutti refuses to read the realities of Hitler's Germany, even when 'Jude' is painted in bold red letters on her windows. Soon, however, Hugo's dreams come true as (presumably on 'Kristallnacht') the salesroom is smashed up, and 'glass splintered, crashed, slid all over the floor in slanting, shining heaps' (p. 42). A nursery song presents images of scarcity (the geese go barefoot) in childish, nonsensical terms. The next day, when Herr Baumgartner is arrested, the description of the stormtroopers is similarly childish: 'Hugo might have been playing a game with his toy soldiers, marching them up, then marching them down' (p. 43). This is no game, however. Herr Baumgartner returns from Dachau only to sign over his business to the not-so-foolish Herr Pfuehl. The following nursery rhyme says it all: 'Fuchs, du hast die Gans gestohlen' (p. 44: Fox, you have stolen the goose).

Confronted with these visible horrors, Hugo's mother's reaction is to retreat, to pay a visit to her childhood friends, the Friedmanns, in the pastoral Grunewald. Here Mutti sings of escape to 'the country where lemons flower' (p. 56 [Goethe]) and reads verses about linden trees, swallows, butterflies, children playing and Rabindranath Tagore.[6] While his mother indulges in nostalgia, recalling a performance of *Lohengrin* in her schooldays, Hugo contemplates real rather than operatic swans, floating on the lake:

> somehow they reminded him of his father's rococo mirrors, gliding as they did upon the shining glass of their reflections in the still water, and he was silenced by the knowledge of their transience.
>
> (p. 46)

Mutti's magical memories of the Swan Knight are replaced by more disquieting, militaristic overtones; the swans' feathers are 'knitted

together like chain mail' (p. 46). For Hugo, childhood provides
little justification for nostalgia. In the woods,

> it seemed he was stumbling through the illustrations of a book
> of fairy stories, the forest where Hansel and Gretel followed a trail of
> breadcrumbs, or in which Sleeping Beauty lay hidden by a wall of
> thorns – beautiful, hushed and vaguely sinister.
>
> (p. 47)

When Albert Friedmann begins to recite a poem about a deer entitled 'The Kaiser of the Woods', doubly anachronistic in both its
political and its pastoral references, Hugo calls his mother back
from the world of texts to the reality of Berlin, where his father is
discovered, a suicide.

From now on, Hugo, isolated at home with Mutti, finds his
copies of 'Der Gute Kamerad' pure fantasy, 'its stories of camping
in the forest and journeys on the sea no more relevant to his life
than a dream is to daytime' (p. 50). Mutti's gift of a monumental
1906 *Kaiserbuch*, inscribed with the imperial motto, is even less
enticing. Virtually a prisoner, Hugo is forced to exist entirely within
the confines of an apartment 'that was beginning to resemble that
Kaiser-coffin of a book' (p. 50). World and books are so identified
that despite her enthusiasm for Tagore, Mutti dismisses the idea of
escape to India as a fairy tale: 'diese Marchen' (p. 56). She is left
behind with only her Goethe for company. Her position recalls the
unpalatable fact, learned after the Holocaust, that 'a man can read
Goethe or Rilke in the evening, that he can play Bach and Schubert
and go to his day's work at Auschwitz in the morning'.[7] All the
polite letters in the world could not prevent the atrocity which now
hangs over Mutti. Baumgartner's Berlin appears to expose all texts
to the irony of history, and underlines the danger of over-immersion in an interior realm of books which may reflect but which fail
to act upon the world about them. Mutti's old fashioned Weimar
high culture no longer bears any relation to its circumambient
society. The world reflected in her mirrors has gone to smash.

In his passage to India, Hugo appears at first to have merely
traded one illusion for another, Hansel and Gretel for Aladdin. In
Venice he feels as if 'already transported to the East' (p. 59). Yet
Desai measures the distance here between her protagonist and his
predecessors. Returning from India, Forster's Fielding saw in Venice
a perfect harmony of nature and culture, and found 'tender romantic fancies' reawakening in him.[8] Baumgartner is travelling in the

opposite direction, and is happy to leave Venice behind: 'he felt himself to be inside a chocolate box, surfeited with sweetness and richness' (p. 60).

When he arrives in India any suggestions of orientalist romance swiftly fade. The Taj Hotel, previously envisaged as an Eastern palace, turns out to be a seedy house with no lighting. It is, of course, the wrong Taj Hotel. Sign and referent do not accord. The proprietor's comment, 'I say Taj Hotel, then this Taj Hotel' (p. 85) introduces a world in which language creates new realities. All at sea, Baumgartner finds himself longing for a guide book: 'Or at least a signboard. In a familiar language. A face with a familiar expression. He could not read these faces' (p. 83). Yet, although Baumgartner feels deceived by India, although his language no longer controls his world, the 'unreadable' quality of Bombay has some positive consequences. If language is no longer mimetic, if it can no longer map the world according to Baumgartner's expectations, it may, none the less, offer a way out of the claustrophobia of Baumgartner's past into a world which is both multiple and syncretic:

> Was it not India's way of revealing the world that lay on the other side of the mirror? India flashed the mirror in your face. ...You could be blinded by it. But if you refused to look into it, if you insisted on walking around to the back, then India stood aside, admitting you where you had not thought you could go. India was two worlds, or ten.
>
> (p. 85)

Although Baumgartner's looking-glass world has given way to a less than enchanting Eastern Wonderland, the blindness of Berlin is not to be repeated.

Baumgartner's individuation remains, however, only potential. When internment interrupts his heterogeneous linguistic and cultural transformation, he finds himself in a society which replicates his childhood. His arrest suggests both an individual state of arrested development, as he is put 'on hold' for the duration of the war, and a more generalised condition of deferred political autonomy. From the mother-country he is transplanted to an all-male environment which is equally infantile. The parodic nature of the camp, which repeats the past in a species of Europe-in-India, provides a sharp critique of Imperial self-replication. With its orchestra, lectures on theosophy, demonstrations of eurythmics, and

opportunites for private study, organised by the 'culture department', the camp provides a facsimile of pre-war German culture up
to and including the hostilities between Nazi and Jewish inmates.
Baumgartner finds the discipline akin to that of childhood, with the
inmates expected to eat, wash, and sleep to a timetable, as if in a
'comical dream – grown men finding themselves returned to their
school' (p. 108). In his spotless white linen, Hugo's friend, Julius,
looks 'like a figure from a pre-war Sunday picnic, or coffee party'
(p. 122). Hugo helps him to sketch furniture, 'recreating his father's
elegant, well-lit, stylish showroom' (p. 124). Within this ersatz
enclave, Baumgartner's own image of Germany becomes progress-
ively distanced from reality. Like all colonisers, he finds himself
yearning for a motherland which he had never really known, represented by a Nordic blonde in the adjoining women's camp:

> she seemed to embody his German childhood – at least, he chose to
> see her as such an embodiment, it was so pleasant to do so, like
> humming a children's song.
>
> (p. 127)

Nor is Baumgartner alone in living in a fantasy world. Cut off from
history, the other inmates resort to fictions of an increasingly fantastic nature, 'No matter how often such carefully constructed
scenes were sent crashing by the truth' (p. 129). Baumgartner's own
illusions are shattered when the 'Norse goddess of the camp'
speaks. Frau Bruckner, a missionary's wife, has adapted so completely to her public role that she has forgotten her original
German. During their internment, Emil Schwarz, a bookish scholar,
comments that the events in the camp have all happened before:
'Mann has described it all ... in *The Magic Mountain*' (p. 132).
Baumgartner, now sceptical of fictions, remains unconvinced: 'it
was just like Schwarz to refer everything in life to books as though
that were the natural solution and end of it all' (p. 132).

Instead of taking refuge in fictions, Baumgartner eschews tale-
telling. Silence becomes his response to events in the camp. When
the Jews refuse to shout 'Heil Hitler', 'Baumgartner gratefully
joined their silence. He realised at that instant that silence was his
natural condition' (p. 117). Yet, although silence can be a weapon,
to submit to the finality of silence is to confirm the nihilism of
Nazism. Mutti has also been silenced; no more letters have arrived
from her. By the time of the novel's opening, Baumgartner has

come to realise that 'the habits of a hermit were growing upon him like some crustaceous effluent; it required an effort, an almost physical effort to crack it, to break through to the liquidity and flow and shift and kinesis of language' (p. 11).

Baumgartner's silence is eventually shattered by Kurt, a young German, who recalls Baumgartner to the world of his youth. Two images of horror are juxtaposed before the close of the novel – the traveller's tales told by Kurt, and the letters from Mutti, presented in flashback. In broad terms they represent the destructive powers of fantasy (Kurt), as opposed to historical reality (Mutti). Initially, Hugo gives Kurt a wide berth. For him, the fair, Teutonic boy in shorts suggests only the horrors of the past in potentially repetitive form:

> The *Lieder* and the campfire. The campfire and the beer.
> The beer and the yodelling. The yodelling and the marching.
> The marching and the shooting. The shooting and the killing.
> The killing and the killing and the killing.
>
> (p. 21)

The explanation for Baumgartner's eventual charity to Kurt may lie in the café-proprietor's introduction of him as one of the 'baby-men' (p. 15) who had come to India 'uninvited' (p. 14) and then turned beggar. In a long disquisition Farrokh describes the young German as representative of a type – 'men who remain children' (p. 13) – who has probably 'kicked his parents in the face' (p. 13) in order to visit India and now expects to be supported by others.

> Soon they need money. Go to post office. Has letter come from my dear mummy, my darling daddy? No? Must have, please look, look again, they must send! No, no letter, no money.
>
> (p. 16)

Baumgartner, similarly uninvited, also came to India in his youth, and has been reduced to begging scraps (for his cats). He, too, left a parent behind, fled to India, waited in vain for letters. Reversing the conventional colonial metaphor of 'mother country' and dependency, Desai pictures Europe once more as child, Europe as the place of illusion, whether tragic (in pre-war Germany) or wilfully cultivated (as in Kurt's use of drugs as a means to an alternative reality). Baumgartner's own arrested development, his paralysis by a European past, reappears in the young German's infantilism. At

Baumgartner's flat he behaves 'like a naughty child' (p. 154), hurling beer about the room. The historical parallels make Baumgartner (a sufferer from 'survival guilt') vulnerable to Kurt, a nightmarish projection of the retribution which he expects. It is this illusion of generalised guilt which exposes Baumgartner to his mirror self, become a mirror enemy. In hard fact, Baumgartner is not at all like Kurt; their specific historical situations are quite different. Baumgartner could not have saved his mother, and was an unwilling victim of the Aryan cult of strength, not, like Kurt, its devotee.

Kurt, however, has little use for fact. Baumgartner's silence is suddenly filled by the German's flood of repetitive Indian horror stories, involving cannibalism, ritual sacrifice, wholesale slaughter, leprosy, flagellation, excesses both erotic and narcotic, and finally, farcically, a yeti. Where the flashback to Berlin illustrated the inefficacy of high culture to defend itself against the grossest forms of inhumanity, demonstrating that books could not prevent atrocity, Kurt's tales dramatise a counter-truth – that those who begin by burning books end by burning men. A would-be Tantric, Kurt has eaten human flesh and burned men (though in Benares in the burning ghats). He is wilfully out of touch with the ordinary world, as his tales demonstrate; they are about as believable as the Giant Rat of Sumatra for which the world is not yet ready. Quite apart from the presence of a yeti, they involve a sword-shaped plant topped with a cockerel's head, sea-serpents, a guest appearance from the devil, and Tibetan magicians flying into the sky on a streak of lightning. Baumgartner's 'mick-muck-mo, make it so' appears to be Kurt's watchword. Kurt's playing fast and loose with material reality, transforming his life into a series of fictions, independent of truth or history, initiates a process of destructive fantasy which culminates in the murder of Baumgartner, appropriately in pursuit of the latter's racing trophies, the symbols of his own past magical desires, in order to procure fresh supplies of illusion-producing substances. The title of the novel, therefore, with its echoes of travelogue (compare *Fodor's Beijing*)[9] is deeply ironic. Baumgartner's Bombay has not been very different from his Berlin after all. He is murdered by an alter ego deeply enclosed within fictions, much as his own earlier self had been. Fairy stories and nursery rhymes have yielded to travellers' tales and thence to a horror story. Fictions appear to have triumphed over fact, and the reader is left with an image of history as textual repetition, and repetition as horror.

A different story is told, however, by the postcards and letters discovered by Baumgartner's body. 'Strangely empty, repetitive and cryptic' (p. 164), they merely repeat the same phrases 'Are you well? I am well. Do not worry. I have enough. Have you enough?' (p. 164). Resistant to textual interpretation, these letters cannot be glossed or decoded. They appear to say nothing. Their explanation, indicated by the numbers on the postcards, which stop abruptly in February 1941, depends upon historical knowledge: in the early days of the war it was possible for the inmates of concentration camps to send and receive mail. The letters thus offer an emblematic opposition between repeated horrors and a paralysed silence, which cannot in the end itself avoid repetition. In themselves the letters have no content (the rules permitted inmates to say very little[10]) but their material reality is crushingly significant, bearing witness to the worst horrors of recent history.

Importantly, it was the discovery of a similar cache of real letters in Bombay, passed to Anita Desai for translation, which triggered the novel. She remarked that, 'Perhaps because they had been so empty they teased my mind. I had to supply the missing history to them.'[11] For the reader the same is now true of Mutti's letters. *Their* history will not pass into oblivion; their gaps and silences, paradoxically, say everything. In the double sense of 'Mutti's letters' – the polite letters (literature) which failed to save her, the correspondence which for all its sparsity bears witness to inhumanity – Desai interrogates the potential importance of European letters in India, as tragically irrelevant or, in their very absences and omissions, historically significant.

It is striking that it is only after the relation of the Indian writer to European literature and history has been problematised, that *Baumgartner's Bombay*, a hitherto freestanding novel, reestablishes a link with Forster which had apparently been broken. It is worth noting that Desai deplored the David Lean film of *A Passage to India* for its divergence from the original. She particularly condemned Lean's rewriting of the ending, in order to make Indian and Englishman clasp hands in friendship. In Desai's opinion, Lean believed he had 'improved' Forster. 'What he is admitting is that he feels he has improved history as well.'[12] When, therefore, Desai rewrites Forster the effect is of a movement away from textual freedom and back to history. In a reprise of the Marabar Caves incident in *A Passage* to India, Baumgartner enters a cave where he hears not a repetitive echo (Forster's 'ou-boum') but an absolute silence. Rather than being presented as a symbolic image of the encounter with a transcendental deity, Desai's cave is fully historic-ised. In the internment camp Baumgartner had tried to keep his mind occupied by watching ants entering a crevice, described as a 'dark cave' (p. 119). But the tactic failed:

> The trouble with such fascinating sights was their silence, their tedium, the endless repetition of forms and actions that blurred and turned into an endless labour of human forms – bent, driven into black caves from which they did not reemerge. *Nacht und Nebel.*
>
> (p. 119)

The German phrase[13] repeats the term applied by the Nazis to pris-oners destined for death, for disappearance into 'Night and Fog' whether in forced labour or camps. When Baumgartner squeezes into the cave, he finds blackness, silence, and a complete absence of explanatory text: 'No voice, no song, not even a dim inscription' (p. 189). Some things are lost to history. The shrine inside is unnamed, unexplained; the cave figures forth the absence, silence and untold horrors of the letters, the night into which Mutti disap-peared. Desai does not, however, expand precise historical horror into totalising negativity. Refusing any vision of nothingness, Baumgartner leaves Forster firmly behind and makes a rapid exit from the cave. Unlike Mrs Moore, 'Baumgartner would not have its no'. Without minimising the real horrors of the past, Desai empha-sises the need not to be complicit with those forces that would erase historical truth, reducing events to myth, fantasy or silence. Although the Holocaust was an enactment of absolute evil, it was so because of particular crimes against particular people. In counter-distinction to the image of history as meaningless repetition, the Cave incident, like the letters, asserts the specificity of history and the necessity of maintaining its silences and omissions in full view, rather than placing past horrors in a generalised history of evil for which nobody in particular, or everyone in general, may be held accountable. After the war, Baumgartner had never been willing to think back to the past: 'That time was a closed book, or like a pack of cards – finite in number' (p. 172). Mutti's letters, however, also a small collection of cards, are finite yet infinite in their implications. For Desai, history cannot be a closed book, a silenced story, but neither can it be reopened and rewritten at random. Some people have been lost to history and to literature, and no amount of 'revisioning' can call them back. Imagination baulks at filling in Mutti's silences, or in fleshing out her untold story; in the words of George Steiner, 'The world of Auschwitz lies outside human speech'. Paradoxically therefore Mutti's letters reveal both the insufficiency of literature in the face of history – and its full necessity.

From *World Literature Written in English*, 30:1 (1990), 37–46.

NOTES

[Judie Newman's essay is a valuable example of new historicist insights into the affinities between historical and literary narratives. The discussion of the historical/literary intertextuality of Desai's Indo-European world of history and letters focuses on the predetermined textuality of its characters and suggests ways of reading literature as a more subtle form of history. The essay, in challenging a universalist approach to history and literature, has many affinities with poststructuralist and feminist positions. Eds]

1. Ramesh K. Srivastava (ed.), *Perspectives on Anita Desai* (Ghaziabad, 1984), p. 3.

2. Anita Desai, *Baumgartner's Bombay* (London, 1988), p. 194. [References in the essay are to page numbers of this edition. Eds]

3. Salman Rushdie, *Midnight's Children* (London, 1982), p. 185.

4. Karl Marx and Friedrich Engels, *Selected Works* (London, 1968), p. 96.

5. Diana Brydon, 'The Myths That Write Us: Decolonising the Mind', *Commonwealth*, 10: 1 (1987), 4–5.

6. Alex Aronson, *Rabindranath Tagore Through Western Eyes* (Calcutta, 1943) accounts for the German vogue for Tagore in the 1930s as part of the evolution towards the irrational and pseudo-mystic.

7. George Steiner, *Language and Silence* (New York, 1967), p. ix.

8. E. M. Forster *A Passage to India* (London, 1969), pp. 275–6.

9. Paul West, 'The Man Who Didn't Belong', *New York Times Book Review*, 9 April 1989, 3.

10. Konnilyn G. Feig, *Hitler's Death Camps* (London, 1981), p. 52. The rules for correspondents from Dachau limited postcard messages to ten lines of legible German.

11. Andrew Robinson, 'Out of Custody', *The Observer*, 3 July 1988, p. 42.

12. Anita Desai, 'The Rage for the Raj', *New Republic*, 25 November 1985, p. 28.

13. Feig notes that a block at Ravensbruck, the women's camp, was known as 'Nacht und Nebel'. See Konnilyn G. Feig, *Hitler's Death Camps* (note 10 above).

14. George Steiner, *Language and Silence*, p. 123.

11

'Divided to the Vein': Patterns of Tormented Ambivalence in Walcott's *The Fortunate Traveller*

CLEMENT H. WYKE

Derek Walcott has said, 'schizoids, in a perverse way, have more personality than the normal person, and it is this conflict of our racial psyche that by irritation and a sense of loss continues to create artists.'[1] He further asserts in the same article that we are 'deprived of what we cannot remember, or what, when we visit its origins never existed the way we imagined, or where we remain strangers, contemptible cousins, the children of indentured servants and slaves.' The picaro in *The Fortunate Traveller* portrays this kind of 'tormented ambiguity', to borrow a term from James Livingston.[2] Because the term 'ambiguity' is usually associated with meaning rather than with personal attitude, as intended here, 'ambivalence' is chosen as the operative word for the purpose of this study.

Poet and persona share this ambivalence, and the artistic process which brings them together is marked by image patterns which map out a journey that simultaneously regresses to the past and advances inevitably into the future. History and memory frequently yield precedence to forward-moving time which eventually becomes apocalyptic vision. A brief consideration of the poet in relation to his consciousness of history, and a sketch of his artistic and psychological involvement with his persona should lead to a more informed analysis of Walcott's artistry in *The Fortunate Traveller*, an artistry that carries the imprint of the author's ambivalence expressed in the poem through a pattern of dual, ambiguous and paradoxical elements integrated by the complex personality of the traveller himself.

Despite Walcott's objections to the 'masochistic recollection' of poets who look to the brutal history of the West Indies for inspiration,[3] he presents in his main persona a quester who is ironically forced to confront his origins and the events of his past in the mirrored reflections of the present. His journey from the old to the new merely provides an unrelenting satire on the evils of the old. Put another way, in *The Fortunate Traveller,* a journey through the modern world of American and European civilization represented, among other things, by the passage across the Mason–Dixon line, is merely a repetition of the old order of victim and victimizer, conquered and conqueror, native dweller and foreign intruder. Walcott, consciously or unconsciously, is negating the statement made in 'Laventille': 'The middle passage never guessed its end.'[4] Instead, *The Fortunate Traveller* illustrates the counter-claim of Brathwaite that the passage has guessed its end. Its end is inextricably bound up in its beginning. The process of the journey and of the quest is not only constructed from the racial memories of the past, but the outcome is shaped by and mirrored in this process.

Not only are the cruel forces of memory projected into the experiences of the present, but there is a tortured convergence of many parallel and divergent elements in Walcott's three-part sequence of poems; the very structure of North–South–North accentuates the contrasting and complementary social realities of the American south with its blatant black–white dichotomies and the north where the lines are more subtly drawn but nevertheless still exist. Throughout *The Fortunate Traveller*, the reader witnesses a convergence of Caribbean, Afro-American and European realities reflected in symbols, myths and geographical landmarks. There is also the contrastive merging of standard language and local dialect, part of what Walcott calls 'that dramatic ambivalence [which] is part of what it means to be a West Indian'.[5] In addition, Walcott brings together the concrete and abstract, the biographical and historical, the physical and spiritual, the social and psychological, the linear and cyclical, and the this-worldly and apocalyptic. All of these conflicting elements reveal a poetic mind in conflict, a man who once described himself as 'a kind of split writer' with one tradition inside him 'going one way, and another going another';[6] in Walcott's memorable phrase, he is 'divided to the vein'. The heartbeat of the fortunate traveller, like that of the creative artist, is also caught between the rhythms of diastole and systole, 'like the pause / between dusk and darkness, between fury and peace'.[7]

The image of the pulsebeat and the vein is not one which is merely used to depict the cultural and linguistic contradictions portrayed in 'A Far Cry from Africa'; the image is also appropriately chosen by Walcott in his poetic collection *Midsummer* (1984) to describe his own tortuous procedure of artistic composition:

> A trembling thought, no bigger than a hurt
> wren, swells to the pulsebeat of my rounded palm,
> pecks at its scratch marks like a mound of dirt,
> oval wings thrumming like a panelled heart.
> Mercy on thee, wren; ...
> ...
> but if you died in my hand, that beak would be the needle
> on which the black world kept spinning on in silence,
> your music as measured in grooves as was my pen's.
> Keep pecking on in this vein and see what happens:
> the red skeins will come apart as knitting does.
> It flutters in my palm like the heartbeat thudding to be gone, ...[8]

It is apparent then that the intense experience of creating poetry is as painfully replete with passionate contradiction and conflict as the quest of the traveller across the rugged landscapes of life. Byron had demonstrated this congruency between art and life and between the artist and literary pilgrim in *Childe Harold,* a work which bears some resemblances to Walcott's *The Fortunate Traveller.* The Miltonic principle of the poet as a poem and as a creator pulled into the very life of the personages of his creation is endorsed by Walcott in one of *The Gulf* poems: 'Resisting poetry I am becoming a poem. / O lolling Orphic head silently howling, / my own head rises from its surf of cloud.'[9] Beyond any notion of the 'egotistical sublime', however, is Walcott's troubled response to deep racial memory which is inextricably linked with both the process and product of his own creative impulses. In poem 50 of *Midsummer,* he speaks of how some of his poems lie 'where stones are deep, in the sea's memory'.[10] The poet associates this memory with his father, Warwick Walcott, whose name is linked with Warwickshire in England. He then speaks of moving his father's grave from the 'blackened headstones / in Castries'.[11] One need not construct autobiography from this poetic commentary to establish the fictional truth which preoccupies Walcott's imagination here. Evidence adduced thus far helps to delineate the poetic personality behind the creation of the principal quester in *The Fortunate Traveller*. The reader is therefore not surprised to see an interesting pattern of tensions and ambiguities between the attitude and behaviour of the traveller himself and the poet who creates him. There are ironic contradictions and unconscious parallels and divisions which define the movements and direction of the poem and its central personage. Opposites and mirror images appear as part of the dynamic between poet, poem and reader. In our observation of this process we must remember Walcott's words in 'What the Twilight Says: An Overture': 'the torment of all self-appointed schizoid saints is that they enact their opposite.'[12]

We must however move from the author to his creation – the traveller. His prototype is the hero of the picaresque novel, the earliest example of which in English is usually ascribed to Thomas Nashe who like Walcott also wrote for the stage, and who entitled his prose work *The Unfortunate Traveller or the Life of Jack Wilton* (1594). Walcott's slight ironic modification of Nashe's title needs no speculation here. Nashe's traveller experiences the same sense of displacement as Walcott's. Jack Wilton describes himself as 'a certain kind of appendix or page, belonging or appertaining in or unto the confines of the English court'.[13] He follows 'the camp or the court, or the court and the camp.' He is 'sole king of the cans and blackjacks, prince of pygmies.' Unlike Walcott's traveller, he indulges in racy invective, but, like Walcott's traveller, he indulges in wit and terse colloquialisms. These colloquialisms, like those of Walcott's main character, can be combined with aureate rhetoric.

One senses, however, that ambivalence in Jack Wilton is a trait which surfaces as a duality of character; he is a phoney who parades as a gentleman who displays mock-erudition and pretentious courtly manners. Walcott's adventurer is more serious and controlled by the burden and destiny of his race and background. Irony through incongruous and opposing patterns of behaviour is nevertheless a strong determinant in the world of both travellers. Jack Wilton invites his reader in Latin, '*Paulo maiora canamus* [let

us sing of somewhat nobler things]',[14] pedantically citing Virgil's
Eclogues; but when he tells of what happens after he departs to
places outside the court, he dwells on the same rogueries and atrocities which characterized his earlier behaviour, so that environmen-
tally court and camp turn out to be the same. Walcott's traveller
often introduces us to Ovid, to Dante and to a catalogue of
European satirists such as 'big-guts Rabelais', Lord Rochester,
Quevedo, Juvenal, Martial, Pope, Dryden, Swift and Lord Byron
('The Spoiler's Return', p. 60), all of whom are a mere supportive
chorus to Spoiler the calypsonian. The journey pursued by the fortunate traveller, like Jack Wilton's, first appears to be diversified as
he moves from place to place, but nothing 'nobler' occurs: from
North to South to North again the traveller encounters an ironic
repetition of the same human hardships and calamities. Walcott's
vision of the future, however, is more sombre and ominously apocalyptic than Nashe's. Some closer, although brief, examination of
the fortunate traveller and of Walcott's poetic interaction with his
character would now be more understandable in [the] light of the
preceding sketch of the author, his creative process and his persona.

The poems of the first section of *The Fortunate Traveller* are sub-
sumed under the title 'North', and introduce us to the territorial
environment first encountered by the traveller – that is, the New
England coastal cities of America. The reader does not, however,
meet the persona through the I-pronoun reference till the second
poem 'Upstate'. The first poem, 'Old New England', reflects in its
title the ironic doubleness of the character's world and the central
paradox of the collection of poems: that the new order is the same
as the old because the former repeats the same evils as the latter.
The visual images of black and white are made to convey meanings
which invert their usual stereotypic symbolism; thus, white, nor-
mally identified with purity and goodness, becomes associated with
violence and destructive victimization. For example, the 'white
church spire whistles into space / like a swordfish' (ll. 3, 4) and the
'white meetinghouse' 'wounds' the hillside with its spire, causing
'brown blood' to trickle down (ll. 14, 15); and God uses 'the white
lance of the church' as his harpoon (ll. 28, 29). Black or brown,
however, are colours which are identified with objects that have
been defiled or damaged or destroyed by other surrounding forces
of influences: for instance, the 'Black clippers' are tarred with
whales' blood (l. 1). This blood, in the second stanza of the poem,
is associated with the wound produced by the spire of the white

meetinghouse (ll. 14, 15). The trail along which the blood is found is 'the Indian trail' (l. 14). These images awaken in the mind of the reader the atrocities of early white American settlers who caused the blood of Indians to flow while controlling them with a hypocritical religious system centralized in the 'white meetinghouse' of the church. In this context, the colour black becomes transferred to the destructive religious world of white colonist settlers, but with the poignant twist of being linked to a nominally good object – the Bible; however, there is a harsh transformation in the meaning of the colour as it assumes the ambiguities of a deceptive, white Christian religion. The good Bible is black, but the reality represented by its use is symbolized by a blackness that is socially stigmatized by those who use the Bible as a weapon. The imagery resonates with these complex meanings:

> The hillside is still wounded by the spire
> of the white meetinghouse, the Indian trail
> trickles down it like the brown blood of the whale
> in rowanberries bubbling like the spoor
> on logs burnt black as Bibles by hellfire.
> ('Old New England', p. 3)

Images and ideas are orchestrated to create a mood of tragedy where violence is directed against the victimized, whether it is the whale, the hunted Indian or the masses of native dwellers harpooned to death by the cruelties of organized religion. Added to this list of victims, in a different though strangely related context, are the 'farm boys back from "Nam"' (l. 7), called at the end of the poem 'our sons home from the East' (l. 33), whom 'the black clippers brought (knotting each shroud round the cross-trees)' (ll. 32, 33). This whole process is ethically rationalized in the consciences of the Old New Englander with the reassurance 'that God is meek but keeps a whistling sword' (ll. 27–8).

'Old New England' is a name that captures all the ironic contrasts and ambiguities of colonialist history: geographically, the ship moves along the coastline of a supposedly independent America, but the names of each port of call recall the cities of the original centre of British colonization: 'New London, New Haven and New Bedford' (l. 2). With this older view of foreign dominance comes all memories of the repeated moments of peaceful contact yielding to bloody belligerence. Hence, the 'spring wind startles an uproar of marching oaks with memories of war' (l. 11). Memory is awakened by the cyclical forces of nature and time. The spring wind suggests the beginning of a new season of life, but that expectation is reversed by the realities of violent warfare and death. By this means, time becomes an annihilating force, using the past to erase the present and leaving the evidence of this obliteration on the landscape by peeling whole counties from the calendar (l. 12). For Walcott, although memory can be awakened, it, like history, inevitably goes through a process of obliteration. In Walcott's play *Remembrance* (1980), Jordan, who sounds like an alter ego of the playwright, emphasizes this principle when he speaks of his son Frederick: 'erase history from your mind and make it your own ... history, gossip, rumor, and what people go say? Blank it out!'[15] This action, however, is paradoxically counterbalanced by remembering the dead 'arranged in your memory, grave after grave, like empty desks in a classroom' (p. 86). The artistic concern with fame and perpetuity that is affected by this paradoxical process can nevertheless be satisfied: 'It doesn't matter where you born, how obscure you are, ... fame and fortune are contained within you. Your body is the earth in which it springs and dies.'[16] Accordingly, we ourselves become the living monuments and receptacles of the dead past and the glorious future.

Moreover in *The Fortunate Traveller*, there are other dualities. Within this environment, the painful ambiguity of the apparently peaceful church spire which reaches into celestial space seems to contrast forcefully with a rocket which 'pierces heaven' (l. 4); but the reader is compelled, like a Metaphysical poet (a breed Walcott greatly admired),[17] to yoke the image of peace violently together with images of hostile destruction, for the spire 'whistles into space' not only 'like a swordfish' (l. 4), but like a rocket. The ambitious thrusts of religion are still linked together with instruments of violence, only now they are augmented by the advancements of technology. The reader witnesses in this process a deconstructive pattern of images collapsing into similarity as an expression of the artistic sensitivities of the poet; these sensitivities are also shaped and activated by the racial memories of a past filled with the dividedness of what may be known as 'the commonwealth experience' portrayed so poignantly by the arrivants of Brathwaite's trilogy. Walcott's Traveller, on the surface of things, is not Brathwaite's Arrivant, but despite Walcott's claim that 'history cannot be ambiguously recorded',[18] we see a tortuous ambiguity underlying the powerful language of his poem.

In the four remaining poems of the first section of *The Fortunate Traveller*, the persona becomes more clearly defined as the first-person pronoun appears for the first time, providing distinguishing features for the speaker. At this point, it is not that Walcott's 'descriptive discipline relents', as Calvin Bedient claims,[19] but that it becomes intensely honest as the persona confesses his inner insecurities before a new and yet strangely familiar cultural environment. The initial sentiment expressed is linked with the artistic impulse: 'Sometimes I feel sometimes / the Muse is leaving, the muse is leaving America' (ll. 13, 14). In direct conflict with this impulse is the attraction to America: 'I am falling in love with America' (p. 6). Compounding the difficulty is the process of cultural acceptance and the thwarted linguistic confusion which Walcott frequently accentuates as a theme of his poetry: 'I must put cold small pebbles from the spring / upon my tongue to learn her language' (p. 6). The experience of adapting linguistically is further complicated by the ancient and contemporary associations of geographical names and the histories which both differentiate and identify them. The Carthage of America triggers rich ancient associations with the African city by the same name and in particular with Cato's ominous words, *Delenda est Carthago* ('Carthage must be destroyed') (p. 11). The ambiguities of ancient and modern history become a veritable montage of names and places which transcend time and location, bringing together Caribbean, American, Greek, African and Middle Eastern recollections. All of these particulars are integrated in the poet's imagination under the counterpointed title 'North and South'.

As McCorkle indicates, 'travelling and mapping' are a process 'where history becomes the knowledge only place can give'. Based on this perspective of history the opening lines of 'North and South' 'state an ambivalence about the very act of naming' places.[20] Moreover, as the journey continues, the vision of the traveller encompasses divergent territory which develops into a Dantean world made from the stuff of Walcott's literary journeys through the great classics of Western Civilization and his real-life travel through memorable spots near island retreats. The poet magically merges inner and outer landscapes as part of his own dual perspective so that snorkeling over the sunken mythical island of Atlantis, travelling like a tourist in Tobago by a glass-bottomed boat to Buccoo Reef and going through the streets of Manhattan are easily integrated with 'the white glare / of the white rose of [Dante's] inferno':

> to snorkel over Atlantis, to see, through a mask,
> Sidon up to its windows in sand, Tyre, Alexandria,
> with their wavering seaweed spires through a glassbottom boat,
> and to buy porous fragments of the Parthenon
> from a fisherman in Tobago, but the fear exists,
> *Delenda est Carthago* on the rose horizon,
>
> and the streets of Manhattan are sown with salt,
> and those in the North all wait for that white glare
> of the white rose of inferno, all the world's capitals.
>
> ('North and South', p. 11)

By collapsing time and place in this way Walcott demonstrates the difficulty of trying 'to compute' what he calls 'the collage of a closing century' (p. 9). He believes 'there is no history, only the history of emotion.'[21] The sense of disorientation which affects the traveller also overtakes the poet and the reader here. 'The mania / of history veils even the clearest air' (p. 14). Language becomes a coiled snake, producing 'paranoid anxiety' (pp. 14, 15); there is a shameful sense of colonialist self-deprecation: 'I accept my function as a colonial upstart at the end of an empire, / a single circling homeless satellite' (p. 11). Exile is a strong sentiment as well: 'I am thinking of an exile farther than any country', and the present environment becomes 'this heart of darkness' (p. 12). The traveller finally identifies with the persecuted fugitive, the Jews of the Diaspora (p. 15) and with the monkey:

> I collect my change from a small-town pharmacy,
> the cashier's fingertips still wince from my hand
> as if it would singe hers – well yes, *je suis un singe*,
> I am one of that tribe of frenetic or melancholy
> primates who made your music for many more moons
> than all the silver quarters in the till.
>
> ('North and South', p. 16)

The monkey as a symbol for Walcott has been explored with complexity in *Dream on Monkey Mountain*, but in his essay on 'What the Twilight Says', the tense ambiguity of the symbol emerges. On one side the mimic quality of the monkey brings human beings into a darkness which is total, but the journey back to the ape is necessary for the artist-actor to articulate his origins. Walcott explains this ambiguous situation of entrapment:

> The noblest are those who are trapped, who have accepted the twilight. If I see these as heroes it is because they have kept the sacred urge of actors everywhere: to record the anguish of the race. To do this, they must return through a darkness whose terminus is amnesia. The darkness which yawns before them is terrifying. It is the journey back from man to ape. Every actor must make this journey to articulate his origins, but for these who have been called not men but mimics, the darkness must be total, and the cave should not contain a single man-made mnemonic object.[22]

For poet then, as for persona, being a monkey is a state of double anguish, one dimension fulfils the demands of our origins, the other the mimetic function of being an artist.

The poems of 'South', the middle section of *The Fortunate Traveller*, develop the same patterns of ambiguity already noticed in 'North'. The complexity of the patterns, however, is increased by paradoxical intepretations of movement, process and time. Space prevents detailed treatment or elaboration here. Walcott juxtaposes the following contending dualities: movement and stasis: 'the tanker that seems still is moving' (p. 38); downward collapse and upward dominance: the fall of the natives' gods, the traditional order, before the ascendancy of the intruder's God:

> Huracan
> You scream like a man whose wife is dead,
> like a god who has lost his race,
> you yank the electric wires with wet hands.
> ('Hurucan', p. 42)

To this suicidal image of fallen deity Walcott adds the ironic contradictions of termination and continuity: 'I decompose, but I composing still' (p. 53). This paradox was introduced in the first section in the poem 'Piano Practice', in the lines: 'perhaps the *fin de siècle* isn't really finished, / maybe there's a piano playing it somewhere' (p. 10). Walcott is well aware of these playful patterns of representing time, both in its linearity and circularity. Both are controlling reflections of 'that tired artifice called history' (p. 38). Moreover, the direction portrayed is linearity which signifies futility; for example, 'The shark racing the shadow of the shark' (p. 54). The pattern may also be circularity which reflects meaninglessness:

> ... my premonition of the scene
> of what passing over this Caribbean.
> Is crab climbing crab-back, in a crab-quarrel,
> and going round and round in the same barrel.
> ('The Spoiler's Return', p. 54)

What exceeds all of this interplay of patterns and this complex network of tensions is Walcott's contrast of tones expressed in the superlative piece of satire among the pieces of the middle section of *The Fortunate Traveller* – 'The Spoiler's Return'. Walcott achieves these contrasts by juxtaposing the formal tone of the three opening lines of Lord Rochester's *The Satire Against Mankind* (1675) with the humorously mocking attitude of Spoiler's calypso on 'The Bedbug' (p. 54), a composition sung originally by a popular Trinidadian calypsonian. In addition, Walcott employs the voice of lament through a parody of Naipaul: 'I see these islands and I feel to bawl, / "area of darkness" with V. S. Nightfall' (p. 54). Tonal shifts are also accomplished through intermittent use of local Trinidad dialect organized according to calypso verbal rhythms: ' "Things ain't go change, they ain't go change at all,"/ to my old chorus: "Lord, I want to bawl" ' (p. 59). Walcott also changes the tone from this semi-humorous sense of light complaint to a tone of satirical lamentation close to that of a Jeremiad or to Robert Burton's passionate but parodic address to the reader in *The Anatomy of Melancholy*. These tonal shifts through an intertextual mingling of literary and oral voices are rooted in the artistic psyche of Walcott, the 'divided child' and 'cultural schizophrenic'.

The middle section concludes with a strong Naipaulian mood which leaves the traveller envying 'the octopus with ink for blood' (p. 83), and becoming a 'mackerel that leap[s] from its element, / trying to be different – ... / married to nothing' (p. 82). Although the outlook is pessimistic here, it is important to remember that for Walcott there is a need at times to regress to nothing as the source of creativity. According to him, 'If there was nothing, there was everything to be made.'[23] As Figueroa concludes, speaking of Walcott's preoccupation with nothing in *Another Life*, 'nothing' is not preoccupation with vacuity but with the concept of 'unhistoricity' applied to the Anglophone Caribbean. 'Nothing' is at once a comment on traditional views and a search for identity based on self-knowledge and real knowledge of history, which 'rejects acceptance of doctrinaire concepts'.[24]

The third and final section of *The Fortunate Traveller* (also 'North') broadens from the narrower canvas of temporal history explored in earlier sections to a timeless apocalyptic world, which is dramatically introduced by a quotation from the book of Revelation describing the advent of famine during the Tribulation period of the end times. The Christian prophetic calendar thus frames the events of colonial history in a future context to show the coalescence and culmination of the cruelties of the past and those of the present age. This cruel environment surrounds a painful but profitable pilgrimage in which the traveller must eventually come to accept the 'twilight' of contradictory and ambivalent experiences as a necessary birthplace for renewed creativity, self-enactment and self-discovery. As Lane argues, Walcott's confrontation with the world results in despair but eventually leads to a renewal which celebrates the power of art and language.[25]

Caught in this Janus-faced environment, the traveller experiences a schizoid perspective of himself and his world. This condition is mirrored in his use of personal pronouns as he moves back and forth from a singular 'I' to a collective 'we': 'I crossed the canal', ... 'I sat on a cold bench', ... 'I remember / a gekko', ... 'We are roaches', ... 'we are the first / to scuttle ... / back to Geneva, Bonn, Washington, London' (pp. 88–90). This collective focus then returns to the personal: 'I cannot bear to watch the nations cry,' and 'I was rehearsing the ecstasies of starvation,' and 'I found my pity, desperately researching / the origins of history' (pp. 90, 91). But this personal emphasis shifts again when the traveller describes himself collectively as 'we savages'; then he returns to a singular focus with 'I envisaged an Africa flooded with ... light' (p. 92). This rapid shifting from an individual to a collective self reflects a self-division which pushes the traveller to search for wholeness of being by 'seeking in all races a common ingenuity' (p. 91). The quest however comes to a powerfully disillusioning conclusion, as is poignantly revealed in the closing verse paragraphs of the title piece 'The Fortunate Traveller'.

The chilling irony of the adjective 'Fortunate' is brought home effectively in the following lines which are recollected as a fragment of dialogue, as the traveller leaves England by sea, having received an 'Iscariot's salary': 'You are so fortunate, you get to see the world – .' The reply, 'Indeed, indeed, sirs, I have seen the world' (p. 92) is weighted with trenchant irony and ambiguity. The meanings are multidirectional in their forcefulness: he has seen the world, but its cataclysmic human tragedies do not make the experience gratifying; if he is fortunate, it is only in the sense that he is not one of the victims, but racial memory may contradict this feeling; he has paid the price to be fortunate – received 'Iscariot's salary', the price of blood. Further, he has seen the world, but the outcome is only a blurred vision ironically underscored by the descriptive line that follows his reply: 'Spray splashes the portholes and vision blurs' (p. 92).

The return to the islands is further marked by a tormented ambivalence as he becomes another Marlow who has peered into the heart of darkness. But unlike Marlow's European capital city of Brussels, the Caribbean setting is the agricultural peasant world of the Africa Kurtz had exploited. Dew is 'on the elephant ears of the dasheen. / Through Kurtz's teeth, white skull in elephant grass' the 'imperial fiction' still sings (p. 93):

> The heart of darkness is not Africa.
> The heart of darkness is the core of fire
> in the white centre of the holocaust.
> The heart of darkness is the rubber claw
> selecting a scalpel in antiseptic light ...
> (*The Fortunate Traveller*, pp. 93, 94)

The forceful transposition of white and black images, with the former given the stereotypic meaning of the latter, recalls the first poem of the collection and brings to full circle the gnawing concern of poet and quester, that the new is merely the old in another form. The truth forces home Walcott's problem with history – it contains in its process an unrelenting determinism which universalizes all particulars, repeats all pasts, confounds all rationales, cancels all conclusions and makes all attempts at closure the seedbed of new beginnings. At every stage of the timeline of history the stream of memory bifurcates in backward and forward movements.

In 'The Season of Phantasmal Peace', the concluding piece of the last section of *The Fortunate Traveller*, the forward movement of the stream of history brings a predictable outcome. This poem is an appropriate climax to a dramatic portrayal of divided pilgrimage; the piece is rightly hailed by one reviewer as 'the best poem in [the] collection'.[26] The third horseman of the apocalypse (the Black horse which symbolizes famine [Revelations 6. 5]) ushers in an age where 'the drawn sword comes in strides' (p. 97). The atmosphere is created in part by absences and presences: love is absent, as we learn from the repeated phrase from 1 Corinthians 13 – 'and have not charity' (p. 97); God is absent; for in the third section of the poem we learn that 'God is dead' (p. 95); time is absent: 'there was no longer dusk, or season, decline of weather' (p. 98). Light is however present, but it is a 'phantasmal light / that not the narrowest shadow dared to sever' (p. 98); there is battle, but paradoxically, it is one in which 'starlings [are] waging peaceful cries' (p. 98); the nations like birds were present with their 'multitudinous dialects and twittering tongues' (p. 98).

More significant than the dualities of absence and presence is the ambiguous merging of light and darkness as a pervasive pattern among the images of this final poem. Following the 'passage of phantasmal light' is the 'icy sunlight'; then there is 'the light / that you will see at evening / in yellow October'. Ultimately, as the poem ends there are 'falling suns' and a seasonal pause between 'dusk and darkness, between fury and peace'. We are however told that this environment is 'as our earth is now, it lasted long' (p. 99). The ambiguity is pervasive here at the very end as well, as the statements in Derridean manner keep undermining their own truths. If the season 'lasted one moment' like a pause, how can it also last long? If the phantasmal light cannot be severed by the narrowest shadow, how can there be dusk and darkness? In fact we were told 'there was no longer dusk' (p. 98). If this is the apocalyptic future, how are things the same as 'our earth is now'? These colliding questions make up the tormenting world of the colonial; it is an inner and outer world of 'fury and peace', but this peace is a phantasmal peace, tangible only in a deceptive way, and quite unsubstantial. Walcott provides some insight into this predicament, which is his as well as his colonialist traveller:

> Colonials, we ... had the theatre of our lives. So the self-inflicted role of martyr came naturally, the melodramatic belief that one was a message-bearer for the millennium, that the inflamed ego was enacting their will. In that simple schizophrenic boyhood one could lead two lives: the interior life of poetry, the outward life of action and dialect.[27]

Accordingly, the action and language of life are captured ambiguously in Walcott's poem, and although he does not see himself as a message-bearer of the millennium, he turns out to be so behind the mask of the central personage of *The Fortunate Traveller*.

There is, however, from this position a sense of light as a motionless point where creative insight is reborn and there is the gift to see things as they are, 'halved by darkness'. The closing lines of 'A Map of Europe' depict this condition of things:

> The light creates its stillness. In its ring
> Everything IS. A cracked coffee cup
> A broken loaf, a dented urn become
> More than themselves, their SELVES, as in Chardin,
> Or in beer-bright Vermeer, Not objects of our pity.
>
> Within it is no *lacrimae rerum*
> No art. Only the gift
> To see things as they are, halved by darkness
> From which they cannot shift.[28]

From this backdrop, the twilight atmosphere of the concluding poem of *The Fortunate Traveller* can be understood with reference to Walcott's metaphysical vision and, in a political sense, to his comments on the figurative use of twilight which 'became a metaphor for withdrawal of Empire and the beginning of our doubt'.[29] This state creates in the artist a dusk-like vision of things:

> ... at every dusk one ignites a city in the mind above the same sad fences where the poor revolve, the theatre still an architectural fantasy, if there is still nothing around us, darkness still preserves the awe of self-enactment as the sect gathers for its self-extinguishing, self-discovering rites.[30]

This emphasis on dusk and twilight as a place of discovery and the starting point of birth and creativity is echoed in the first chapter of *Another Life*, where Walcott asserts that we must 'begin with twilight', a 'twilight eager to complete itself'.[31] This environment is appropriate to beginning life *in medias res*, a process through which a 'divided child' develops into a poet.

Walcott advances to a more succinct conclusion: 'the noblest are those who are trapped, who have accepted the twilight.' The fortunate traveller in this sense is a trapped hero for Walcott, who, as artist, has kept the sacred urge 'to record the anguish of the race'.[32]

From *Ariel: A Review of International English Literature,* 20: 3 (July 1989), 55–71.

NOTES

[Clement Wyke's essay combines psychoanalytical criticism and a new historicist approach in what is an articulate intertextual analysis of the mapping of an old/new world and the tensions at play in Derek Walcott's writings. Eds]

1. Derek Walcott, 'His is the Pivotal One About Race', *Trinidad Guardian*, 1 Dec. 1963, p. 23.

2. James T. Livingston (ed.), *Caribbean Rhythms* (New York, 1974), p. 208.

3. Gordon Rohlehr, ' "This Past I Borrowed" ... : Time, History, and Art in Brathwaite's Masks', *Caribbean Studies*, 17 (1977), 10.

4. Derek Walcott, *Collected Poems* (New York, 1986), p. 86.

5. Derek Walcott, 'Some West Indian Poets', *London Magazine*, 5 (1965), 15–30; cited in Robert Hamner, 'Derek Walcott: his Works and his Critics: An Annotated Bibliography, 1947–80', *Journal of Commonwealth Literature*, 16 (1981), 156.

6. Mervyn Morris, 'Derek Walcott' in *West Indian Literature* (London, 1979), ed. Bruce King, p. 145.

7. Derek Walcott, *The Fortunate Traveller* (London, 1982), p. 99. References to this poem are given in parentheses in the essay.

8. Derek Walcott, *Midsummer* (London, 1984), XXVII, p. 50.

9. Derek Walcott, *The Gulf and Other Poems*, 1969 (London, 1974), 'Moon', Metamorphoses, p. 12.

10. Walcott, *Midsummer*, p. 70.

11. Ibid.

12. Derek Walcott, *Dream on Monkey Mountain and Other Plays* (New York, 1970), p. 32.

13. Thomas Nashe, *The Unfortunate Traveller* in *Tudor Poetry and Prose* sel. and ed. J. W. Hebel et al. (New York, 1953), p. 966.

14. Ibid.

15. Derek Walcott, *Remembrance* and *Pantomime* (New York, 1980), p. 75.

16. Ibid., p. 86.

17. Dennis Jones, 'Derek Walcott', *Dictionary of Literary Biography Yearbook*, ed. Karen Rood et al. (Detroit, 1982), p. 273.

18. Derek Walcott, 'The Muse of History', in O. Coombers (ed.), *Is Massa Day Dead?* (New York, 1974), p. 11.

19. Calvin Bedient, 'Derek Walcott, Contemporary', *Parnassus*, 9: 2 (Fall/Winter, 1981), 32.

20. James McCorkle, 'Re-Mapping the New World: The Recent Poetry of Derek Walcott', *Ariel*, 17: 2 (1986), 3, 4.

21. Derek Walcott, 'What the Twilight Says: An Overture', in *Dream on Monkey Mountain and Other Plays* (New York, 1970), p. 5.

22. Ibid.

23. Ibid., p. 4.

24. John Figueroa, 'A Note on Derek Walcott's Concern with Nothing', *Revista/Review of Interamericana*, 4: 3 (1974), 422–8.

25. Travis M. Lane, 'A Different "Growth of a Poet's Mind": Derek Walcott's *Another Life*', *Ariel*, 9: 4 (1978), 65–78.

26. Helen Vendler, 'Poet of Two Worlds', Review of *The Fortunate Traveller*, by Derek Walcott, *The New York Review of Books*, 4 March 1982, p. 26.

27. 'What the Twilight Says' in *Dream on Monkey Mountain*, p. 4.

28. Derek Walcott, *Selected Poems* (New York, 1964), p. 79.

29. 'What the Twilight Says', in *Dream on Monkey Mountain*, p. 4.

30. Ibid., pp. 4, 5.

31. Derek Walcott, *Another Life* (New York: Farrar, 1972), pp. 3, 4.

32. 'What the Twilight Says', in *Dream on Monkey Mountain*, p. 5.

12

Cultural Imperatives in Derek Walcott's *Dream on Monkey Mountain*

DAIZAL R. SAMAD

To Derek Walcott in 'What the Twilight Says', the West Indies is a splintered stage upon which the discontinuous lines of culture have become contaminated, itemized, and commercialized on the altar of politics and tourism:

> Every state sees its image in these forms which have the mass appeal of sport, seasonal and amateurish. Stamped on that image is the old colonial grimace of the laughing nigger, steelbandsman, carnival masker, calypsonian and limbo dancer ... the folk arts have become the symbol of a carefree accommodating culture, an adjunct to tourism, since the state is impatient with anything it cannot trade.[1]

Even here, then, in densities of the folk, there is no exemption from contamination. Again, the West Indian is being manipulated to enact the role that has been assigned him by other 'cultures' through the ages, a role which he has uncritically assumed. The West Indian has become a 'mimic man'. The result is escape into hallucinations in which home is constructed on some dubious model outside the cultural/actual landscape of the West Indies. In this sense, the West Indian's gaze 'is filmed with hope of departure'[2] either to North America, Europe, Asia or Africa.

For Walcott, the search for home involves a profound quest for the Word, in much the same way that Wole Soyinka's Professor in

The Road (1965) searches for the Word.[3] But Walcott goes even further back along the corridors of time, towards that dark prehistoric place where man was ape, where 'the voice must grovel in search of itself, until gesture and sound fuse and the blaze of their flesh astonishes them.'[4] With this return to the origins of language and being, the West Indian may dramatize his authentic role as a New World Adam, a role plagued and blessed with a paradoxical joy and anguish.

The enactment of self as heterogeneous entity upon the landscape of home should be done with a realization of the problems which constantly emerge to address those who live in a 'mixed' milieu like the West Indies. Certainly, one of the most important of these dilemmas is the need to find some social/cultural/artistic model which would elicit the participation of the heterogeneous aspects of the region. The West Indian may then stand upon a 'ground of hiatus' and be released from the consolidated postures and anxieties which debilitate and plague the individual and social consciousnesses of the people. The need is for participation and release in order that we may achieve a sense of self and community and exorcize the demon of alienation and homelessness.

Derek Walcott's plays address themselves to this problem and his particular striving is for some imaginative archetype that will encompass the multiplicity of paradoxes that plague this anxiety-ridden age of ours, and that will involve or afford a vision of reconciliation and reconstruction.

Home for Derek Walcott involves beheading the illusions of belonging offered by authoritarian models; it involves the invocation of the sleeping spirits that lay within the actual and metaphorical archipelagal landscape of the West Indies. A sense of self and a home for that self, suggests Walcott, depend upon a resolution within the West Indian's schizoid consciousness and upon a restatement or a redramatization of the history of humanity in which hackneyed schisms between 'religious' evolution and 'Darwinian' evolution reveal themselves as partial statements which may be imaginatively, if unpredictably, resolved.[5] Arriving out of this necessarily powerful grope come new fusions and applications of archetypes and myths to the birth/ death/ rebirth of the Caribbean person; archetypes, myths and legends pertaining to processes of birth, death and rebirth are allowed intimate intercourse with the muse of the Caribbean.

Dream on Monkey Mountain, begun while Walcott was in the United States in 1959, attempts a fusion of those traditionally conflicting elements which have resulted in a sense of disorientation and homelessness. The traditions of Europe and Africa, for instance, enacted a psychic tug-of-war in the consciousness of the West Indian; it is this inner conflict which elicits Walcott's painful query in 'A Far Cry from Africa':

> I who am poisoned with the blood of both
> Where shall I turn, divided to the vein?[6]

This dichotomy is the legacy of the history of the region, and it results in the dangerous illusion within the West Indian sensibility that home lies in any direction away from the region. But to give up any of the other 'wholenesses' so necessary for reintegration would be to deny essential fragments of the splintered stage upon which a sense of home may be constructed in the West Indies itself. In *Dream on Monkey Mountain*, the central character, Makak, attempts to rediscover the discontinuous links between the multiplicity of archetypes that reside in the oceanic layers of West Indian culture.

The stage setting at the beginning of the play itself tends toward a fusion of dualities of principles and traditions:

> *A spotlight warms the disc of an African drum until it glows like the round moon above it. Below the moon is the stark silhouette of a volcanic mountain. Reversed, the moon becomes the sun.*
>
> (p. 212)

The face of the firmly planted African drum reaches up to reflectively associate itself with the celestial moon. At the same time, this traditionally feminine symbol, reversed, becomes the traditional male-oriented sun. Because the symbol of the moon in Walcott's work often suggests Whiteness and therefore Europe, the implications are that the traditional African symbol of the drum is addressed by other ethno-cultural densities which contain both male and female possibilites. There is yet another symbol – that of the volcanic mountain – a jutting pre-ejaculatory phallic symbol. Also in the Prologue, there appears the trickster figure of Ananse whose form is composed of the dancer and a character 'like the figure of Baron Samedi'. Makak's dream, then, is set amidst a combination of potentially fertile images and contrasting perspectives.

The play begins with Tigre and Souris in one cell and Makak in the other, the three presided over by Corporal Lestrade. Makak has been arrested for 'mashing up' Alcindor's Cafe. Lestrade, a mulatto, is as split as Makak himself; he is presented as the worst possible kind of extreme: a self-deluded representative of law and order, doing the 'white people work', and condemning the Blacks as 'animals, beasts, savages, cannibals, niggers' whom he sees as dedicated to the task of 'turning this place into a stinking zoo' (p. 216). Makak's responses to Lestrade's formal queries indicate, through their ironic implication, that the former is nameless, belongs to a tired race, and takes as his religion, Roman Catholicism.

Both Tigre and Souris oscillate between slight sympathy for Makak and flattery toward Lestrade; by playing one against the other, they seek to satisfy their need for sensationalism. Responding to flattery, Lestrade dons the garments of justice, its superfluous trappings. Souris and Tigre tell him to put on the wig and gown, and he responds with: 'I can both accuse and defend this man' (p. 220). As he launches into his prosecution/defence, Lestrade reveals his tragic/humorous misuse of language: the Word itself has become eclipsed, ineffectual. Significantly, Makak at this stage is silent; he is not a party to the slaughter of language. Lestrade says:

> I will spare you the sound of that voice which have come from a cave of darkness, dripping with horror, these hands are the hands of Esau, the fingers are like roots, the arteries as hard as twine, and the palms seamed with coal. But the animal, you observe, is tamed and obedient.
>
> (p. 222)

Although Lestrade is unaware of this, he is stressing the organic, elemental, recreative force that Makak embodies. In his first long speech, Makak tells about his isolation and degradation;

> Is thirty years now I have look in no mirror,
> Not a pool of cold water, when I must drink,
> I stir my hands first, to break up my image.
> (p. 226)

The speech indicates that Makak refuses to confront the nature of his human image not only because he is Black and thinks himself ugly, but also because he cannot confront what he really is – fragmented and eclipsed. But, paradoxically, he is true to himself at the same time – true to the fragmentation, the breaking up of a human image.

As Makak recalls his dream, he invokes a mystical setting in the minds of his audience that reiterates the dualities that are implicit in the initial backdrop. The environ of Monkey Mountain itself assumes animate proportions, wrapping Makak in a Madonna-like, vapour-like embrace and gives birth to him at the moment he sees the spectral White woman. But the image of birth works inversely too, for the 'manscape' of Makak's consciousness also gives birth to the woman: Europe 'discovers' the West Indies, and the child constantly gives birth to the mother:

> As I brush through the branches, shaking the dew,
> A man swimming through smoke,
> And the bandage of smoke unpeeling my eyes,
> As I reach to this spot,
> I see the woman singing
> And my feet grow roots. I could move no more.
> A million silver needles prickle my blood
> Like a rain of small fishes.
> The snakes in my hair speak to one another
> The smoke mouth open, and I behold this woman
> The loveliest thing I see on this earth
> Like the moon walking along her own road.
>
> (p. 227)

Either way, there is something sinister in this rebirth and the images of birth are fairly obvious – because the 'feet growing roots', while positive in terms of rootedness, is qualifed by that statement of stasis: 'I could move no more.' Also, there is the image of the small fishes – a sinister pirannah-like image of self-annihilation; but this fear is counterpoised by a certain passion. Moreover, one cannot ignore the reference to Medusa, the snake-haired Gorgon of Greek mythology; yet, this may be a reference to the hair of the Black man, an unconscious echo of the very image which Makak attempts to deny by stirring the water. His use of the superlative to describe the woman's beauty points to Makak's illusion that this is a vision of implacable identity; and this is strengthened by his perception of her as being 'like the moon walking along her own road', which is certainly a static image that assumes the illusion of dynamic tension. The moon, feminine, impermanent, cannot stand or walk on her own road and come into fertile dialogue with herself. She is, in actual fact, what Makak points to in the prison, 'nothing'. Yet this illusion is real in the sense that Makak's obsession is a real one: the West Indian's obsession with Whiteness and Europe. Ironically, Lestrade, Souris and Tigre see this:

> **Corporal**   I can see nothing. (*To the judges*)
>   What do you see?
> **Judges**   Nothing. Nothing.
>
> (p. 228)

Lestrade's summing up of the vision as an insane one is derogatory: 'Is this rage for whiteness that does drive niggers mad.' While the statement does have obvious sexual connotations, there is a deeper psychological truth which involves the Europeanization of the West Indian and the simultaneous submergence of the transplanted and transformed values and cultures of Africa. At the same time, 'nothing' expresses the need for creation: 'If there was nothing there was everything to be made.'[7]

Scene i shifts the action of the play to Monkey Mountain itself, as Makak recollectively introduces the figure of the 'practical realist' Moustique, the character that offers balance to Makak's fantasy. The parasitic Moustique ('mosquito' or 'flea')[8] is necessary in every sense: the mosquito has its place in the biological, ecological hierarchy of things; and Moustique helps keep Makak grounded in the practical world. However, Moustique's tendency towards extreme materialism is a dangerous one:

> **Makak**   I going mad, Moustique.
> **Moustique**   Going Mad? Go mad tomorrow, today is market day. We have three bags at three-and-six a bag, making ten shillings and sixpence for the week and you going mad?
>
> (p. 232)

There is a further frightening thing about Moustique. He is described as 'a little man with a limp', and he himself speaks of 'this twist foot God give me'. The anatomy of Satan has often been recorded in the 'Pan-ic' terms: 'Often He (Satan) has been described as limping, a symbol of impotence, according to some writers, and He is frequently black in colour.'[9]

Now a strange thing is occurring here: if, as Diana Lyn says, Walcott creates a 'universal situation' (her argument stems from

Lestrade's 'In the beginning was the ape, and the ape had no name, so God call him man'. She emphasizes, 'not black, not white but man'), then the figure of the Pan-like Moustique is incorporated into the consciousness of man.[10] This seems to come into direct conflict with Laurence Breiner's stipulation that the West Indian condition is 'Adamic, not Satanic'.[11] On one hand, Diana Lyn implicitly denies the importance of racial/cultural heterogeneity that is so central to *Dream on Monkey Mountain*; on the other hand, both Breiner and Lyn fall prey to that which Walcott warns against – the appeal of total, implacable models – the total model of Adam or Satan, the total model of God or the universe. Both critics ignore Walcott's vision of the West Indian as the expelled/admitted Adam who consists of a variety of partial elements. As Walcott himself puts it in 'The Sea is History':

> First there was heaving oil,
> heaving as chaos;
> Then, like the light at the end of a tunnel ...
> and that was Genesis.
> Then there were the packed cries,
> the shit, the moaning:
> Exodus.[12]

As well as being the expelled/admitted Adam, therefore, the genesis of the West Indian is compared with the exodus of Hebrews from Egypt, the Middle Passage to the journey across the desert. He arrives through the time and expanse of actual/ metaphorical sea and desert upon the Caribbean shores. In this sense Moustique is Makak's alter ego and it is Makak's compassion for him that allows them to live with each other. Moustique reminds the old man:

> You find me in the gutter, and you pick me up like a wet fly in the dust, and we establish in this charcoal business. You cut, burn and so on, and I sell, until we make enough to buy the donkey.

> (p. 233)

There is a bond of compassion between them, but this is undermined when Moustique abandons a fair commercial alliance for commercial exploitation. Now, as Makak recalls his vision of the woman about which he has already told Lestrade, Souris and Tigre (as he had told it to Moustique in the first place), there is an important addition: 'She call out my name, my real name. A name I do not use.' Because she is a figment of his imagination, 'a banana of his mind', she has access to deeply hidden facts about Makak:

> She did know my name, my age, where I born, and that it was charcoal I burn and selling for a living. She know how I live alone, with no wife and no friend ...
> **Moustique**   No friend ...
>
> (pp. 235–6)

The actor who plays Moustique would, of course, need to express the particular hurt that the little man must be feeling at his exclusion from Makak's emotional circle. It is important to see that Moustique, whether out of his curious perspective and insight or whether out of hurt, sees the spectral White woman as a 'diablesse'. There is, therefore, a poignant irony in Moustique's short soliloquy: 'The misery black people have to see in this life. ... A man not only suppose to catch his arse in the daytime but he have to ride nightmares too' (p. 238). The rest of the scene – indeed, the play itself – is a battle for the 'soul' of Makak by both 'devil' and 'diablesse'. She uses sexuality and an appeal to irrationality; he uses forceful practicality, cringing fear (of the spider) and tears, and appeals to the old man's compassion. Makak is being tempted into forming a relationship with either the fantastic or the materialistic. To establish this, though, he must allow one of them to 'possess' him fully. The danger is that should he yield to such temptations, Makak would be like a Christ/artist/Adam giving up his innocence, integrity, recreative potential, and fulfilling balance between the physical and spiritual. The West Indian would betray his own humanity.

The irony is, of course, that the White woman wishes to consolidate the romanticized vision he has of himself and Africa; Moustique wants him to compromise belief and truth for greed. Both invade – 'visit' – him on Monkey Mountain: one resides in the psychological realm, the other in the actual landscape.

Scene ii of *Dream on Monkey Mountain* shows Makak as a Jesus-like healer and Moustique as a Judas-like exploiter of the former's spiritual strength. Now, we are also introduced to the figure of Basil, the death-figure drawn from Haitian mythology.[13]

Moustique encounters a procession that is taking a dying man to the hospital. He joins in the prayers:

And give us this day our daily bread ... and is that self I want to
talk to you about, friend. Whether you could spare us a little bread ...
for thine is the Kingdom and the power and the glory ...
for our stomach sake, stranger.

(p. 244)

As much as this is comic, there is a serious element here because
Moustique points to the necessity of balancing spiritual food with
actual food, matters of the soul with bread and butter issues. He gets
his 'bread' (the pun here on money is unmistakable) and then brings
Makak to the scene. As Makak puts a living coal in his palm, 'a soul
in my hand', he invokes his own organic and spiritual beginnings:

Like the cedars of Lebanon,
like the plantains of Zion,
the hand of God plant me
on Monkey Mountain.
(p. 248)

From this spiritual height, he sees the rest in their homeless, rootless
state, 'like a twisted forest, / like trees with no roots', and encourages them to sing out of the depths of their historical anguish and
faith: 'Sing as you sing / in the belly of the boot.'

Makak eventually saves the sick Josephus and Moustique pro-
claims him God's messenger, and himself 'like St Peter self ...
Secretary Treasurer'. He then asks the people, as he opens his
haversack, to 'further the cause'. It is here that Moustique comes
into conflict with Basil, the overseeing death-figure. Also, out of the
argument between Moustique and Makak comes the realization
that the White apparition appeals to the woodcutter's sensuality as
well as to his psychological obsession with 'whiteness' and all that
that implies. The materialistic Moustique, on the other hand,
exploits Makak's spiritual power as well as their friendship in order
that his commercialism be gratified. Moustique is, in every sense,
dealing with death, and that is why Basil threatens him, 'We go
meet again, stranger' (p. 252).

Scene ii takes us back to the cells as Lestrade's recollection begins
to merge with and complement Makak's. Lestrade shows once
again that he has succumbed to the temptations of European postures and consequently has eclipsed a segment of his psychologi-
cal/cultural make-up. His concept of self and home resides in the
total and static mimicking of European concepts and biases and in

the denial of the Black aspect of his mulatto legacy. Fittingly adorned in wig and gown, he tells Souris and Tigre:

> This is our reward, we have borne the high torch of justice through darkness to illuminate with vision the mind of primeval peoples, of back-biting tribes. We who have borne with us the texts of the law, the Mosaic tablets, the splendour of marble in moonlight, the affidavit and the water toilet ...
>
> (p. 256)

There is a startling resemblance to Kurtz's sentiments in Joseph Conrad's *Heart of Darkness*: the colonizer sees himself as the bearer of the torch of civilization and salvation to the 'darkness' of Africa. Theodore Colson in his 'Derek Walcott's Plays: Outrage and Compassion' also sees this connection and deals with it in some detail.[14] As memory takes Lestrade strolling through the market-place, much like a supervising planter – he is armed, over-confident and comfortable in his knowledge of the suffering of the 'slaves' (he says of the vendors, 'they paralyse ... because they born slaves and they born tired') – he recalls the rumours of Makak's healing powers. Into this vision/recollection comes Moustique, equally over-articulate, similarly masquerading, but as the 'Abyssinian Lion', Makak.

Moustique unveils the official's nakedness by exposing the lie inherent in 'the colour of (his) English (which) is "white"', and which is spoken by the 'usual voice of small-time authority' (p. 267). The Corporal in turn exposes the fear and insecurity that lie behind Moustique's facade of over-confidence and power. As Moustique, in fear of the spider, drops the bowl, the Corporal loudly asks: 'A spider? A man who will bring you deliverance is afraid of a spider?' (p. 268). But it is Basil who ultimately exposes Moustique's deception to the people, that his 'tongue on fire, but the eyes are dead' (p. 269). In impotent anger, Moustique confesses a truth that is applicable to both himself and Lestrade: 'All that I have is this, black faces, white masks!' The crowd, incensed, beats Moustique while the Corporal, in fear and complacency, stands idly by. Makak enters as Moustique lies alone, dying amidst the spoils of his deceit. The little man confesses: 'I take what you had, I take the dream you have and I come and try to sell it. I try to fool them, and they fall on me with sticks, everything, and they kill me' (p. 273).

It is Makak's longing for self-respect, psychical wholeness, and a sense of home that makes him fantasize; and it is out of Moustique's confession that he is able to confront the materialist aspect of himself. Moustique's final advice reverberates with a portentous, prophesying ring: 'Go back, go back to Monkey Mountain. Go back.' But this advice is unheeded because the vision of the White woman dominates Makak's consciousness. Finally, Makak looks into the dead man's eye and sees there a vision that 'darkens his (own) vision', and he 'lets out a terrible cry of emptiness' (p. 274).

Clearly, Makak has seen the horrifying possibility of what he himself could become should this aspect of self be allowed to dominate – 'nothing', a profound zero. Ironically, Moustique had told him earlier, 'You is nothing ... man together two of us is minus one' (p. 270); Basil had earlier told Moustique, 'I want nothing, partner' (p. 237). Death needs life to gratify its womb, and the sum total of Moustique's life is nothing. But Moustique is the materialistic aspect of Makak, which, extreme and untempered, becomes a sinister, devilish thing: the vision of life itself culminating in a sum total of nothing is a terrifying thought, and so Makak, though brave enough to confront it, screams out of the depths of self. In this sense, Moustique is a Black reflection of the 'nothing' that is the White apparition. These are both symbolic ghosts of the past that haunt the West Indian, leaving him a flesh-coated void.

This psychic tug-of-war which these two worlds of Black and White, Africa and Europe, play on Makak's consciousness is starkly mentioned in the quotation from Frantz Fanon's *The Wretched of the Earth* that Walcott uses to introduce part two of *Dream on Monkey Mountain*: 'Two worlds; that makes two bewitchings; they dance all night and at dawn they crowd into the churches to hear mass; each day the split widens ...' (p. 277).

Walcott follows Fanon's cue and shows that either choice would inevitably result in a denial of self, because both invest in the consolidation of a sense of cultural and psychological emptiness rather than in the reintegration and fulfilment of self. Initially, Lestrade mimics the values and attitudes of White colonizers; simultaneously, the ghostly White woman tempts Makak to choose a romanticized, illusory vision of his African heritage. With Lestrade, it amounts to a horrifying cultivation of hubris. When Makak offers him money, the Corporal screams hysterically:

I am incorruptible, you understand? Incorruptible. The law is your salvation and mine, you imbecile, you understand that. This ain't the bush. This ain't Africa. This is not another easy-going nigger you talking to, but an officer. A servant and an officer of the law! Not the law of the jungle, but something the white man teach you to be thankful for.

(p. 280)

Lestrade believes that his salvation and home lie in the White world. He tells the thieves, 'Remind me to ask for a transfer to civilization' – a definite reference to the departure syndrome that plagues the West Indies. Tigre sums Lestrade up like this:

Corporal Lestrade, the straddler, neither one thing nor the next, neither milk nor coal, neither day nor night, neither lion nor monkey, but a mulatto, a foot-licking servant of marble law.

(p. 283)

This, curiously, might apply to Makak as well, whose very consciousness is split, mulatto. Tigre, on hearing that Makak has money hidden away, also attempts to exploit the tormented old man. His plan is to get Makak to break them out of jail and have him show where the money is hidden on Monkey Mountain. Incensed by Tigre, Makak stabs Lestrade and says in horror and frustration: 'O God, O gods! What am I, I who thought I was a man? What have I done? ... Christian, cannibal, I will drink blood. You will drink with me' (p. 286). The reference to the Christian ceremony is clear;[15] but there is another level of reference, for the communion comes into symbolic coincidence with 'jungle law'. Both involve the ritual drinking of 'blood', both satiate a certain kind of hunger, and both presuppose a certain freedom. But it is important to see that the 'killing' of Lestrade springs not from a ritual concept of sacrifice, but from the selfish motivation of revenge and profit.

Nevertheless, in the break-out from prison Lestrade is only injured, and his words as he plucks the knife from his shoulder are at once ironically prophetic and true to his peculiar complex. He sees that he must play 'another part'. This implies his self-imposed role as descendant of the White slave master who often appears in the history books as hunter of runaway slaves (the hunting of the Maroons of Jamaica, for instance); but 'another part' also carries an underlying meaning which foreshadows his change in the rest of the play. His sentiments echo, with frightening precision, the final words of Kurtz's manifesto in Conrad's *Heart of Darkness:* 'Exterminate all the brutes!'[16] Lestrade says:

> There's nothing quite so exciting as putting down the natives. Especially after reason and law have failed. So I let them escape ... I'll have good reason for shooting them down .... Attempting to escape the prison of their lives. That's the most dangerous crime. It brings about revolution.
>
> (p. 286)

He fails to see that the tyrant who dehumanizes is involved in a complex self-degradation: the enslavement and persecution of any people engenders in the human race itself a profound sense of guilt and torment.

As the dream progresses, the victimized and hunted Makak becomes more and more obsessed with life-denying violence. He talks to his imaginary army: 'I want to tell them this. That now is the time. The time of war. War. Fire, fire and destruction. The sky is one fire. Makak will destroy' (p. 295). It is Lestrade's entrance in his role of hunter/explorer/ravager/conquistador, that disturbs Makak's frenzied speech. Makak and his two generals hide, and Lestrade, his own consciousness in turmoil, alone, is confronted by Basil. Cornered by the figure of death, who uses the same concepts of law, logic, and reason that Lestrade himself was adept at, the Corporal quickly becomes cognizant of his other part, his Blackness. Lestrade now confesses his burdened conscience and fragmented consciousness:

> I jeered thee because I hated half of myself, my eclipse. But now in the heart of the forest at the foot of Monkey Mountain I kiss your foot, O Monkey Mountain. ... Was that my voice? My voice. O God, I have become what I mocked. I always was. I always was.
>
> (pp. 299–300)

But even as Makak welcomes him into the flock, Tigre and Souris vent their hate and revenge on the prodigal. Makak, out of his own disillusionment, also thirsts for revenge: 'I have brought a dream to my people, and they reject me. Now they must be taught, even tortured, killed. I will break up their tribes' (p. 304). This, again, resembles the darkness that Kurtz embodies. He too has the skulls of his victims decorating his fence; so that all these tendencies toward

obsession culminate in Kurtz's abysmal darkness: Lestrade's obsession with his inherited 'Whiteness', Moustique's tendency toward
commercial extreme, and Makak's toward a 'Black' extreme.

Tigre interrupts Makak's tirade by picking up the gun and saying
what his motives were in the first place. Souris asks him, 'Are you
sure where you are, Tigre, are you sure who you are?' And his
response is, 'I am a criminal with a gun, in the heart of the forest
under Monkey Mountain. And I want his money' (p. 303). This, of
course, shatters Makak who asks dumbfoundedly: 'Money ... that
is what you wanted? This is what it is all about ... Money ... ?' The
shock jolts and almost aborts Makak's vision. He is disoriented not
only in the realm of dream, but also in the physical/psychical area
of Monkey Mountain which he knows so well but which now
looms up before him as a strange and frightening place. The characters around him lose their identity. He gropes forward and stops,
saying, 'I am lost. I have forgotten the way.' From the depths of
tired disillusionment Makak says: 'I was a king among shadows.
Either the shadows were real, and I was no king, or it is my own
kingliness that created the shadows. Either way, I am lonely, lost,
an old man again' (p. 304).

But his hopelessness is not irrevocable, for Makak is beginning an
unconscious rejection of the static moon image, precursor of the
image of the cultural stasis and nothingness symbolized by the
White woman:

> I wanted to leave this world. But if the moon is earth's friend, eh,
> Tigre, how can we leave the earth? And the earth self? Look down
> and there is nothing at our feet. We are wrapped in black air, we are
> black, ourselves shadows in the firelight of the white man's mind.
>
> (p. 304)

What Makak is pointing to here is the inchoate nature of the
spheres of the cosmos itself. One thing lends reality to the other:
should it be asked to revolve alone, without the companionship of
sun, moon and other spheres, then the earth itself would be an illusion. The White world must coexist with the Black, the lunar and
solar alongside the earthly; without their dialogue with each other,
the cosmos itself is confounded: a void, a nothing is created.

In the next scene, Makak takes up his position as African
monarch, sitting on what would be the Ashanti golden stool;
Lestrade sheds his colonial uniform and dons African robes. It is he
who, in actual fact, controls:

Corporal Inventor of history! (*kisses Makak's foot*)
Makak I am only a shadow.
Corporal Shh. Quiet, my prince.

(p. 311)

As the 'enemies of Africa' are called, the list includes historical as well as fictional figures. All those who have committed art or good deeds, 'whether of genius or geography', are condemned to death. 'Their crime ...', says Basil, '... is that they are indubitably White' (p.312).

Having finished with all Whites, the tribunal now turns to Black enemies of the cause. Moustique is resurrected to appear before the court, accused by Lestrade of having 'betrayed our dream'. But Moustique counters to Makak:

> Look around you, old man, and see who betray what. Is this what you wanted when you left Monkey Mountain? Power or love? ... Oh, I remember you in those days long ago, you had something there (*touching his breast*), but here all that gone. All this blood, all this killing, all this revenge.

(pp. 314–15)

Makak, nevertheless, yields to popular pressure and condemns Moustique to death. But the Moustique he has condemned contains the knowledge of life and death; he has already been absolved from his burden of guilt, has already died. The killings represent a perversion of ritual sacrifice into legalized public murder built on the brutal premises of hatred and revenge. But this is all self-destruction because man's inhumanity to man is a correlative of man's own impotence: the ineffectuality of the tyrant is mirrored in the death of his victim. The tyrant himself becomes less than human. As Moustique tells Makak: 'That is not your voice, you are more of an ape now, a puppet' (p. 315).

The final figure that is brought before Makak is that of the apparition who has herself enticed him into this role. Makak's demand that he be alone with the woman is important; it demonstrates his refusal to sensationalize this issue. Lestrade, Souris, and Basil remain long enough for the first two, who were formerly blind to her presence, to now see her as 'Plain as the moon' (p. 317). They, too, have been possessed by her. The killing of the White woman, though, is done by Makak in ritual aloneness; it becomes a kind of suicide. When Makak kills her, he does not kill the authoritarian White aspect of his consciousness at all – he has done that already with Moustique by seeing the death of the mer-cantile mentality; on the contrary, what he kills is the polarized and static romanticized vision of his ancestral past – a vision which has itself arisen out of Makak's obsession with Whiteness. This is precisely why he removes his African robe, pronounces himself free, 'Now, O God, now I am free', then he beheads her.

Both tempting models of home have now been finally repudiated by the West Indian who has learned that to choose one over the other is to indulge in self-abuse, self-denial and self-annihilation. Home lies, rather, in the animated milieu of Monkey Mountain itself, amidst which whirl and exist the intangible but real spectres of the past. Walcott's philosophy is that nothing should be allowed to go to waste; each relic of the West Indian's past, however appar-ently insignificant, is necessary for reintegration. Nothing must be lost or forgotten; the fragments of the past must be patiently gath-ered, confronted, resisted and creatively reassembled and reused. No single fragment should be allowed total control lest the West Indian become – remain – a mimic man.

The hint that Monkey Mountain is home comes from early in the play. The very first scene, set on Monkey Mountain, begins like this:

> **Moustique**   Makak, Makak, wake up. Is me, Moustique. You didn't hear me calling you from the throat of the gully?
>
> (p. 231)

Makak is in a coma, with the apparition still in his mind. Moustique enters; the ingredients for the rebirth of the Word are there. The stage directions are important here: '*We hear a cry far off, echoing.*' This is the authentic and initial scream that comes from the West Indian, the New World expelled/embraced Adam who is central to the all-embracing and releasing archetype that Walcott is attempting. The 'throat' of the gully amalgamates the images of voice and birth: giving birth to voice and being, as it were. Interestingly enough, Susan Beckman has responded in a similar but less specific way to this subterranean amalgamation; she actually speaks of '... forging a new language that could speak his (Walcott's) New World into life'.[17]

Atop Monkey Mountain resides the Muse of the Caribbean who insists on the participation – social, cultural, and artistic[18] – of all the selves that reside in the West Indian. But each self, as *Dream on Monkey Mountain* shows, threatens dictatorship and the demise of the others because each attempts to consolidate its own peculiar perspective. Makak's dream involves the repudiation of the models of racial/cultural superiority; and, having rejected them, Makak may voice his real name, Felix Hobain; and he may change his 'denomination affiliation' from a stammered singular 'Cat'olique' to 'I believe in my God'.

In his final speech, Makak, as if in strange recall of his oscillation between the setting sun of Empire and the eclipsed, sinking moon of Africa, in vague memory of his adherence to one cultural imperative or the other says:

> The branches of my fingers, the roots of my feet, could grip nothing, but now, God, they have found ground ... now this old hermit is going back home, back to the beginning, to the green beginning of this world. Come, Moustique, we going home.
>
> (p. 326)

And to the song, 'I going home' Makak and Moustique, both having confessed their obsessions within the dream, walk towards home, towards Monkey Mountain. As they walk home and the dream fades, we realize that the conflicts wrought from the multi racial, multi-cultural, multi-lingual milieu of the West Indies create a complex heterogeneous socio-cultural body. The excellence of Derek Walcott's *Dream on Monkey Mountain* resides in this poet's awareness of conflicting variables within the West Indies and the West Indian; its excellence rests upon his complex vision and hope for reintegration/resolution/rebirth.

For Walcott, home is the Caribbean, fragmented but potent. We live there, and strangely the Caribbean lives in a manifestly splintered presence within the oceanic layers of our psyche: a presence which will arise in us and address us in rainbow ways which we may not always comprehend, but which we must always put to creative use as we attempt to grapple with a tortured existence.

From *Commonwealth Essays and Studies*, 13: 2 (1991), 8–21.

NOTES

[Daizal Samad's essay examines the way Walcott has striven to address psychic divisions within the Caribbean consciousness, and his attempt in *Dream on Monkey Mountain* to create in the character of Makak an 'imaginative archetype' which might reconcile these oppositions, and provide the possibility of healing. It tends at times to be acquiescent in its exegesis of

Walcott's male-centred myth, and its commentary on the problematical beheading of the White Goddess might be contrasted with that provided by Elaine Savory, in the essay that follows. Eds]

1. Derek Walcott, 'What the Twilight Says: An Overture', *Dream on Monkey Mountain* (New York, 1970), p. 7. [All references to the play *Dream on Monkey Mountain* are in parentheses within the text.]

2. Walcott, 'What the Twilight Says,' p. 5.

3. Wole Soyinka, *The Road* (London, 1971).

4. Walcott, 'What the Twilight Says,' p. 5.

5. This philosophical position closely approximates Wilson Harris's.

6. Derek Walcott, *In A Green Night* (London, 1962).

7. Walcott, 'What the Twilight Says,' p. 4.

8. Walcott seems to use 'Moustique' with 'mosquito' in mind, but I am told by Dr Anthony Boxill that the patois word translates more accurately into 'flea'.

9. R. E. L. Masters, 'The Anatomy of the Devil,' *Eros and Evil* (Maryland, 1962), p. 12.

10. Diana Lyn, 'The Concept of the Mulatto in Some Works of Derek Walcott', *Caribbean Quarterly*, 26: 1 & 2 (March–June 1980), 51.

11. Laurence Briner, 'Tradition, Society, the Figure of the Poet', *Caribbean Quarterly*, 26: 1 & 2 (March–June 1980), 11.

12. Derek Walcott, *Star Apple Kingdom* (New York, 1979), p. 25.

13. Derek Walcott, 'Meanings', *Savacou*, 2 (September 1970), 47.

14. Theodore Colson, 'Derek Walcott's Plays: Outrage and Compassion', *World Literature Written in English*, 12: 1 (April 1973), 88–91.

15. Mark, 13: 22–3.

16. Joseph Conrad, *Heart of Darkness* (London, 1967), p. 118.

17. Susan Backman, 'The Mulatto of Style: Language in Derek Walcott's Drama', *Canadian Drama*, 16: 1 (Spring 1980), 71.

18. Robert Hamner, 'Conversation with Derek Walcott', *World Literature Written in English*, 16: 1 (November 1977), 46.

13

Value Judgements on Art and the Question of Macho Attitudes: the Case of Derek Walcott

ELAINE SAVORY

'Madeline, you cannot as a woman know a man'
Malcochon

In the late-twentieth-century ferment of critical debate, there are many schools which represent particular socio-political directions, such as Marxist, or philosophical theses, such as those of the Phenomenologists, Structuralist et al. Feminist criticism, whatever that means at this point, when the term feminist is itself highly debatable and even unacceptable within the community of progressive women,[1] is one more critical direction which reflects a special interest. The collective effect of these differing and often conflicting critical theories/groups has been at least helpful to the realization by some in the Western countries that much of what passes for universal criteria of taste are actually merely culturally and class-dictated opinions. More than that, in Third World critical circles the interconnections between anti-racist and anti-colonialist perspectives and those of the women's movements are beginning to be closely examined. This is nowhere more important than in the work of masculinist male writers in Third World societies who often unthinkingly reflect mass male prejudice/myth about women. We are aware that some of these atttudes are so widespread as to amount to a cultural bias in the male culture of a particular society, but they nevertheless receive special reinforcement and endorsement when a talented and mainly effective writer includes them in his major work.

The argument of this paper seeks to demonstrate that not only is the work of Derek Walcott, a deservedly celebrated poet, dramatist and theatre practitioner in the Caribbean, inclusive of strong prejudices about women but that these are often associated with weakening of power in his writing. It seems reasonable to assume, after all, that prejudices which deflect the individual from exploration and growth, will have that same effect on those areas of writing which are centred in them. Fortunately, given his attitudes to women, Walcott's creative world is a predominantly male one, in which men have close and important understanding of one another. He also deals with racism, colonialism and the situation of the poor masses with intelligence, anger and originality. But his treatment of women is full of clichés, stereotypes and negativity. I shall seek to show how some of his worst writing is associated with these portraits of women, which sometimes lead him to the brink of losing verbal control, or give rise to a retreat into abstract, conventional terms which prevent any real treatment of the subject.

A good deal of recent thinking about literary activity has focused on the relation between reader and writer through the text, and there is an importance now given in a good deal of Third World literary analysis to the issue of clashes between the writer's reality/prejudices and those of the reader.[2] It is no longer possible to deny that certain attitudes expressed in literary works are bound to alienate the reader in unconstructive ways (as opposed to healthy provocation of thought/issues). Racism, class prejudice, sexism and colonialist attitudes are endemic in so many cultures that it might seem unfair to ask that writers control/eliminate them in themselves, but that is indeed the issue as we continue to look to serious art for moral sensitivity and the expansion of our conceptual horizons.

The philosophical position which links aesthetic achievement to moral sensitivity is a bold one, but the British philosopher Hugo Meynell has stated such a case:

> good art satisfies characteristically by showing us what it is to experience, to understand, to judge, or to decide. ... Its effect is to militate against those limitations of our consciousness which are due to our

physical and social environment. Bad art is to a great extent, when not merely technically incompetent, that which imposes or reinforces such limitations.[3]

He goes on to say that bad art also does not permit the reader to experiment with feeling, sensation and moral judgement. Good art, he suggests, produces a complex state of mind in the reader, a state in which both condemnation and sympathy are equally difficult or easy, and responses are therefore highly likely to be thought-provoking, tentative and to therefore lead to further consideration and to resistance to facile opinions. Good art, then, would lead a reader out of the enclosures of perception which she/he has inherited and into exploratory thought. What I suggest in this paper is that relative technical incompetence (or, alternatively, aesthetic limitation, over-control or linguistic evasion) arises out of limitations of perception as much as of the artist's talent and training. Complexity of perception must surely challenge the artist to think of new ways of shaping the form which in turn leads to growth. There is a delicate balance in very good writing between tensions and contradictions and the resolution of these into a secure conclusion which is destroyed by excessively simple emotional directive from the writer. Basically, the writer cannot afford to be afraid of an important aspect of the experience she/he describes: fear leads to a desire to control/ evade which damages the possibility of aesthetic development. For whatever reason, Walcott's most recent work has been disappointing.[4] I shall not deal with that, but rather with the serious implications of the treatment of women in his earlier works.

Walcott's Caribbean region is a place of tensions between the sexes. Single mothers, still very numerous, and often in economic difficulty, are still somehow perceived often by men as powerful, despite their social and economic powerlessness. Men talk about women in hostile ways (although the younger educated man is beginning to respond to the strength of the women's movement in the region). The degree of female autonomy, leadership, and sexual independence which has been forced to develop in many Caribbean women as a result of male behaviour is not recognised as an advantage to the region, but as a reason for men to resist change being advocated by feminists. The good husbands and lovers of the Caribbean are also too often silent and invisible: the creative literature at present available for young women to read abounds with portraits of difficult male–female relations and with stereotypical attitudes towards women, depicting them as victims of male violence or in other ways as losers or marginal figures.

Walcott's work reflects this world. Some portraits of women will first make it clear how his vision of women focuses on fear/disgust on the part of the man. In a poem about Othello and Desdemona, the association of sexuality and violence is very explicit, interwoven of course in this case with racial tension. The quality of the writing betrays a failure to hold these elements together in a creative way. The overblown emotional crudity of the following passage will serve to illustrate how Walcott can rely upon images from the world of sexist prejudice and racial myth:

> And yet, whatever fury girded
> on that saffron-sunset turban, moon-shaped sword
> was not his racial, panther-black revenge
> pulsing her chamber with raw musk, its sweat
> but horror of the moon's change,
> of the corruption of an absolute,
> like a white fruit
> pulped ripe by fondling but doubly sweet.[5]

The technical competence is here stretched so taut that it collapses. In the centre of this passage, there is a tension between idealism and disgust which characterizes another portrait of woman's sexuality in *Another Life*. Here a beautiful woman is unfaithful to her husband and although this is indeed an immorality which might justify moral rebuke, Walcott's choice of language once more reveals powerful resentments against a woman less than devoted to her husband, and furthermore sexually adventurous, and insinuates that her son is damaged by her nature.

> Next day her golden face seemed shrunken,
> then, when he ulysseed, she bloomed again ...
> Dressed in black lace, like an impatient widow,
> I imagined that skin, pomegranate, under silks
> the sheen of water, and that
> sweet-sour smell vixens give off.[6]

This passage presents a tension between woman's loveliness (golden) and her sexual nature (pomegranate skin, sweet-sour smell, vixens) which create a repulsive intimacy with the woman, which is what happens also in the passage on Desdemona and Othello, and again, in the play *Joker of Seville* (where of course male infidelity is treated lightly and stylishly), Juan's attitude to women is tinged with disgust:

> For if there's nothing in that cleft,
> that little Delphic mystery,
> but God, there's very little left
> to die for, between you and me.
> Two graves, one life, the second grave
> no more than an indifferent slit
> to take another stiff.[7]

In the portrait of Anna, youthful love of the poet-persona in *Another Life*, there is a threatening quality which Edward Baugh has considered:

> I see her stride
> as ruthless as that flax-bright harvester
> Judith, with Holofernes' lantern in her hand.

This too is a kind of idealisation, as Judith by her murder of Holofernes proved herself a partner and heroine; but the connotations which adhere to her when she is seen from Holofernes' point of view are inescapable, complicating Anna's connotations of simplicity and truth.[8]

This image of Anna as murderous female (perceived via the freemasonry of maleness rather than through the role she plays in her culture by her action), comes after a description of her sexual energy in a mildly threatening context:

> For one late afternoon, when again she stood
> in the door of a twilight always left ajar,
> when dusk had softened the first bulb
> the colour of the first weak star,
> I asked her, 'Choose',
> the amazed dusk held its breath,
> the earth's pulse staggered,
> she nodded, and that nod
> married earth with lightning ...
> I hear that open laugh,
> I see her stride ...[9]

The images of Anna here are idealized, romanticized (something of the famous bathos of Hemingway's 'the earth moved' for orgasmic experience in his novel *For Whom the Bell Tolls* lurks in 'the earth's pulse' and the 'amazed dusk'), but there is a sense of the energy of this young woman being part of natural forces which could be hostile to the poet. The fear of strong female sexuality which characterizes patriarchy is present here: Anna is young and innocent but there is that about her which will be powerful, and it is this quality which creates conflict in the poet-persona.

Of all these passages, the first one discussed (from 'Of Goats and Monkeys') is the weakest, from an aesthetic point of view, but all the passages are relatively slack. Both descriptions of the Captain's wife and Anna have a facile quality, produced in the former by an urgency of tone which disturbs the rhythm of the lines in a breathless hostility couched in nearly abusive language, and in the latter by a choice of conventional 'poetic' words/phrases which seem to evade Anna as much as they describe her, and are woven into a conversational, all too easy, tone. In none of these passages is there that wonderful tightness of rhythm and unorthodoxy of word, image and idea which marks Walcott at his best. It is as if woman has little reality in Walcott's imagination, and that there is little between romanticism on the one hand and appalled rejection on the other in her treatment in his works.

One of the most powerful and revealing descriptions of woman as ideal which he offers comes in his prose essay which prefaces the collection of plays *Dream on Monkey Mountain:*

> The last image is of a rain-flushed dawn, after a back-breaking night of filming, in a slowly greying field where the sea-wind is like metal on the cheek. In the litter of the field among tarpaulins, stands a shawled girl caught in that gesture which abstractedly gathers cloth to shoulder, her black hair lightly lifting, the tired pale-skin flushed, lost in herself and the breaking camp. She was white, and that no longer mattered. Her stillness annihilated years of anger. His heart thanked her silently from the depth of exhaustion, for she was one of a small army of his dreams. She was a vessel caught at the moment of their Muse, her clear vacancy the question of a poem which is its own answer. She was among the sentries who had watched till dawn.[10]

The elements in this description are important. Once more there is use of conventional images, romantic aspects of woman in conjunction with romanticisms about nature. The woman is white, and Walcott's attitude to that is honest and important: her whiteness is no longer a source of anger because her passivity and service to the poet have absolved her of her colour (but what images this conjures of the passive, serving white wife being able only through her service to transcend the history of her race's guilt). Here the underlying violence in the Othello–Desdemona poem and the underlying fear of Anna in *Another Life* are explained: woman is ideal if she is an extension of the man's imagination, a servant of his will and quiescent figure in his world. Let her set out with a stride (like Anna) towards her own goals, and she becomes dangerous. Though the passage from the preface to *Dream* is overwritten and highly removed from the reality of the real woman it describes (who was in fact anything but a merely passive handmaiden of the poet), it does contain some important elements for our study. The woman described is used to aggrandize the poet's (male artist's) need for female support/inspiration for his work, and also is perceived through a romantic distancing.[11]

Women who step out in life have often been the subject of male writers' tragic stories, stories which put the blame on the unusual spirit of the woman and not on the fecklessness of the male saboteurs of her life. Three of the most tragic victims of male-dominated societies are the male-created figures of Pasternak's Lara, and Thomas Hardy's Tess and Bathsheba Everdene. Walcott uses these in a poem which is again expressive of fear of woman:

> I feared the numbing kiss
> of those women of winter
> Bathsheba, Lara, Tess
>
> whose tragedy made less
> of life, whose love was more
> than love or literature.[12]

Once again the poetic vision here is diffuse, the poetry pretending to a philosophical grandeur which under examination proves to be a shallow statement. The real 'danger' in these women of northern fiction is that they each tried to be a real person as opposed to a male fantasy (although they are also, of course, myths as well). Once the idealism which makes woman controllable goes away, there lurks underneath a raw anger:

> When I left the madhouse I tried other women
> but, once they stripped naked, their spiky cunts
> bristled like sea-eggs and I couldn't dive.[13]

Walcott's work contains many images of beautiful, desirable women as passive creatures who await the male decision/appreciation. But these women are often described in near-cliché, pretty images which belong in popular myths of femininity. Walcott is rarely near to the originality and sturdiness of his portraits of men when he deals with women although he is sometimes negatively innovative, as with the image of the 'spiky cunts'. Often the woman is associated with conventional images like the moon, treated conventionally. The moon and the sea become (as in other poets ambivalent about women, like T. S. Eliot and Christopher Okigbo) convenient ways of showing abstract approval to women. When Walcott wants to describe sexual happiness, he looks for a conventionally pretty word:

> K with quick laughter, honey skin and hair,
> and always money. In what beach shade, what year
> has she so scented with her gentleness
> I cannot watch bright water but think of her ...[14]

Sometimes, his writing conjures up more of the coy and calculated sexuality of a *Playboy* centrefold:

> I knew when dark-haired evening put on
> her bright silk at sunset, and folding the sea,
> sidled under the sheet with her starry laugh,
> that there'd be no rest, there'd be no forgetting.[15]

There is one powerful female image which is not attacked, because it is perceived as a maternal force, and that is the goddess-moon, a symbol which has brought out the masochistic side of macho maleness in a number of poets (again, notably Okigbo). It is only sexually active/possible women who are required to be passive to be approved, but a mythic symbol can represent the dominating and yet sustaining aura of a mother who loves her child:

> happy the earth is still changing
> that the full moon can blind me with her forehead
> this bright foreday morning ...[16]

The writing here is good, because here the language blends sounds and rhythmic patterns freely and is positive and full of energy, expressing a confidence and an original vision (the moon's 'forehead'). In the same poem, 'The Morning Moon', he says he is 'still haunted by the cycle of the moon' and that 'I gasp at her sane brightness'. Although Walcott overworks the word 'bright' in relation to his positive images of woman, the adjective 'sane' lifts it in this context into something fresh. Again, in *Another Life,* the moon is a maternal force which, like Anna, is associated with the cosmic power of lightning, but here there is no rejection as a result:

> The moon came to the window and stayed there.
> He was her subject, changing when she changed ...
> His dun flesh peeled white by her lightning strokes![17]

Walcott's ultimate refinement of woman takes her out of the world altogether:

> I live on the water,
> alone. Without wife and children ...
>
> Now I require nothing,
> from poetry, but true feeling,
> no pity, no fame, no healing. Silent wife,
> we can sit watching grey water ...[18]

Woman becomes art, and a certain resolution settles over the poetry.[19]

This whole context of woman as image in Walcott's work contrasts abruptly with the creations for which he is justifiably known and admired: the male pairs who abound in his work, like Makak and Moustique, or the odd couple of Pantomime, and the individual male creations like the Devil in *Tijean* or Afa in *Sea at Dauphin,* or the poet-persona in *Another Life* are all living beings precisely because they are complex, perceived with tolerance, wryness, compassion and a bold honesty, a blend of realism and romanticism which makes the characterization close to archetype but not in the least unconvincing. The characters seem to absorb their creator's full attention, and ours: their language is subtle, containing a true balance between opposites held together in a creative tension. The fictive personality of the Devil for example, is a marvellously entertaining character, as well as a racist white Planter and the archetype of evil. He longs to feel and is clearly condemned by his nature to be unhappy. Walcott's Devil is a serious philosophical comment on evil, on the effect evil has on the individual, and at the same time a strong socio-political comment on Caribbean racism and colonialism. He is also a witty individual. Such complex and creative perception never marks Walcott's women characters who are linear by comparison: the Captain's wife, for example, is said to be 'formidable' and 'obliquely masculine' and her son is terrified of life: her adventuring is therefore placed in a negative context and the possibility for a living, contradictory character is ignored. The reader is asked for a relatively simplistic emotional response.

What I am arguing here is that since Walcott is clearly capable of superb characterization and writing, it is a pity that when he depicts women his aesthetic achievement falls to a level of relative banality. His portrait of the Black woman, for example, bears no relation to the feisty, emotionally various, strong, vulnerable and generally complex picture emerging by Black women themselves:

> a black rose of sorrow, a black mine of silence
> raped wife, empty mother, Aztec virgin. ...[20]

In *Dream on Monkey Mountain,* he offers an archetype of the White woman which owes something to Jean Genet's *The Blacks,*[21] and which despite the obvious relevance of a symbol of whiteness being destroyed to release the hero of the play from his own psychic enslavement to self-hate, presents a stage image of justified violence against woman. Man revolts against the tyranny of his own fantasies/desires, choosing to destroy that which he cannot otherwise resist. It is important that this image of white racism is presented as a woman, justified object of hate and violence which lies just under the surface of the adoring lover (as we graphically saw in 'Goats and Monkeys', in the portrait of Othello). Clearly, the White woman was not the only oppressor in the slavery-colonial period in the Caribbean, but the White man seems less culpable in Walcott's world, for both the Devil in *Tijean* and the grand failure Harry in *Pantomime* are perceived as human despite their evident capacity for tyranny. Perhaps Walcott only makes allowances for male evil, out of the freemasonry of maleness which regardless of race, culture or history, can unite against woman. It is also perhaps important that the White woman predominates as a symbol over the Black woman in Walcott's work, possibly because she is more distant and unknowable as a person (because of the male resistance to reality in woman, and because of racial tensions), and therefore is easier to evade as a reality than a woman of the community with which Walcott predominantly identifies, i.e. the African majority.

Women writers, critics and philosophers are at work at this time trying to undo the damage which has been done to women and to relations between women and men, by the refusal of male society to cope with the reality of woman's resources and strengths. Of course, just as the slave/servant knows the master better than the master can know her/him, so the woman knows male culture better than the man knows hers. Adrienne Rich, the poet and feminist writer, has said that woman must re-see and re-vise: once the ability to see properly is achieved then many things change. It is then not a minor issue that Walcott's women are so limited. Whether a woman watches *Joker of Seville* and sees women as creatures of limited perception and intelligence, or hears the honestly strong wife of Jordan in *Remembrance* called a Xanthippe and a Delilah[22] (the old clichés of the 'shrew' and the 'bitch'), or accepts an unrealistic image of sexual womanhood (in the mermaid image in 'Anadyomene'),[23] she is absorbing negative images of her gender to no productive end. Furthermore, Walcott's creative achievement falters very often when he presents these limited images. If he explored the tensions and contradictions inherent in the images of women he chooses, perhaps some really great writing would ensue. But it is time the old clichés were put away: regardless of culture, we have been fed a propagandist list of images of woman which reinforce male hegemony (notions that all good women are devoted mothers, passive virgins or noble old grandmothers; that exciting and independent women with some creative ability are mermaids or Helen of Troy or goddesses only useful if they help male inventiveness; that women who know themselves and are capable of adventure are witches and murderesses). It is time for male writers to explore the idea that women have a humanity at least as complex as that of men and as worth exploring. It may not be important to a male mind that women do not like his images of them, but it ought to be important that he is filling his creative work with outworn and evasive rhetoric which weakens his achievement.[24]

From *Journal of Commonwealth Literature*, 21: 1 (1986), 109–19.

NOTES

[Elaine Savory's essay provides a useful example of a feminist perspective providing alternative readings and insights in the deconstruction of archetypal male representations of women. At the same time she adopts a traditional humanist position in linking questions of artistic accomplishment with moral value, arguing that Walcott's poetry sometimes suffers technically and aesthetically because of a habitual misreading of /insensitivity to women within the author and the dominant male culture of his – and many another – region. Eds]

1. Despite the Caribbean Association of Feminist Research and Action having been formed and having determined 'feminist' in its own terms as someone who is male or female with a commitment to ending the oppression of women, feminist is still a difficult term for many Third World women to accept because of the American/ European emphasis which it has long had.

2. 'Meaning was not something which all men and women everywhere intuitively shared, and then articulated in their various tongues and scripts: what meaning you were able to articulate depended on what script or speech you shared in the first place.' Terry Eagleton on the Structuralists, *Literary Theory* (Oxford, 1983), p. 107. See also, for an excellent study of the implications of colonialist ideology in creative literature, Abdul JanMohamed, *Manichean Aesthetics: the Politics of Literature in Colonial Africa* (Amherst, MA, 1983).

3. Hugo Meynell 'Aesthetic Satisfaction' paper read at the Eighth National Conference of the British Society of Aesthetics in 1973, pp. 7–8.

4. *Midsummer* (London, 1984) and *The Fortunate Traveller* (New York, 1981) both have a facility with words which is disturbingly superficial. Dr Michael Gilkes remarked on this in a paper (as yet unpublished) delivered at the Fifth Conference on West Indian Literature in the Caribbean held May 1985 at the College of the Virgin Islands, on Walcott's *Midsummer*. In the poem, many of the images of woman discussed in my paper reappear: the Muse as woman, Helen, woman used as superficial illustration ('Lift up that old Greek skirt, / and every girl sees what philosophy is about', *Midsummer,* p. 22), woman as the sea, mother et al. The point is that well-worn images of woman as mother, moon, water, etc. are needed in new and striking contexts to have a poetic vitality.

5. 'Goats and Monkeys', *The Castaway* (London, 1965), pp. 27–8.

6. *Another Life* (London, 1973), p. 31.

7. *The Joker of Seville* and *O Babylon* (New York, 1981).

8. This entire extract is taken from the text of Edward Baugh, *Derek Walcott: Memory as Vision: Another Life* (London, 1978), p. 56.

9. *Another Life,* pp. 8–9.

10. *Dream on Monkey Mountain and Other Plays* (London, 1972), p. 39.

11. It is interesting to note that many male artists owe their productivity to the domestic support of a woman/women, whereas female artists are often either alone or supporting children as they struggle to make time to work. There are few references to supportive male Muses in female literature as a result.

12. *The Gulf* (London, 1969), p. 47.

13. *The Star-Apple Kingdom*, p. 8.

14. *In a Green Night* (London, 1972), p. 56.

15. *The Star-Apple Kingdom*, p. 4.

16. *Sea-Grapes* (London), p. 92.

17. *Another Life*, p. 6.

18. *Sea-Grapes,* p. 91.

19. Perhaps it is this languid quality of resolution which makes the most recent poetry seem flaccid: 'I could offer her nothing but the predictable / pale head-scarf of the twilight's lurid silk' seems festooned with sound/would-be richness, but fails to penetrate a potential area of self-examination as to the use of cliché in relation to women. See *The Fortunate Traveller,* p. 10.

20. *The Star-Apple Kingdom*, p. 57.

21. See Elaine Savory (Fido) 'Images of Dream: Walcott, Soyinka and Genet', *African Theatre Review*, 1: 1 (May 1985).

22. *Remembrance* and *Pantomime* (New York, 1980).

23. *In a Green Night*, p. 57.

24. See Carole Boyce Davies, 'Maidens, Mistresses and Matrons: Feminine Images in Selected Soyinka Works' in *Ngambika: Studies of Women in African Literature* (Trenton, NJ, 1986), pp. 75–88. This essay was written in complete isolation from mine but comes to very similar conclusions about Soyinka and the principle of female stereotyping in male literature. 'Skill at female portraiture is not automatic but requires sensitivity and insight in all writers, and particularly in male writers. The writer must also recognise when he is creating negative images' (p. 86).

14

An Empire of Poetry

SIDNEY BURRIS

Adam Smith, the eighteenth-century political economist best known for his treatise *The Wealth of Nations*, described in 'Essay on Colonies' the peculiar problem that confronted Christopher Columbus as he sailed into the uncharted territories that would become known as the West Indies. These lush, heavily forested islands bore little resemblance to the Eastern world that Marco Polo had described, but Columbus persevered in his illusion, confident that he had made landfall in the vicinity of the Ganges river. Eventually Columbus realized that Oriental wealth had eluded him; but he could not elude Isabella. Attempting to satisfy his Queen, Columbus faced a problem of marketing and advertising, one of the earliest instances of the socio-cultural practice that dominates our own century. Over two hundred years ago Smith precisely described its Columbian appearance:

> But the countries which Columbus discovered either in this or in any of his subsequent voyages, had no resemblance to those which he had gone in quest of. ... It was of importance to Columbus, however, that the countries which he had discovered, whatever they were, should be represented to the court of Spain as of very great consequence; and, in what constitutes the real riches of every country, the animal and vegetable productions of the soil, there was at that time nothing which could well justify such a representation of them.[1]

Faced with an intractable dilemma, Columbus was forced to characterize the island culture in the most alluring terms that he could conjure, terms that neatly, prophetically encapsulate the informing structure of colonialist thought: 'They [the islanders] exhibit great

259

affection to all,' Columbus wrote, 'and always give much for little, content with very little or nothing in return.'[2] According to Columbus' rhetoric of profit, these islands offered good prospects for a sound investment.

Derek Walcott's sprawling new poem, *Omeros*, attempts to provide for his Caribbean homeland the definitive strengths and comforts of a national narrative, and it is keenly aware of the ways in which the Columbian perspective survives in the late twentieth century. Part of the poem's herculean ambition lies in its effort to counter the fragmentary representations encouraged by the colonial vision and emblematized briefly but pointedly throughout the poem by the camera, that simplifying tool of the tourist who comes to capture on film, as the saying goes, the exotic images that have been judiciously disseminated to titillate his Columbian wanderlust. The first tercet of the poem, in fact, finds Philoctete, one of the main characters, smiling for the tourists, 'who try taking / his soul with their cameras',[3] and as the poem closes, Achille, another of its main characters, is raging 'at being misunderstood / by a camera' (LIX, iii).

Imperial culture in the West Indies, which Walcott does not consider an entirely pernicious one, practices an art of deception that can be psychologically debilitating to its subjects, and it is a deception as old as Columbus. Determined, often deceived by the argumentative strategies, even the visual imagery, of colonial promotion, village life occasionally fashions itself around this authorized narration, accepting in the process an imposed history. In his essay 'What the Twilight Says: An Overture' (included in the 1970 collection *Dream on Monkey Mountain and Other Plays*), Walcott addresses this problem:

> Every state sees its image in those forms which have the mass appeal of sport, seasonal and amateurish. Stamped on that image is the old colonial grimace of the laughing nigger, steelbandsman, carnival masker, calypsonian and limbo dancer. These popular artists are trapped in the State's concept of the folk form, for they preserve the colonial demeanour and threaten nothing.[4]

Speaking of one of the villages in which much of the poem takes place, Walcott develops this idea in *Omeros*, writing that the village 'had become a souvenir / of itself', a degrading accommodation that ultimately sanctions a subliteracy deemed quaint and a poverty deemed exotic, or 'photogenic':

... Its life adjusted to the lenses

of cameras that, perniciously elegiac,
took shots of passing things – Seven Seas and the dog
in the pharmacy's shade, every comic mistake

of spelling, like *In God We Troust* on a pirogue,
BLUE GENES, ARTLANTIC CITY, NO GABBAGE
DUMPED HERE.
The village imitated the hotel brochure

with photogenic poverty, with atmosphere.
(LXII, i)

Walcott's poem immediately takes its place among those richly tessellated works of colonialism whose sense of cultural solidity is shot through with an array of diverse allegiances. But notes of severe skepticism and weariness now and again pervade the narrative, and even though they are largely resolved by the exuberant historiography that continuously engages the poet, they never entirely vanish from his score. The muscular persuasion of Walcott's line – overwhelming, exhausting – aptly reenacts, whenever it chooses to do so, the baroque *ennui* of island life.

A portion of the fundamental structure of this historiography derives from the two classical epics popularly attributed to Homer. In 'What the Twilight Says' Walcott stated categorically that the writers of his generation were 'assimilators' and that they 'knew the literature of Empires, Greek, Roman, British, through their essential classics'.[5] Walcott, who grew up on St Lucia, received a sound colonial education, and in interviews he has expressed his gratitude to the system that carried this literature to a small island in the Caribbean. Commentators on *Omeros*, then, will understandably busy themselves in tracking down the Homeric parallels in Walcott's poem – after Joyce, there are many practiced hands waiting in the wings – but this seems a particularly ill-fated approach because part of the poem's task, its attempt to recreate the original authenticity of Walcott's Caribbean culture, lies in its deliberate deflation of analogy.

Central to much contemporary Irish poetry, for example, the analogical imagination searches for similitude in the historical events that have given rise to other political structures in other countries, hoping to find there a conceptual basis for its own response to its own dilemma. Walcott, on the other hand, often sets up an obvious parallel between one of his characters and its

Homeric equivalent only to punctuate it with a kind of slapstick disregard – a Joycean technique – as when Machaon, who heals Philoctete's wound in the Odyssey, becomes Ma Kilman, who heals Philoctete's ulcerous wound in *Omeros*. Or in Book Seven, the last book of the poem, the narrator cavalierly confesses to Omeros that he never read the *Odyssey* 'all the way through' (LVI, iii). Finally, the narrator's ultimate pronouncement on Helen, who stands at the center of the narrative, arrives late in the poem and encapsulates the most trenchant commentary on the enticing but frustrating, even fruitless business of tracking down the Homeric parallel:

> ... Names are not oars
>
> that have to be laid side by side, nor are legends;
> slowly the foaming clouds have forgotten ours.
> You were never in Troy, and, between two Helens,
>
> yours is here and alive; their classic features
> were turned into silhouettes from the lightning bolt
> of a glance. These Helens are different creatures,
>
> one marble, one ebony. One unknots a belt
> of yellow cotton slowly from her shelving waist,
> one a cord of purple wool, the other one takes
>
> a bracelet of white cowries from a narrow wrist;
> one lies in a room with olive-eyed mosaics,
> another in a beach shack with its straw mattress. ...
>
> (LXII, ii)

Here is Walcott's deft revision of what Eliot identified as the 'mythic method' in his review of Joyce's *Ulysses* (the work that in all likelihood will emerge as the most generous sponsor of *Omeros*). Instead of advocating the contemporaneity of mythic structures, thereby establishing the linear clarities of a tradition, Walcott gradually reveals the failure of such structures to represent adequately the multifarious tensions of his own culture, thereby establishing its sovereign integrity. The most persuasive approach to Walcott's mythic method would find, particularly in Helen, the gradual sloughing of the Homeric associations until, in the case of Helen, for example, she stands at the end of the poem, a figure, fully Caribbean, of ebony (LXII, ii).

Walcott's deepest organizational structures, both formal and conceptual, lie buried in his developing sense of the theater, and like Yeats before him, his poetry and plays participate in a fecund network of cross-fertilization. Walcott published his first collection of verse in 1948, and two years later, *Cry for a Leader*, one of his earliest dramatic pieces – there is still some question concerning the bibliography – was produced in St Lucia. Since that time over thirty plays have been staged, and Walcott continues his involvement in the dramatic arts, a genre whose engaged social function Walcott acknowledged when he established the Trinidad Theatre Workshop in 1959. In 'What the Twilight Says', Walcott speaks to the two ingredients that informed his colonial boyhood, two perspectives that, when combined, lead directly to the world of the theater:

> Colonials, we began with this malarial enervation: that nothing could ever be built among these rotting shacks, barefooted backyards and moulting shingles; that being poor, we already had the theater of our lives. ... In that simple schizophrenic boyhood one could lead two lives: the interior life of poetry, the outward life of action and dialect.[6]

Action and dialect, balanced by a sustaining poetic sensibility, provided Walcott with the basis for his notion of a Caribbean theater that would legitimate the life and language of this people, and *Omeros* represents an elaborate extension of this project.

Over twenty-five characters, each varying considerably in importance, appear throughout this poem comprising seven books, sixty-four chapters, and roughly eight thousand lines. Achille and Philoctete, two fishermen, occupy the foreground of the narrative with Hector, another fisherman, who abandoned his career to become a taxi driver and who 'paid the penalty of giving up the sea' (XLV, iii) by losing his life in a wreck; the English Empire is represented by Major Dennis Plunkett, who fought with Montgomery's Eighth Army in North Africa and who, when we first meet him, is drinking a Guinness and wiping away 'the rime of gold foam freckling his pensioned moustache / with a surf-curling tongue' (V, i). His wife, Maud, is Irish in the old style, 'framed forever in the last century' (LXI, i), and her association with Glendalough in County Wicklow further connects her, as does her Christian name, with the Gonne family (Iseult lived at Laragh, a few miles away) and with Yeats's lyric 'Stream and Sun at Glendalough'. And Helen heavily influences the lives of these five characters, even when she is not present in the narrative; brooding over the events, giving them their particular cast and hue, she becomes the tutelary spirit of her home, 'selling herself like the island, without / any pain' (XXI, i).

The poem tracks these characters through their daily lives, sometimes hinting at their varied relationships, sometimes describing baldly the arc of each biography. Monologues are unimportant to Walcott, unless we consider the narrator's voice monologic, because the essence of his technique involves the steady revelation of character through dialogue with other characters, real or imagined, and this is a technique fundamental of course to dramaturgy. But even dialogue for Walcott is fraught with social and historical implication. The linguistic fragmentation of the Caribbean islands, caused by the various colonizers imposing their native languages, has in turn created the kind of cultural *insularismo* that has led each island group to become, as David Lowenthal has argued in *Social and Cultural Pluralism in the Caribbean*, 'a museum in which archaic distinctions [are] preserved'.[7] Walcott's verse marshals these fencing energies effectively, as in the following passage when the narrator meets Major Plunkett in the bank soon after Maud's funeral. The passage cries out to be staged:

> 'Our wanderer's home, is he?'
>   I said: 'For a while, sir,'
> too crisply, mentally snapping to attention,
> thumbs along trousers' seam, picking up his accent
>
> from a khaki order.
>   'Been travellin' a bit, what?'
> I forgot the melody of my own accent,
> but I knew I'd caught him, and he knew he'd been
>   caught,
>
> caught out in the class-war. It stirred my contempt.
> He knew the 'what' was a farce, I knew it was not
> officer-quality, a strutting RSM,
>
> Regimental Sarn't Major Plunkett, Retired.
> Not real colonial gentry, but spoke like
> them from the height of his pig farm, but I felt as tired
>
> as he looked. Still, he'd led us in Kipling's requiem.
> 'Been doin' a spot of writing meself. Research.'
> The 'meself' his accommodation.
>   (LIV, i)

The deeply ceremonial nature of this confrontation, reminiscent of the 'tundish' episode in Joyce's *A Portrait of the Artist as a Young Man*, derives its definitive energy from the spoken language's ability to demarcate cultural hierarchies and political allegiances, and

Walcott's insistence on situating these verbal exchanges within heavily plotted contexts aligns one predominant strain of this poem's structure with the renovative Caribbean theater that has engaged him for years.

Walcott's deepest hopes for the artistic enfranchisement of his community are bound up in his concept of a local theater that gradually assumes international acceptance. 'The future of West Indian militancy', he wrote in 'What the Twilight Says', 'lies in art.'[8] These are large claims, but not unrealistic ones as long as the stage continues to define itself as resistive, as continually aligned against an indigenous diffidence that arises from the native inhabitants who are uncertain about their abilities to participate in the grand ritual of theater: 'there was in the sullen ambition of the West Indian actor a fear that he lacked proper weapons, that his voice, colour and body were no match for the civilised concepts of theater.' Walcott's new poem, with its deep fund of history inflected through its melodious and regional song, deploys in great abundance an array of proper weapons.

But the consoling grace of theater lies in the simple reconciliation of the falling curtain, in the sense that the social environment of the stage has reached its purposeful conclusion. However revolutionary the intention of the play, the last word of the last scene of the last act envisions more than an audience, it imagines a community, and it is from this deeply felt resolution that some of the most stirring scenes of *Omeros* derive. In Book Two, Plunkett and Achille, each moving through their radically different social spheres, pause to look at the night sky. The discursive dimension of language requires, of course, that we view these episodes sequentially, but Walcott has typically conceived the two vignettes dramatically, as if they took place on a split stage. As in the first scene of the fourth act in *Othello* where the Moor is allowed to overhear Cassio and Iago, with both parties in plain view of the audience, and with each party unaware of the other, so Plunkett 'counted the stars / like buttons through the orchids' (XXI, ii), while Achille in another part of the village is viewing the same sky:

> From night-fishing he knew the necessary ones,
> the one that sparkled at dusk, and at dawn, the other.

> All in a night's work he saw them simply as twins.
> He knew others but would not call them by their given
> names, forcing a silvery sweb to link their designs,

> neither the Bear nor the Plough, to him there was heaven
> and earth and the sea, but Ursa or Plunkett Major,
> or the Archer aiming? He tried but could not distinguish
>
> their pattern, nor call one Venus, nor even find the
> pierced holes of Pisces, the dots named for the Fish;
> he knew them as stars, they fitted his own design.
>
> (XXI, ii)

Although the divisive histories that stand behind these two mis-aligned characters have resigned them to their hierarchical positions in Caribbean culture, their passing engagement with the constella-tions, their beguiling ignorance of their astronomical names, briefly unites them in their vision. Theatrically conceived, such moments never entirely assuage the conflicts – linguistic, social, political – that Walcott addresses in this poem, but they do assert the promi-nence of the Caribbean's locale, its overwhelming environment. It is in this alone that Walcott often locates, perhaps paradoxically, much of the trenchant interrogation that sustains this national nar-rative. In Chapter XXII, Walcott finds for Plunkett a peculiar attraction, 'something unexpected' (XXII, iii) in the colonial experi-ence, and it adumbrates the final words of the poem where the sea, like the two opposing histories represented by the Major and Achille, is 'still going on' (LXIV, iii)

> ... The Plunketts quietly continued,
>
> parades continued, cricket resumed, and the white feathers
> of the proconsul's pith-helmet, and the brass and red
> of the fire engines. Everything that was once theirs
>
> was given to us now to ruin it as we chose,
> but in the bugle of twilight also, something unexpected.
> A government that made no difference to Philoctete,
>
> to Achille. That did not buy a bottle of white kerosene
> from Ma Kilman, a dusk that had no historical regret
> for the fishermen beating mackerel into their seine,
>
> only for Plunkett, in the pale orange glow of the wharf
> reddening the vendors' mangoes, alchemizing the bananas
> near the coal market, this town he had come to love.
>
> (XXII, iii)

Plunkett has become absorbed by the diurnal rhythms of life on the island, but even more than his absorption, he relishes the colonizer's freedom, the oddly liberating sense of displacement that strengthens him whenever he realizes that he has fallen in love with a town whose welfare he can, if the need arises, safely disregard. Now and again, uneasy truces are worked out in Walcott's poem between the native inhabitants of the island and the governing class, but these are truces whose terms have historically misrepresented the magnificent biographies of islanders like Achille, Philoctete, and Helen. Recording the evidence to correct such a misrepresentation is one of the most fundamental purposes of *Omeros,* and in this endeavor Walcott has succeeded wildly, providing for his region a deeply assimilative work that immediately becomes essential to further assessments of the Caribbean literary tradition.

From *Southern Review,* 27: 3 (1991), 558–74.

NOTES

[Sidney Burris's brief essay examines the ideological enterprise behind Walcott's poetry and drama, comparing them with James Joyce's attempts to create indigenous narratives, in part by reworking and recasting established fictions. Although he describes Helen as the 'tutelary spirit' of *Omeros,* interestingly in the light of Elaine Savory's essay, he devotes more space and attention to the exiled figure of Major Plunkett.

The following notes, and the references to *Omeros* within the essay, have been compiled by the editors. The essay was originally published as a review study without notes. Eds]

1. Adam Smith, *An Enquiry into the Nature and Causes of the Wealth of Nations* (1776), vol. 2, ed. R. H. Campbell and A. R. Skinner (Oxford, 1976), pp. 559–60.

2. Columbus's account of what he believed to be part of the Asian landmass was sent by letter to Ferdinand and Isabella of Spain in February 1493. He based his cartography on Ptolemaic maps. Washington Irving quoted Columbus at length in his *Columbus: Voyages of Discovery* (1828), especially focusing on the impression Columbus received on seeing the peoples of the islands for the first time.

3. Derek Walcott, *Omeros* (first publ. New York, London, 1990) ch. I, i.
    [*Omeros* is divided into seven books consisting of sixty-four chapters, each chapter divided into three sections. Further chapters and sections are given in parentheses in the essay – Roman numerals for chapters, Arabic for sections. Eds]

4. Derek Walcott, 'What the Twilight Says: An Overture', in *Dream on Monkey Mountain and Other Plays* (first publ. 1970; London, 1972), p. 7.

5. 'What the Twilight Says', p. 4.

6. Ibid., p. 6.

7. For a detailed account of pluralism in the West Indies see David Lowenthal, *West Indian Societies* (London, 1972), pp. 87ff.

8. 'What the Twilight Says', p. 18.

9. Ibid.

Further Reading

BOOKS ON POSTCOLONIAL LITERATURE AND THEORY

G. S. Amur, V. R. N. Prasad, B. V. Nemade and N. K. Nihalani, *Indian Readings in Commonwealth Literature* (New Delhi: Sterling Publishers Private, 1985).

Chidi Amuta, *The Theory of African Literature: Implications for Practical Criticism* (London: Zed Books, 1989).

Bill Ashcroft, Gareth Griffiths and Helen Tiffin, *The Empire Writes Back: Theory and Practice in Post-Colonial Literatures* (London and New York: Routledge, 1989).

Firdous Azim, *The Colonial Rise of the Novel* (London: Routledge, 1993).

Homi K. Bhabha, *Nation and Narration* (London: Routledge, 1990).

Daniel Bivona, *Desire and Contradiction: Imperial Visions and Domestic Debates in Victorian Literature* (Manchester: Manchester University Press, 1990).

David Cook, *African Literature: A Critical View* (London: Longman, 1977).

Carole Boyce Davies and Anne Adams Graves (eds), *Ngambika: Studies of Women in African Literature* (Trenton NJ, Africa World Press, 1986).

Charles T. Davis and Henry Louis Gates, Jr (eds), *The Slave's Narrative* (Oxford: Oxford University Press, 1985).

Geoffrey V. Davis and Hena Maes-Jelinek (eds), *Crisis and Creativity in the New Literatures in English* (Amsterdam: Rodopi, 1990).

Cheikh Anta Diop, *The African Origin of Civilization: Myth or Reality* (first publ. in French, 1955; Westfort, USA: Lawrence Hill, 1974).

James Donald and Ali Rattansi (eds), *'Race', Culture and Difference* (London: Sage and Open University, 1992).

Dennis Durden and Cosmo Pieterse (eds), *African Writers Talking* (London: Heinemann, 1972).

Frantz Fanon, *The Wretched of the Earth*, trans. Constance Farrington (first publ. as *Les Damnés de la Terre*, 1961; Harmondsworth: Penguin, 1990).

Frantz Fanon, *Black Skin, White Masks* (New York: Grove Press, 1967).

Henry Louis Gates, Jr, *Figures in Black: Words, Signs, and the 'Racial' Self* (Oxford: Oxford University Press, 1989).

Simon Gikandi, *Reading the African Novel* (London: James Currey, 1987).

Georg M. Gugelberger (ed.), *Marxism and African Literature* (London: James Currey, 1985).

K. Holst-Petersen and A. Rutherford (eds), *A Double Colonization: Colonial and Post-Colonial Women's Writing* (Aarhus: Dangaroo, 1985).

Adeola James (ed.), *In Their Own Voices: African Women Writers Talk* (London: James Currey, 1990).

Abdul R. JanMohamed, *Manichean Aesthetics: The Politics of Literature in Colonial Africa* (Amherst: University of Massachusetts Press, 1983).

Abdul R. JanMohamed and David Lloyd (eds), *The Nature and Context of Minority Discourse* (Oxford: Oxford University Press, 1990).

Hazel Johnson and Henry Bernstein (eds), *Third World Lives of Struggle* (Oxford: Heinemann/Open University, 1982; rpt. 1988).

Eldred Durosimi Jones, Eustace Palmer and Marjorie Jones (eds), *Women in African Literature Today* (London: James Currey, 1987).

Rana Kabbani, *Europe's Myths of Orient: Devise and Rule* (London: Macmillan, 1986).

Jomo Kenyatta, *My People of Kikuyu* (Nairobi: Oxford University Press, 1966).

Bruce King (ed.), *Post-Colonial English Drama: Commonwealth Drama since 1960* (London: Macmillan, 1992).

Bruce King (ed.), *The Commonwealth Novel since 1960* (London: Macmillan, 1991).

Viney Kirpal (ed.), *The New Indian Novel in English: A Study of the 1980s* (New Delhi: Allied Publishers, 1990).

Bernth Lindors, *Critical Perspectives on Nigerian Literature* (London: Heinemann, 1975).

Gerald Moore, *The Chosen Tongue: English Writing in the Tropical World* (London: Longmans, 1969).

Pamela Mordecai and Betty Wilson (eds), *Her True-True Name: An Anthology of Women's Writing from the Caribbean* (London: Heinemann, 1989).

Meenakshi Mukherjee, *Realism and Reality: the Novel and Society in India* (Oxford and New Delhi: Oxford University Press, 1985).

Satendra Nandan (ed.), *Language and Literature in Multicultural Contexts* (Suva, Fiji: University of the South Pacific and Association for Commonwealth Language and Literature Studies, 1983).

Susheila Nasta (ed.), *Motherlands: Black Women's Writing from Africa, the Caribbean and South Asia* (London: Women's Press, 1991).

Emmanual Obiechina, *Culture, Tradition and Society in the West African Novel* (Cambridge: Cambridge University Press, 1975; repr. 1980).

Eustace Palmer, *An Introduction to the African Novel: A Critical Study of Twelve Books* (London: Heinemann, 1972; repr. 1987).

Carolyn A. Parker, Stephen H. Arnold, A. M. Porter and H. Wylie (eds), *When the Drumbeat Changes* (Washington, DC: Three Continents Press, 1981).

Kenneth Ramchand, *An Introduction to the Study of West Indian Literature* (London: Faber, 1976).

Jeffrey Richards, *Imperialism and Juvenile Literature* (Manchester: Manchester University Press, 1989).

Salman Rushdie, *Imaginary Homelands* (London: Granta/Penguin, 1991).

Edward W. Said, *Orientalism: Western Conceptions of the Orient* (London: Routledge, 1978).

Edward W. Said, *The World, the Text, and the Critic* (London: Faber, 1984).

Edward W. Said, *Culture and Imperialism* (London: Chatto & Windus, 1993).

K. K. Sharma (ed.), *Indo-English Literature: A Collection of Critical Essays* (Ghaziabad: Vimal Prakashan, 1977).
Wole Soyinka, *Myth, Literature and the African World* (Cambridge: Cambridge University Press, 1976).
Wole Soyinka, *Art, Dialogue and Outrage: Essays on Literature and Culture* (Ibadan: New Horn Press, 1988).
Gayatri Chakravorty Spivak, *The Post-Colonial Critic: Interviews, Strategies, Dialogues*, ed. by Sarah Harasym (London, New York: Routledge, 1990).
Avadesh K. Srivastava (ed.), *Alien Voice: Perspectives on Commonwealth Literature* (Lucknow, India: Print House, 1981).
Florence Stratton, *Contemporary African Literature and the Politics of Gender* (London: Routledge, 1994).
William Walsh, *Indian Literature in English* (London: Longman, 1990).
Jane Wilkinson, *Talking with African Writers* (London: James Currey, 1992).

ARTICLES AND ESSAYS ON POSTCOLONIAL LITERATURE AND THEORY

Kofi Anyidoho, 'African Creative Fiction and a Poetics of Social Change', *Komparatistische Hefte*, 13 (1986), 67–81.
Adebayo Bolaris-Williams, 'Marxian Epistemology and the Criticism of African Literature', *Ufahamu*, 13: 1 (1983), 84–103.
Aimé Césaire, 'World Congress of Black Writers', *Black Orpheus*, 1 (Sept.1957).
Barbara Christian, 'The Race for Theory', *The Nature and Context of Minority Discourse*, ed. Abdul R. JanMohamed and David Lloyd (Oxford: Oxford University Press, 1990), pp. 37–49.
Christopher Dailly, 'The Novelist as a Cultural Policy-Maker', *Présence Africaine*, 125 (1983), 201–13.
Carole Boyce Davies, 'Motherhood in the Works of Male and Female Igbo Writers: Achebe, Emecheta, Nwapa and Nzekwu', *Ngambika: Studies of Women in African Literature*, ed. Carole Boyce Davies and Anne Adams Graves (Trenton, NJ: Africa World Press, 1986), pp. 241–56.
Raoul Granqvist, 'Orality in Nigerian Literature', *Moderna Sprak*, 77: 4 (1983), 329–43.
Trevor Griffiths, ' "This Island's Mine": Caliban and Colonialism', *Yearbook of English Studies*, 13 (1983), 159–78.
Georg M. Gugelberger, 'Decolonizing the Canon: Considerations of Third World Literature', *New Literary History*, 22 (1991), 505–24.
Benedict M. Ibitokun, 'The Dynamics of Spatiality in African Fiction', *Modern Fiction Studies*, 37: 3 (Autumn 1991), 409–26.
Djelal Kadir, 'The Survival of Theory and the Surviving Fictions of Latin America', *Modern Fiction Studies*, 32: 3 (Autumn 1986), 383–96.
Chidi T. Maduka, 'The Black Aesthetic and African Bolekaja Criticism', *Ufahamu*, 14: 3 (1985), 139–55.
The Massachusetts Review (Summer 1986), 241ff: whole volume consists of 'Essays on Ethnicity and Literature'.

Kyalo Mativo, 'Criteria for the Criticism of African Literature', *Ufahamu*, 13: 1 (1983), 65–83.

Victoria Earle Matthews, 'The Value of Race Literature: an Address Delivered at the First Congress of Colored Women of the United States, at Boston, Mass., July 30th, 1895', *The Massachusetts Review* (Summer 1986), 170–85.

Vijay Mishra and Bob Hodge, 'What is post(-)colonialism?', *Textual Practice*, 5: 3 (Winter 1991), 399–414.

Michael Valdez Moses, 'Caliban and his Precursors: the Politics of Literary History and the Third World', in *Theoretical Issues in Literary History*, ed. David Perkins (Cambridge, MA: Harvard University Press, 1991), pp. 206–26.

J. I. Okonkwo, 'Cultural Revolution and the African Novel', *Ufahamu*, 14: 3 (1985), 104–13.

Kayode Omole, 'Linguistic Experimentation in African Literature', *The Literary Review*, 34: 4 (Summer 1991), 589–600.

Anthony Pagden, 'The Savage Critic: Some European Images of the Primitive', *The Yearbook of English Studies: Colonial and Imperial Themes*, Special Number ed. G. K. Hunter and C. J. Rawson, 13 (1983), 32–45.

Dianne Schwerdt, 'Deconstructing Cultural Imperialism: African Literature and the Politics of Language', *Southern Review: Literary and Interdisciplinary Essays*, 24: 1 (1991), 57–68.

Jai Shyam, 'Plights of Contemporary Life in Recent African Fiction', *Arizona Quarterly*, 42: 3 (1986), 248–60.

Eric Sellin, 'Reflections on Linguistic and Literary Colonization and Decolonization in Africa', *Studies in Twentieth Century Literature*, 15: 1(Winter 1991), 43ff.

Wole Soyinka, 'The Critic and Society: Barthes, Leftocracy and Other Mythologies', *Black Literature and Literary Theory*, ed. Henry Louis Gates, Jr (New York: Methuen, 1984).

EURO-AMERICAN CRITICAL THEORY

Louis Althusser, *Lenin, Philosophy and Other Essays*, trans. Ben Brewster (London: New Left Books, 1971).

Mikhail Bakhtin, *The Dialogic Imagination*, ed. M. Holquist, trans. C. Emerson and M. Holquist (Austin: University of Texas Press, 1981).

Roland Barthes, *Mythologies*, trans. A. Lavers (London: Cape, 1972).

Hélène Cixous, 'The Laugh of the Medusa', *New French Feminisms*, ed. Elaine Marks and Isabelle de Courtivron (Brighton: Harvester, 1981).

Jonathan Culler, *On Deconstruction: Theory and Criticism after Structuralism* (London: Routledge & Kegan Paul, 1975).

Paul de Man, *Allegories of Reading* (New Haven, CT.: Yale University Press, 1979).

Jacques Derrida, *Of Grammatology*, trans. Gayatri Chakravorty Spivak (first publ. in French, 1967; Baltimore: Johns Hopkins University Press, 1976).

Michel Foucault, *Madness and Civilization* (London: 1967).

Michel Foucault, *The Order of Things: The Archaelogy of the Human Sciences*, trans. A. M. Sheridan (London: Tavistock, 1966).

Fredric Jameson, *Marxism and Form: Twentieth Century Dialectical Theories of Literature* (Princeton, NJ: Princeton University Press, 1971).

Fredric Jameson, *The Prison-House of Language* (Princeton, NJ: Princeton University Press, 1972).

Julia Kristeva, *Desire in Language: A Semiotic Approach to Literature and Art*, ed. Leon S. Roudiez, trans. Thomas Gora, Alice Jardine, and Leon S. Roudiez (New York: Columbia University Press, 1980).

Julia Kristeva, 'Women's Time' (1981); repr. in *The Feminist Reader*, ed. Catherine Belsey and Jane Moore (London: Macmillan, 1989).

Claude Lévi-Strauss, *The Savage Mind* (London: 1966).

Pierre Macherey, *A Theory of Literary Production* (London: Henley & Boston, 1978).

Karl Marx and Friedrich Engels, *On Literature and Art*, ed. L. Baxandall and S. Morawski (New York: International General, 1974).

Toril Moi, *Sexual/Textual Politics: Feminist Literary Theory* (London: Methuen, 1987).

Toni Morrison, 'Rootedness: The Ancestor as Foundation', in *Black Women Writers* (1950–1980): *A Critical Evaluation*, ed. Mari Evans (New York: Anchor Books, 1984), pp. 339–45.

P. Stallybrass and A. White, *The Politics and Poetics of Transgression* (London: Methuen, 1986).

Leon Trotsky, *Literature and Revolution* (Ann Arbor: University of Michigan Press, 1971).

Raymond Williams, *Marxism and Literature* (Oxford: Oxford University Press, 1977).

CHINUA ACHEBE: WRITINGS AND INTERVIEWS

There are numerous editions of Chinua Achebe's works. The following selection lists the original editions:

Things Fall Apart (London: Heinemann, 1958); *No Longer at Ease* (London: Heinemann, 1960); *Arrow of God* (London: Heinemann, 1964); *A Man of the People* (London: Heinemann, 1966); *Girls at War and Other Stories* (London: Heinemann, 1972); *Beware Soul Brother* (London: Heinemann, 1972); *Morning Yet on Creation Day: Essays* (London: Heinemann, 1975); *The Trouble with Nigeria* (Enugu: Fourth Dimension, 1983); *Anthills of the Savannah* (London: Heinemann, 1987); *Hopes and Impediments: Selected Essays 1965–1987* (London: Heinemann, 1988); Chinua Achebe in Interview, 'The Writer's Role in Society', *African Concord*, 20 Oct. 1987; in Conversation with J. O. J. Nwachukwu-Agbada, *Commonwealth Essays and Studies*, 13: 1 (1990). 117–24; Jane Wilkinson (ed.), Talking with African Writers (London: James Currey, 1992).

Books on Chinua Achebe
David Carroll, *Chinua Achebe: Novelist, Poet, Critic* (London: Macmillan, 1980).

Holger G. Ehling, *Critical Approaches to 'Anthills of the Savannah'* (Amsterdam, Atlanta, GA: Rodopi, 1991).

Simon Gikandi, *Reading Chinua Achebe* (London: James Currey, 1991).

C. L. Innes, *Chinua Achebe* (Cambridge: Cambridge University Press, 1990).

C. L. Innes and Bernth Lindfors, *Critical Perspectives on Chinua Achebe* (Washington, DC: Three Continents Press, 1978).

G. D. Killam, *The Writings of Chinua Achebe: A Commentary* (London: Heinemann, 1969; rev., repr. 1983).

Benedict Chiaka Njoku, *The Four Novels of Chinua Achebe: A Critical Study* (New York: Peter Lang, 1984).

Robert M. Wren, *Achebe's World: The Historical and Cultural Context of the Novels of Chinua Achebe* (Washington, DC: Three Continents Press, 1980).

Articles on Chinua Achebe

Edna Aizenberg, 'Cortazar's Hopscotch and Achebe's *No Longer at Ease*: Divided Heroes and Deconstructive Discourse in the Latin American and African Novel', *Orike: An African Journal of New Writing*, 25–26 (1984), 10–26.

C. A. Babalola, 'A Reconsideration of Achebe's *No Longer At Ease*', *Phylon: The Atlanta University Review of Race and Culture*, 47: 2 (1986), 139–47.

Lloyd W. Brown, 'Cultural Norms and Modes of Perception in Achebe's Fiction', in *Critical Perspectives on Nigerian Literature*, ed. Bernth Lindfors (London: Heinemann, 1975), pp. 127–41.

Mbye B. Cham, 'Language as Index of Character, Humor and Conflict in *Arrow of God* and *A Man of the People*', *A Current Bibliography on African Affairs*, 17: 3 (1984–85), 243–65.

Simon Gikandi, 'Rereading the African Novel: Myth, Language and Culture in Chinua Achebe's *Arrow of God* and Elechi Amadi's *The Concubine*', in his *Reading the African Novel* (London: James Currey, 1987), pp. 149–70.

Abdul JanMohamed, 'Sophisticated Primitivism: The Syncretism of Oral and Literate Modes in Achebe's *Things Fall Apart*', *Ariel: A Review of International Literature Written in English*, 15: 4 (1984), 19–39.

B. Eugene McCarthy, 'Rhythm and Narrative Method in Achebe's *Things Fall Apart*', *Novel: A Forum on Fiction*, 18: 3 (Spring 1985), 243–56.

Russell McDougall, 'Achebe's *Arrow of God*: The Kinetic Idiom of an Unmasking', *Kunapipi*, 9: 2 (1987), 8–24.

D. Ibe Nwoga, 'The Igbo World of Achebe's *Arrow of God*', *Literary Half-Yearly*, 27: 1 (1986), 11–42.

Samuel B. Olorounto, 'The Notion of Conflict in Chinua Achebe's Novels', *Obsidian II: Black Literature in Review*, 1: 3 (1986), 17–36.

Kofi Owusu, 'The Politics of Interpretation: the Novels of Chinua Achebe', *Modern Fiction Studies*, 37: 3 (Autumn 1991), 459–70.

Angela Smith, 'The Mouth With Which to Tell of Their Suffering: The Role of Narrator and Reader in Achebe's *Things Fall Apart*', *Commonwealth Essays and Studies*, 7: 1 (Autumn 1988), 77–90.

Joseph Swann, 'From *Things Fall Apart to Anthills of the Savannah*: the Changing Face of History in Chinua Achebe's Novels', in *Crisis and Creativity in the New Literatures in English*, ed. Geoffrey V. Davis and Hena Maes-Jelinek (Amsterdam: Rodopi, 1991), pp. 191–203.
Onyemaechi Udumukwu, 'Achebe and the Negation of Independence', *Modern Fiction Studies*, 37: 3 (Autumn 1991), 471–91.

NGUGI WA THIONG'O: WRITINGS AND INTERVIEWS

Works by Ngugi have appeared in various editions: the following selection gives the first appearance of his works.

A complete list of Ngugi's early journalism of the 1960s is given in Bernth Lindfors, 'Ngugi wa Thiongo's Early Journalism', *World Literature Written in English*, 20 : 1 (1981), 36–41; *Weep Not Child* (London: Heinemann, 1964); *The River Between* (London: Heinemann, 1965); under the name James Ngugi, *A Grain of Wheat* (London: Heinemann, 1967); under the name James Ngugi, *The Black Hermit* (London: Heinemann, 1968); *Homecoming: Essays on African and Caribbean Literature* (London: Heinemann, 1972); *Secret Lives and Other Stories* (London: Heinemann, 1975); *Petals of Blood* (London: Heinemann, 1977); *The Trial of Dedan Kimathi* – with Micere Mugo (London: Heinemann, 1976); *Devil on the Cross* (first Gikuyu edition publ. East Africa: Heinemann, 1980; English edition, London: Heinemann, 1982); *Detained: A Writer's Prison Diary* (1981); with Ngugi wa Mirii, *I Will Marry When I Want* (London: Heinemann, 1982) – translation of the play *Ngaahika Ndeenda* (1977); *Writers in Politics – Essays* (London: Heinemann, 1981); *Decolonising the Mind* (Harare: Zimbabwe Publishing House, 1986); 'Moving the Centre: Towards a Pluralism of Cultures', *The Journal of Commonwealth Literature*, 26 : 1 (1991), 198ff; Interview – 'Language as Carrier of People's Culture: An Interview with Ngugi wa Thiong'o', with Hansel N. Eyoh, *Ufahamu*, 14: 3 (1985), 156–60; repr. in *Journal of Commonwealth Literature*, 21: 1 (1986), 162–6; Interview with Will Acworth, *Ufahamu*, 18: 2 (1990), 41ff; 'The Language of Struggle: Ngugi wa Thiong'o on the prisonhouse of language', in conversation with Feroza Jussawalla, *Transition: An International Review*, 54 (1991), 142–54.

Books on Ngugi wa Thiong'o

David Cook and Michael Okenimpke, *Ngugi wa Thiong'o: An Explanation of his Writing* (London: Heinemann, 1982).
G. D. Killam, *An Introduction to the Writings of Ngugi* (London: Heinemann, 1980).
G. D. Killam (ed.), *Critical Perspectives on Ngugi wa Thiong'o* (Washington, DC: Three Continents Press, 1984).
C. B. Robson, *Ngugi wa Thiong'o* (London: Macmillan, 1979).
Carol Sichermann, *Ngugi wa Thiong'o: The Making of a Rebel – A Source Book in Kenyan Literature and Resistance* (London: Hans Zell Publishers, 1990).

Articles on Ngugi wa Thiong'o

P. A. Aborisade, 'National and Revolutionary Consciousness: Two Phases of Ngugi's Artistic Praxis', *Ufahamu*, 18: 2 (1990), 59–74.

Irene Assiba d'Almeida, 'The Language of African Fiction: Reflections on Ngugi's Advocacy for an Afro-African Literature', *Présence Africaine*, 120 (1981), 82–92.

Jacqueline Bardolpho, 'Ngugi wa Thiong'o's *A Grain of Wheat* and *Petals of Blood* as Readings of Conrad's *Under Western Eyes* and *Victory*', *The Conradian*, 12: 1 (1987), 32–49.

Lisa Curtis, 'The Divergence of Art and Ideology in the Later Novels of Ngugi wa Thiong'o: A Critique', *Ufahamu*, 13: 2–3 (1984), 186–214.

Jennifer Evans, 'Women and Resistance in Ngugi's *Devil on the Cross*', *African Literature Today*, 15 (1987), 131–9.

Ian Glenn, 'Ngugi wa Thiong'o and the Dilemmas of the Intellectual Elite in Africa: a Sociological Perspective', *English in Africa*, 8: 2 (September 1981), 53–66.

Thomas H. Jackson, 'Orality, Orature, and Ngugi wa Thiong'o', *Research in African Literature*, 22: 1 (Spring 1991), 5–15.

Rustum Kozain, 'Form as Politics, or the Tyranny of Narrativity: Re-Reading Ngugi wa Thiong'o's *Petals of Blood*' *Ufahamu*, 18: 3 (1990), 77–90.

Tobi Levin, 'Women as Scapegoats of Culture and Cult: An Activist's View of Female Circumcision in Ngugi's The *River Between*', *Ngambika: Studies of Women in African Literature*, ed. Carole Boyce Davies and Anne Adams Graves (Trenton, NJ: Africa World Press, 1986), pp. 205–21.

Bernth Lindfors, 'Ngugi wa Thiong'o's Early Journalism', *World Literature Written in English*, 20: 1 (1981), 23–41.

Bernth Lindfors, '*Petals of Blood* as a Popular Novel', *Commonwealth Novel in English*, 6: 1 (1982), 49–55.

Peter Nazareth, 'The Second Homecoming: Multiple Ngugi's in *Petals of Blood*', in *Marxism and African Literature*, ed. Georg M. Gugelberger (London: James Currey, 1985), pp. 118–29.

Gichingiri Ndigirigi, 'Character Names and Types in Ngugi's *Devil on the Cross*', *Ufahamu*, 19: 12/13 (1991), 96–111.

Chimalum Nwankwo, 'Women in Ngugi's Plays: From Passivity to Social Responsibility', *Ufahamu*, 14: 3 (1985), 85–91.

Femi Ojo-Ade, 'Mugo, the "Stranger" Hero: Madness in Ngugi's *A Grain of Wheat*', *Pacific Quarterly*, 6: 3–4 (1981), 133–45.

Bayo Ogunjimi, 'Language, Oral Tradition and Social Vision in Ngugi's *Devil on the Cross*', *Ufahamu*, 14: 1 (1984), 56–70.

Carol M. Sicherman, 'Ngugi wa Thiong'o and the Writing of Kenyan History', *Research in African Literatures*, 20: 3 (Fall 1989), 347–70.

D. Salituma Wamalwa, 'The Engaged Artist: the Social Vision of Ngugi Wa Thiong'o', *Africa Today*, 1st Quarter (1986), 9–18.

ANITA DESAI: WRITINGS AND INTERVIEWS

The following is a selection:

    Cry the Peacock (first publ. 1963; repr. Delhi: Orient Paperbacks, 1990);
    Voices in the City (first publ. 1965; repr. Delhi: Orient Paperbacks,

1992);*Bye-Bye Blackbird* (Delhi: Hind Pocket Books, 1971); *Where Shall We Go This Summer?* (first publ. 1975; repr. Delhi: Orient Paperbacks, 1991); *Fire on the Mountain* (London: Heinemann, 1977); *Games at Twilight* (London: Heinemann, 1978); *Clear Light of Day* (London: Heinemann, 1980); *The Village by the Sea* (London: Heinemann, 1982); *In Custody* (London: Heinemann, 1984); *Baumgartner's Bombay* (London: Heinemann, 1988); Interview – 'An Interview with Anita Desai', by Atma Ram, *World Literature Written in English*, 16: 1 (November 1977), 95–104;. Interview – 'Anita Desai at Work: An Interview', by Ramesh K. Srivastava, *Perspectives on Anita Desai*, ed. Ramesh K. Srivastava (Ghaziabad: Vimal Prakashan, 1984); Interview – 'An Interview with Anita Desai', Pascale Seguet, *Commonwealth Essays and Studies*, 10: 2 (Spring 1988), 43–50; Interview – 'Against the Current: A Conversation with Anita Desai', ed. Corinne Demas Bliss, *The Massachusetts Review* (Fall 1988), 521–37; Interview – 'An Interview with Anita Desai 1 August, 1989: Cambridge, England', *World Literature Written in English*, 30: 1 (Spring 1990), 47–55.

Books on Anita Desai
Usha Bande, *The Novels of Anita Desai* (New Delhi: Prestige Books, 1988).
Jasbir Jain, *Stairs to the Attic: The Novels of Anita Desai* (Jaipur: Printwell, 1987).
Vincy Kirpal, *The New Indian Novel in English* (New Delhi: Allied Publishers, 1990) – also includes other Indian authors.
B. Ramchandra Rao, *The Novels of Anita Desai – A Study* (New Delhi: Kalyani Publishers, 1977).
R. S. Sharma, *Anita Desai* (New Delhi: Heinemann, 1981).
Ramesh K. Srivastava (Ed.), *Perspectives on Anita Desai* (Ghaziabad: Vimal Prakashan, 1984).

Essays and Articles on Anita Desai
S. Krishnamoorthy Aithal and Rashmi Aithal, 'Indo-English Fictional Experiments with Interrracial and Intercultural Relationships', *Alien Voice: Perspectives on Commonwealth Literature*, ed. Avadhesh K. Srivastava (Lucknow, India: Print House, 1981), pp. 84–100.
S. Krishnamoorthy Aithal, 'The Ballad of East and West Updated: Anita Desai's *Bye-Bye, Blackbird*', *Perspectives on Anita Desai*, ed. Ramesh K. Srivastava (Ghaziabad: Vimal Prakashan, 1985), pp. 156–61.
Peter Alcock, 'Rope, Serpent, Fire: Recent Fiction of Anita Desai', *Language and Literature in Multicultural Contexts*, ed. Nandan Satendra (Suva, Fiji: University of South Pacific, 1983), pp. 11–22.
Uma Alladi, 'To Accept or Reject: The Woman as Wife', *The Literary Criterion*, 20: 4 (1985), 79–90.
Shyam M. Asnani, 'Anita Desai's Fiction: A New Dimension', *Indian Literature*, 24: 2 (March–April 1981), 44–54.
Shyam M. Asnani, 'Desai's Theory and Practice of the Novel', *Critical Perspectives on Anita Desai*, ed. Ramesh K. Srivastava (Ghaziabad: Vimal Prakashan, 1985), pp. 5–16.

Alamgir Hashmi, 'Clear Light of Day between India and Pakistan', *The New Indian Novel in English*, ed. Viney Kirpal (New Delhi: Allied Publishers Limited, 1990), pp. 65–71.

Jasbir Jain, 'The Use of Fantasy in Anita Desai's Novels', *Explorations in Modern Indo-English Fiction*, ed. R. K. Dhawan (New Delhi: Bahri, 1982), pp. 227–37.

Jasbir Jain, 'Airing the Family Ghosts: Anita Desai's *Clear Light of Day*', *World Literature Written in English*, 24: 2 (Autumn 1984), 496–522.

Viney Kirpal, 'An Image of India: A Study of Anita Desai's *In Custody*', *Ariel: A Review of International Literature in English*, 17: 4 (1986), 127–38.

Shantha Krishnaswamy, 'Anita Desai – The Sexist Nature of Sanity', *The Woman in Indian Fiction in English* (1950–80) (New Delhi: Ashish Publishing House, 1982).

Malashir Lal, 'The Shift from Female Centred to Male Centred Narrative in the Novels of the 1980s: A Study of Anita Desai and Nayantara Sahgal', *The New Indian Novel in English*, ed. Viney Kirpal (New Delhi: Allied Publishers, 1990), pp. 279–86.

Bipin B. Panigrahi and Viney Kirpal, 'The Dangling Man: Deven in Anita Desai's *In Custody*', *The New Indian Novel in English*, ed. Viney Kirpal, pp. 271–8.

Dieter Riemenschneider, 'History and the Individual in Anita Desai's *Clear Light of Day* and Salman Rushdie's *Midnight's Children*', *The New Indian Novel in English*, ed. Viney Kirpal (New Delhi: Allied Publishers, 1990), pp. 187–99; first publ in *World Literature Written in English*, 23: 1 (1984), 196–207.

Som P. Sharma and Kamal N. Awasthi, 'Anita Desai's *Cry the Peacock*: A Vindication of the Feminine', *Perspectives on Anita Desai*, ed. Ramesh K. Srivastava (Ghaziabad: Vimal Prakashan, 1985), pp. 138–49.

Brijraj Singh, 'Desai's *Clear Light of Day: A Study*', *Perspectives on Anita Desai*, ed. Ramesh Srivastava (Ghaziabad: Vimal Prakashan, 1984), pp.189–93.

M. Sivaramkrishna, 'From Alienation to Mythic Acceptance: The Ordeal of Consciousness in Anita Desai's Fiction', *Perspectives on Anita Desai*, ed. Ramesh K. Srivastava (Ghaziabad: Vimal Prakashan, 1985), pp. 17–30.

Ann Lowry Weir, 'The Illusion of Maya: Feminine Consciousness in Anita Desai's *Cry the Peacock*', *Journal of South Asian Literature*, 21: 2 (Summer–Fall 1981), 1–41.

DEREK WALCOTT: WORKS AND INTERVIEWS

The following is a chronological selection:

During the 1960s Walcott reviewed the arts for the *Trinidad Guardian*: cf. details in Robert D. Hamner, 'Derek Walcott: his Work and his Critics – An Annotated Bibliography, 1947–1980', *Journal of Commonwealth Literature*, 16: 1 (1981), 142–84; *In A Green Night* (London: Cape, 1962); *Selected Poems* (New York: Farrar, Straus, 1964); *The Castaway* (London: Cape, 1965); *Drums and Colours*,

Caribbean Quarterly, Special Issue, 7: 3 (1969); The Gulf (London: Cape, 1969); 'Meanings', *Savacou*, 2 (September 1970), 45–53; *Dream on Monkey Mountain and Other Plays* (New York: Farrar, Straus & Giroux, 1970); 'What the Twilight Says' included in *Dream on Monkey Mountain*, pp. 3–40; *Another Life* (New York: Farrar, Straus & Giroux, 1973); article, 'The Caribbean: Culture or Mimicry?', *Journal of Interamerican Studies*, 16: 1 (Feb. 1974), 3–13; 'The Muse of History', essay in Orde Coombs (ed.), *Is Massa Day Dead* (New York: Anchor, 1974), pp. 1–27; *Sea Grapes* (New York: Farrar, Straus & Giroux, 1976); *The Joker of Seville* and *O Babylon!* (New York: Farrar, Straus & Giroux, 1978); *The Star-Apple Kingdom* (New York: Farrar, Stauss & Giroux, 1979); *Remembrance and Pantomime: Two Plays* (New York: Farrar, Straus & Giroux, 1980); *The Fortunate Traveller* (New York: Farrar, Straus & Giroux, 1981); *Midsummer* (New York: Farrar, Straus & Giroux, 1984); Interview with Robert Hamner – 'Conversation with Derek Walcott', *World Literature Written in English*, 16: 1 (November 1977); *Collected Poems 1948–1984* (New York: Farrar, Straus & Giroux 1986); *Omeros* (New York: Farrar, Straus & Giroux, 1990); Interview with David Montenegro – 'An Interview with Derek Walcott', *Partisan Review*, 57: 2 (1990), 202–14.

Books on Derek Walcott

Edward Baugh, *Derek Walcott: Memory as Vision* (London: Longman, 1978).

Stewart Brown (ed.), *The Art of Derek Walcott* (Bridgend: Seren, 1991). This book contains a very useful and extensive bibliography.

R. D. Hamner, *Derek Walcott* (Boston: Twayne, 1981).

Articles on Derek Walcott

Peter Allcock, ' "... some deep amnesiac blow": Amnesia in the Poetic Development of Derek Walcott', *SPAN: Journal of the South Pacific Association for Commonwealth Literature and Language Studies*, 21 (October 1985), 75–95.

Robert Bensen, 'The New World Poetry of Derek Walcott', *Concerning Poetry*, 16: 2 (Fall 1983), 29–42.

Paul Breslin, ' "I Met History Once, But He Ain't Recognize Me": The Poetry of Derek Walcott', *TriQuarterly*, 68 (Winter 1987), 168–83.

Stephen P. Breslow, 'Trinidadian Heteroglossia: A Bakhtinian View of Derek Walcott's Play *A Branch of the Blue Nile*', *World Literature Today: A Literary Quarterly of the University of Oklahoma*, 63: 1 (Winter 1989), 36–9.

Joseph Brodsky, 'The Sound of The Tide' in *Less Than One: Selected Essays* (Harmondsworth: Penguin, 1987), pp. 164–5.

Stewart Brown, 'Derek Walcott: Poems', in *A Handbook for Teaching Caribbean Literature*, ed. David Dabydeen (London: Heinemann, 1988), pp. 96–104.

Robert Crawford, 'Homing', *Poetry Review*, 80 : 4 (Winter 1990/91), 8–10.

Rita Dove, 'Either I'm a Nobody, or I'm a Nation', *Parnassus: Poetry in Review*, 14: 1 (1987), 49–76.

Robert Elliot Fox, 'Derek Walcott: History as Dis-Ease', *Callaloo: An Afro-American and African Journal of Arts and Letters*, 9: 2 (Spring 1986), 331–40.

Robert D. Hamner, 'The Art of Chiaroscuro: Caliban Confronts the White World', *International Literature in English: Essays on the Major Writers*, ed. Robert L. Ross (New York: Garland, 1991), pp. 703–16.

Seamus Heaney, 'The Murmur of Malvern' in *The Government of the Tongue* (London: Faber, 1990), pp. 23–9.

Patricia Ismond, 'Walcott's Later Drama: from *Joker* to *Remembrance*', *Ariel: A Review of International Literature in English*, 16: 3 (1985), 89–101.

Patricia Ismond, 'North and South: A Look at Walcott's Midsummer', *Kunapipi*, 8: 2 (1986), 77–85.

Patricia Ismond, 'West Indian Literature as an Expression of National Cultures: The Literature of St Lucia', *World Literature Written in English*, 29: 2 (Autumn 1989), 104–15.

Biodun Jeyifo, 'On Eurocentric Critical Theory: Some Paradigms from the Texts and Sub-Texts of Post-Colonial Writing', *Kunapipi* (11: 1 (1989), 107–18.

David Mason, 'Derek Walcott: Poet of the New World', *The Literary Review: An International Journal of Contemporary Writing*, 29: 3 (Spring 1986), 269–75.

James McCorkle, 'Re-Mapping the New World: The Recent Poetry of Derek Walcott', *Ariel: A Review of International Literature Written in English*, 17: 2 (1986), 3–14.

Russell McDougall, 'Music, Body, and the Torture of Articulation in Derek Walcott's "Sainte Lucie"', *Ariel: A Review of International Literature in English*, 23: 2 (April 1992), 65–83.

Erskine Peters, 'The Theme of Madness in the Plays of Derek Walcott', *College Language Association Journal*, 32: 2 (1988), 148–69.

J. A. Ramsaran, 'New World Mediterranean Poet', *World Literature Written in English*, 21: 1 (Spring 1982), 133–47.

Bin Ramke, ' "Your words is English, is a different tree": On Derek Walcott', *Denver Quarterly*, 23:2 (Fall 1988), 90–9.

John Thieme, 'A Caribbean Don Juan: Derek Walcott's *Joker of Seville*', *World Literature Written in English*, 23: 1 (1984), 62–75.

John Thieme, '*Ti-Jean and his Brothers* and *Dream on Monkey Mountain*', in *A Handbook for Teaching Carribean Literature*, ed. David Dabydeen (London: Heinemann, 1988), pp. 86-95.

Helen Vendler, 'Poet of Two Worlds', *The New York Review of Books*, 4 March 1982, pp. 23–7.

Susan Willis, 'Caliban as Poet; Reversing the Maps of Domination', *The Massachusetts Review*, 29: 3 (Winter, 1982), 615–30.

USEFUL PERIODICALS

Whilst many literary journals devote special numbers to postcolonial literatures, the following international reviews feature essays in this field, some exclusively specialising in the subject:

Ariel: A Review of International Literature Written in English, Canada: University of Calgary.

ACLALS Bulletin: The Association for Commonwealth Language and Literature Studies.

Carib, published by the West Indian Association for Commonwealth Literature and Language Studies, University of the West Indies.

Commonwealth Essays and Studies.

Commonwealth Novel in English.

Current Bibliography on African Affairs.

The Journal of Commonwealth Literature, Hans Zell Publishers, London.

Journal of Indian Writing in English.

Kunapipi, Aarhus, Denmark: Dangaroo Press.

Modern Fiction Studies, Purdue Research Foundation, Canada: especially 37: 3 (Autumn 1991) devoted to 'Postcolonial African Fiction'.

New Literature Review, Australia: University of Wollongong.

Présence Africaine: Revue Culturelle du Monde Noir, bilingual series, published by Société Africaine de Culture, 25 bis, rue des écoles, 75005 PARIS.

Research in African Literatures, ed. Bernth Lindfors, University of Texas Press, PO Box 7819, Austin, TX 78712.

Ufahamu: Journal of the African Activist Association, African Studies Center, University of California, Los Angeles, California 90024.

World Literature Written in English, published in Guelph, Canada.

Notes on Contributors

F. Odun Balogun is Assistant Professor of English at the University of Benin, Nigeria.

Sidney Burris is Associate Professor of English at the University of Arkansas, and has published one book of verse, *A Day at the Races*, and a critical study of Seamus Heaney's work, *The Poetry of Resistance: Seamus Heaney and the Pastoral Tradition*.

Elleke Boehmer is the author of the novels *Screens Against the Sky* and *An Immaculate Figure*, and the critical work, *Migrant Metaphors: Colonial and Postcolonial Literature* (forthcoming 1995). She has published widely on postcolonial literature and lectures in English at the University of Leeds.

Stewart Crehan is a lecturer in English at the University of Transkei, and formerly taught at Manchester Polytechnic and the University of Swaziland. He is the author of *Blake in Context* (1984), an essay on Blake in the Penguin *History of Literature*, vol. V (1995) and has written articles on African Popular Theatre for *RAL*.

Bettina Knapp is a Professor in the department of Romance Languages and Comparative Literature at Hunter College, City University of New York. She has published extensively on French and American literature, and among her most recent books are *Images of Chinese Women: A Westerner's View* and *Images of Japanese Women: A Westerner's View*, published by the Whitston Press, New York.

Neil Ten Kortenaar is an Assistant Professor of English at Concordia University in Montreal. He researches into African and Caribbean literature and postcolonial literature generally. Others essays he has written on Achebe have appeared in *Research into African Literatures* and *PMLA*.

Harveen Sachdeva Mann is an Assistant Professor of English at Loyola University, Chicago, and has published articles on postcolonial literature in a number of journals including *Aerial, Modern Fiction Studies* and *New Orleans Review*.

Judie Newman is a Lecturer in the School of English at the University of Newcastle. An expanded version of her essay will appear in a book entitled *Postcolonial Fictions*, to be published by Edward Arnold in 1995/6.

Chidi Okonkwo is a lecturer in English at Chester College of Higher Education, and has been a Visiting Scholar at Cambridge University and held a fellowship at the University of Wales. The author of many journal articles and book chapters on African and Postcolonial literature, he is currently writing a book entitled *Postcoloniality, Decolonisation and the Novel as Socio-Political Agonistics* for Macmillan Press.

Philip Rogers is Associate Professor of English at Binghamton University, and taught for two years at the University of Nigeria (Nsukka). He has written extensively on nineteenth-century fiction for such journals as *Nineteenth Century Literature, Comparative Literature, Slavic and East European Review* and on Chinua Achebe's poetry for *The Journal of Commonwealth Literature.*

Daizal R. Samad is attached to the Department of English at the National University of Malaysia, and was previously Assistant Professor at St Thomas University in Canada. A Canadian, brought up and educated in the Caribbean, he has published articles in scholarly journals in Barbados, Canada, Britain, France, Guyana, India, Malaysia and the United States.

Elaine Savory taught at the University of the West Indies, Barbados, from 1974 to 1990, where she was one of the team which established Women's Studies. She has published widely on African, Caribbean and Indian women writers, and co-edited *Out of the Kumbla: Women and Caribbean Literature* with Carole Boyce Davies. She is currently writing a study of Jean Rhys for Cambridge University Press and finishing work on her first play, *spirit.* Elaine Savory used to write as Elaine Savory Fido.

Clement Wyke is Professor of English at The University of Winnipeg, Manitoba, Canada.

Index